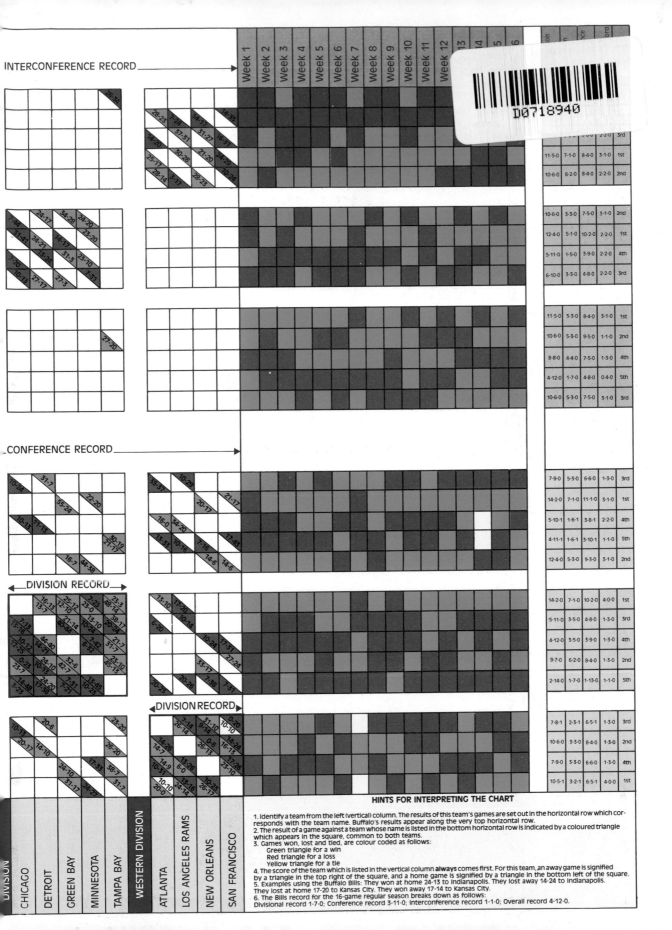

INTERCONFERENCE RECORD

CONFERENCE RECORD

DIVISION RECORD

DIVISION RECORD

DIVISION

CHICAGO
DETROIT
GREEN BAY
MINNESOTA
TAMPA BAY
WESTERN DIVISION
ATLANTA
LOS ANGELES RAMS
NEW ORLEANS
SAN FRANCISCO

Week 1 · Week 2 · Week 3 · Week 4 · Week 5 · Week 6 · Week 7 · Week 8 · Week 9 · Week 10 · Week 11 · Week 12 · Week 13 · Week 14 · Week 15 · Week 16

HINTS FOR INTERPRETING THE CHART

1. Identify a team from the left (vertical) column. The results of this team's games are set out in the horizontal row which corresponds with the team name. Buffalo's results appear along the very top horizontal row.
2. The result of a game against a team whose name is listed in the bottom horizontal row is indicated by a coloured triangle which appears in the square, common to both teams.
3. Games won, lost and tied, are colour coded as follows:
    Green triangle for a win
    Red triangle for a loss
    Yellow triangle for a tie
4. The score of the team which is listed in the vertical column **always** comes first. For this team, an away game is signified by a triangle in the top right of the square, and a home game is signified by a triangle in the bottom left of the square.
5. Examples using the Buffalo Bills: They won at home 24-13 to Indianapolis. They lost away 14-24 to Indianapolis. They lost at home 17-20 to Kansas City. They won away 17-14 to Kansas City.
6. The Bills record for the 16-game regular season breaks down as follows:
Divisional record 1-7-0; Conference record 3-11-0; Interconference record 1-1-0; Overall record 4-12-0.

INTERPRETING THE 1986 RESULTS CHART (See inside front cover)

The chart colour-codes the result of every game in the 1986 regular season. For each club, the results of its games are listed in the horizontal row which corresponds both with its name in the left (vertical) column and the name of its opponent in the bottom (horizontal) row.

The result of every game is indicated by a triangle, coloured green for a win, red for a loss and yellow for a tie. In every square, the position of the triangle indicates either a home or an away game. For a home game, the triangle is at the bottom left of a square, while for an away game it is at the top right.

Looking at the results for Buffalo, we see that they won only one game, at home to Indianapolis, against teams from the AFC East. Against the AFC Central, again their only win was at home to Pittsburgh. Against Kansas City (AFC West) they lost at home and won away. Finally, Buffalo won at home to St Louis and lost away to Tampa Bay.

In the 1986 season there were two tied games, Atlanta at home to San Francisco, and Philadelphia at home to St Louis.

INTERPRETING THE ALL-TIME HEAD-TO-HEAD CHART (See inside back cover)

The numbers in the boxes represent the all-time won-lost-tied record of the team in the left (vertical) column against the team in the top (horizontal) row. Thus, Buffalo has won seven, lost thirty-four and tied one game in the series against Miami. The colour of the box indicates the current status.

A green box indicates that the team is leading in the series.

A pink box indicates that the team is behind in the series.

A yellow box indicates that the series is tied.

Thus, Buffalo is tied with Indianapolis, trails Miami and is ahead against Denver.

AMERICAN FOOTBALL
BOOK 5

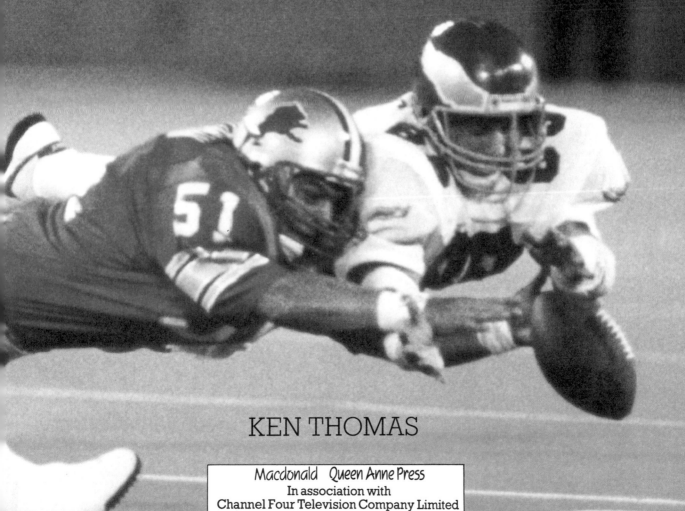

AMERICAN FOOTBALL
BOOK 5

KEN THOMAS

Macdonald Queen Anne Press
In association with
Channel Four Television Company Limited

ACKNOWLEDGEMENTS

I remember the time when I used to write a book on American Football and two enthusiastic lads would look over my shoulder, point out a few errors and make the odd suggestion. Such has been the passage of time that the lads have become young men, whom veteran readers of this Annual will know as Nick Wridgway and Roger Smith. In the five years over which this Annual has been published, they have become an inseparable part of its production.

Roger, who was the first British fan of the Dallas Cowboys, arrives armed with the statistics, and I no longer need ask if they are correct. Roger, I am extremely grateful. Nick is no ordinary proof reader – on the subject of American Football, he is the best – and that's only part of it, for, this side of the Atlantic, as a researcher he is without equal. Thanks Nick.

Then there's the American connection. My grateful thanks go to Larry Eldridge, Jr., of ABC TV, who kindly granted permission to use information on the New York Giants, which he had researched in his capacity as an NFL historian of some standing. Pete Abitante, who combines being a real gentleman with his official role as the AFC Information Director, has been of great assistance. Thanks, Pete. As for Beau Riffenburgh, of NFL Properties Inc., I'll start by apologising for misspelling his name in last year's effort. I was the last person to see the funny side of it but, fortunately, he was one of the first. He's that kind of fellow and he also gives freely of his vast expertise on the subject of American Football. Thanks, Beau.

The bulk of the photographic material came from NFL Properties Inc., Los Angeles. Kevin Terrell did the research and Sharon Kuthe did the rest. My thanks go to a super duo.

Speaking of duos, I couldn't wish for a more considerate pair of professionals than Celia Kent and Simon Webb. Simon is the designer and Celia makes sure that I don't slip up on my use of gerunds, and the like. To Myles Hartley and Terry Briggs, I am most grateful for permission to use charts which previously appeared in *Touchdown* magazine.

Ever tactful and always charming, Mrs Susanna Yager, the Publishing and Merchandising Manager of Channel Four Television, orchestrates the entire production and has my sincere thanks.

Finally, there's my wife, Janie, who plays an increasingly important role in the whole project. I couldn't possibly do the things I do – have a damned good time with my mates while somebody else shoulders the responsibilities of running a home – without Janie's support. Thanks love.

K.T. June 1987

A Queen Anne Press Book

© Ken Thomas 1987

First published in Great Britain in 1987 by
Queen Anne Press, a division of
Macdonald & Co (Publishers) Ltd
3rd Floor, Greater London House
Hampstead Road
London NW1 7QX

A BPCC plc Company

The American Football Book is associated with Channel Four Television's coverage of the sport produced by Cheerleader Productions Limited.

British Library Cataloguing in Publication Data

Thomas, Ken
   The American football book 5.——
   (Channel Four book).
   1. Football
   I. Title
   796.332   GV951

ISBN 0-356-14712-6

Typeset by SX Composing Ltd

Printed and bound in Great Britain

PHOTOGRAPHS
All photographs have been supplied by courtesy of the NFL with the exception of All-Sport 2-3, 6, 8, 27R, 46, 51, 74T, 89, 125, 139.

CONTENTS

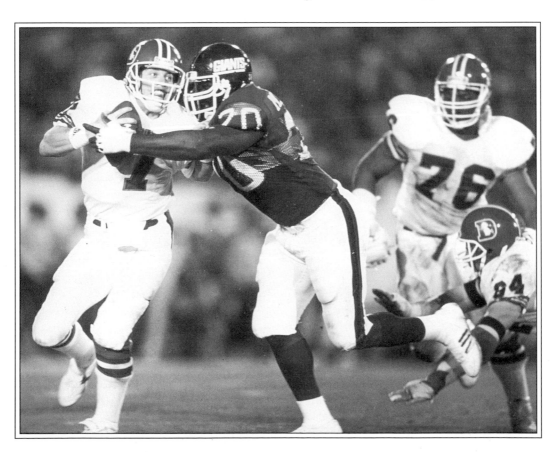

INTRODUCTION

1986 will be remembered as the year the Cowboys and the Bears came to town. A full-house throng at Wembley Stadium sang, 'Here we go,' and off we went into the NFL's 67th campaign. It came to a conclusion in Pasadena, California, where the New York Giants crushed the Denver Broncos in Super Bowl XXI.

On the domestic scene, the rival organisations completed their separate seasons before abandoning their conflicting self-interests and merging under the heading of the Budweiser League. How many teams are there? Hundreds and still counting. The league does have a chance to make it, but it will not be easy. Maybe they ought to follow the line of Joe Carr, who, in the early 1930s, correctly saw that the NFL's future lay in the concentration of excellence. In the terminology of the 1980s, that would mean the formation of a Super League containing, say, eight teams.

The British movement attracts, perhaps, 200,000 people, players, loyal servants and fans, whereas, on a good Sunday evening, Channel Four attracts four million viewers. There's no doubt where the weight of interest lies, and that's in the NFL. Cheerleader Productions made a quantum leap in presentation by hiring Frank Gifford to anchor the programme. An articulate, polished presenter, Gifford also is a member of the Pro Football Hall of Fame. A key figure in the team which first brought Monday Night Football to the American viewing public, here he was, sixteen years later, doing the same on Sundays for the Brits.

Way back then, the 1970 season, when your writer was untangling the subtleties of 'man-for-man defense' and debating the new 'zones', Detroit beat both Chicago and the Rams while St Louis hammered the Cowboys 38-0. These days, the balance of power has shifted some-what, but your writer remains unchanged in his ambition which, simply, is to share his pleasure, the nostalgia and the excitement of this beautiful game. This series of books is part of a package which includes *A Guide to American Football* and, written in collaboration with Nick Wridgway and Roger Smith, two volumes of *Who's Who in American Football*. The style of Book 5 is the same as usual except for the odd addition, such as the inclusion of leading sackers in the statistical sections. I hope that it continues to meet with the satisfaction of the reader.

Left: Jay Schroeder, quarterback of the Washington Redskins.

Contents page: Denver's John Elway sacked by George Martin of the New York Giants in Super Bowl XXI.

☆☆☆☆☆☆ CHAPTER ONE ☆☆☆☆☆☆

A REVIEW OF THE 1986 SEASON

Prologue

Ask most British pro football fans what they were doing on July 28th, 1986, and they probably couldn't give you an answer. But ask them about the evening of the 29th and most would describe tuning in to AFN for news about *the* lawsuit.

The story goes back to early 1983 and the formation of the United States Football League. Being a Spring-Summer league, it was supposed to fill the gap in the pro football calendar but, inevitably, there was conflict with the NFL. Perhaps having learnt from the experiences of a good half-dozen previous challenges, stretching back over sixty years, the NFL's clubs withstood the temptation to engage in an inter-league bidding war for players. It had meant that several potential superstar draftees opted for playing in the USFL, but that notional loss was felt little. Even when the USFL had announced its intention to go head-to-head with the NFL, by playing an Autumn schedule in 1986, it was not a serious worry.

But, increasingly, the USFL cried 'dirty pool', amongst other things accusing the NFL of using its monopoly position to influence the national television networks, on whose support the future prosperity of the USFL depended. Also, there was the small matter that the USFL had lost a reported $169 million over its first three seasons. And it came as no surprise when they multiplied their losses by ten and went to court seeking damages of $1.69 billion.

The verdict came through somewhere around 10:30 GMT that night, July 29th. The NFL had been cleared of all charges, except the application of its monopoly position. The rub was that the jury, in its wisdom or perhaps its contempt, awarded damages of just $1, trebled to $3. For all intents and purposes, the USFL ceased to exist though, at the time of writing, an appeal is pending.

Even before the court proceedings had begun, several of the USFL's best players, such as Mike Rozier, Reggie White, Anthony Carter and Steve Young, had drifted into the NFL. Now the rest would

Jim Kelly was expected to revitalise the Bills.

follow. Remember the excitement? Jim Kelly, Kelvin Bryant and Herschel Walker – they were all going to come and play football in our street.

Jim Mora had been the USFL's most successful head coach, his Philadelphia/Baltimore Stars having played in all three USFL Championship Games, twice winning the title. In 1986, he would be attempting to guide the New Orleans Saints to their first net-winning season. Having put things in order up in

Minnesota, Bud Grant handed over to his close friend and professional colleague of eighteen years, Jerry Burns, for whom it would be the first campaign at the helm. Gene Stallings, who became the head coach of the St Louis Cardinals, had impeccable credentials, having served as an assistant under Alabama's Paul 'Bear' Bryant and the 'Dean' of head coaches, Dallas's Tom Landry. Much was expected of Buddy Ryan, who was widely seen as the architect, sometime father figure, of that terrifying Chicago Bears defense which represented the current state of the art. Ryan took charge of a Philadelphia Eagles club which, one felt, had the talent to respond to his style of coaching. Both Hank Bullough (Buffalo) and Jerry Glanville (Houston) were entering their first full seasons as head coaches after having stepped into the breach during the 1985 campaign.

The 1986 collegiate draft was particularly strong in running backs and for both the offensive and defensive lines, and players in those three categories were taken with nineteen of the twenty-seven selections in the first round. There was, however, a disappointment of huge proportions when the first player selected overall, Auburn running back Bo Jackson, opted for a career with major league baseball's Kansas City Royals. Jackson, who won the 1985 Heisman Trophy, had been compared with the great O.J. Simpson and would surely have helped the Tampa Bay Buccaneers, the NFL's second-weakest club in 1985, who saw their prime position in the draft go to waste. (The weakest club in 1985, Buffalo, had exercised its option in a previous trade which gave Cleveland the opportunity to select Bernie Kosar in the 1985 supplemental draft.)

As a further move in the search for perfection, the NFL adopted the limited use of instant television replay, to help out in cases where the on-field officials were unsighted. Innovation always has had its detractors and this one would prove to be no different.

Of course, the big question was, 'Who's going to win the Super Bowl?' Here, the Chicago Bears had the strongest claim, after having dismissed their opponents with consummate ease in the 1985 play-offs. Injuries meant that they would be without two key players, wide receiver Dennis McKinnon and cornerback Leslie Frazier, but they had drafted well. Their most serious challengers from within the NFC appeared to be the Rams, San Francisco, Washington, the Giants and, as always, Dallas. Of the AFC clubs, there was good reason to expect that the Patriots would come back strongly after their learning experience at the hands of the Bears in Super Bowl XX. That Eastern division, including Miami and

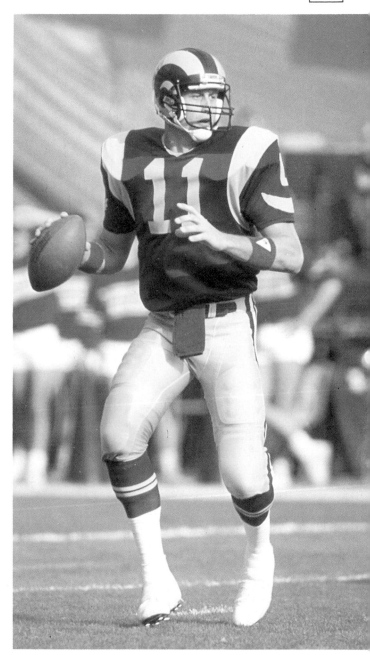

Jim Everett was the first quarterback selected in the draft.

the Jets, looked the most competitive of the three, by a whisker over the AFC West. People always fancy the Raiders - and the Raiders always fancy themselves - while the Broncos looked very solid. The Central appeared to be a contest between the orthodoxy of the Cleveland Browns and the free expression of the Cincinnati Bengals.

This writer liked the Rams and Miami – there's honesty for you!

WEEK ONE

American Football Conference
Cincinnati 14 at Kansas City 24
Indianapolis 3 at New England 33
Los Angeles Raiders 36 at Denver 38
Miami 28 at San Diego 50
New York Jets 28 at Buffalo 24
Pittsburgh 0 at Seattle 30

National Football Conference
Atlanta 31 at New Orleans 10
Detroit 13 at Minnesota 10
Los Angeles Rams 16 at St Louis 10
New York Giants 28 at Dallas 31
Philadelphia 14 at Washington 41
San Francisco 31 at Tampa Bay 7

Interconference Games
Cleveland 31 at Chicago 41
Houston 31 at Green Bay 3

Interconference Play
AFC 1 – NFC 1

The league's use of instant replay was called into action on only the third play of the game between Cleveland and the reigning Super Bowl Champion Bears. Cleveland safety Al Gross recovered possession in the Chicago end zone after a bad snap from Chicago center Jay Hilgenberg. The officials on the field said, 'maybe,' and the man in the booth said 'yes.' But Cleveland's elation was short lived as Chicago's Dennis Gentry returned the ensuing kickoff 91 yards for a touchdown. And though the Browns stayed in touch, even closing to 31-34 with six minutes remaining, a Matt Suhey touchdown settled the issue in favour of a slightly-shaken Bears team which, perhaps, needed stirring.

There was no joy for the four new head coaches, all of whom lost. Eric Dickerson rushed for 193 yards on a Rams club-record 38 carries, but Gene Stallings' Cardinals had driven down to the one-yard line when time ran out, leaving them just six points adrift. Jerry Burns' Minnesota, too, fell foul of a powerhouse display of running, against Detroit, for whom James Jones equalled the club record with 36 carries and gained a career-best 174 yards. In that game, Eddie Murray's fourth-quarter 44-yard field goal was the difference. For both Stallings and Burns it had been close, but Jim Mora's New Orleans Saints were never in it against Atlanta, and Buddy Ryan's team, Philadelphia, slipped to a heavy defeat against Washington. Interestingly, in that game, Washington's long-range kicker, Steve Cox, kicked a 55-yard field goal. And even more interestingly, it was the shortest of his career. (Coming into the season, he had kicked just two field goals, covering distances of 60 and 58 yards.)

Over in the AFC West, Denver couldn't have wished for a better start to the campaign, as they scored ten fourth-quarter points to overhaul the Raiders 38-36. But there were early suggestions that they wouldn't have things all their own way, as Kansas City nipped Cincinnati, San Diego bombed Miami and Seattle shut out Pittsburgh for the second time in their six-game series.

It's becoming a tradition for Dallas to open in the full glare of Monday Night Football – they've played in six of the last seven – and it was wholly in context when they shared a thriller with the Giants. 'Why didn't we pick him when we had the chance?' the other clubs must have reflected, when the Cowboys' Herschel Walker took over in the second half from the injured Tony Dorsett and ran ten yards for the winning touchdown with only 1:16 remaining.

Left: Marcus Allen (L.A. Raiders) set a new NFL record with his tenth consecutive 100-yards-rushing game.

Right: Dennis Gentry on the way to opening Chicago's account against Cleveland.

STANDINGS

AFC East	W	L	T	PF	PA		NFC East	W	L	T	PF	PA
New England	1	0	0	33	3		Dallas	1	0	0	31	28
N.Y. Jets	1	0	0	28	24		Washington	1	0	0	41	14
Buffalo	0	1	0	24	28		N.Y. Giants	0	1	0	28	31
Indianapolis	0	1	0	3	33		Philadelphia	0	1	0	14	41
Miami	0	1	0	28	50		St Louis	0	1	0	10	16
AFC Central							**NFC Central**					
Houston	1	0	0	31	3		Chicago	1	0	0	41	31
Cleveland	0	1	0	31	41		Detroit	1	0	0	13	10
Cincinnati	0	1	0	14	24		Green Bay	0	1	0	3	31
Pittsburgh	0	1	0	0	30		Minnesota	0	1	0	10	13
AFC West							Tampa Bay	0	1	0	7	31
Denver	1	0	0	38	36		**NFC West**					
Kansas City	1	0	0	24	14		Atlanta	1	0	0	31	10
San Diego	1	0	0	50	28		L.A. Rams	1	0	0	16	10
Seattle	1	0	0	30	0		San Francisco	1	0	0	31	7
L.A. Raiders	0	1	0	36	38		New Orleans	0	1	0	10	31

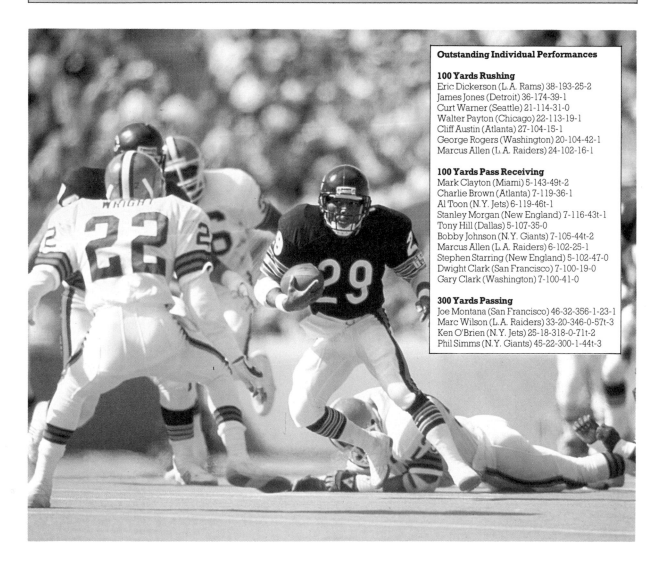

Outstanding Individual Performances

100 Yards Rushing
Eric Dickerson (L.A. Rams) 38-193-25-2
James Jones (Detroit) 36-174-39-1
Curt Warner (Seattle) 21-114-31-0
Walter Payton (Chicago) 22-113-19-1
Cliff Austin (Atlanta) 27-104-15-1
George Rogers (Washington) 20-104-42-1
Marcus Allen (L.A. Raiders) 24-102-16-1

100 Yards Pass Receiving
Mark Clayton (Miami) 5-143-49t-2
Charlie Brown (Atlanta) 7-119-36-1
Al Toon (N.Y. Jets) 6-119-46t-1
Stanley Morgan (New England) 7-116-43t-1
Tony Hill (Dallas) 5-107-35-0
Bobby Johnson (N.Y. Giants) 7-105-44t-2
Marcus Allen (L.A. Raiders) 6-102-25-1
Stephen Starring (New England) 5-102-47-0
Dwight Clark (San Francisco) 7-100-19-0
Gary Clark (Washington) 7-100-41-0

300 Yards Passing
Joe Montana (San Francisco) 46-32-356-1-23-1
Marc Wilson (L.A. Raiders) 33-20-346-0-57t-3
Ken O'Brien (N.Y. Jets) 25-18-318-0-71t-2
Phil Simms (N.Y. Giants) 45-22-300-1-44t-3

WEEK TWO

American Football Conference
Buffalo 33 at Cincinnati 36 (OT)
Cleveland 23 at Houston 20
Denver 21 at Pittsburgh 10
Indianapolis 10 at Miami 30
Kansas City 17 at Seattle 23
New England 20 at New York Jets 6

National Football Conference
Dallas 31 at Detroit 7
Green Bay 10 at New Orleans 24
Minnesota 23 at Tampa Bay 10
Philadelphia 10 at Chicago 13 (OT)
St Louis 13 at Atlanta 33
San Francisco 13 at Los Angeles Rams 16

Interconference Games
Los Angeles Raiders 6 at Washington 10
San Diego 7 at New York Giants 20

Interconference Play
AFC 1 – NFC 3

Walter Payton carrying the Bears to victory against Philadelphia.

They called it the 'Buddy Bowl' when Buddy Ryan returned to Chicago, seeking the one victory for which he'd probably have settled over the entire campaign. And his Eagles gave the mighty Bears almost all they could handle. Walter Payton had Philadelphia reeling, as he rushed for a game total of 177 yards, taking his career total to 15,150 and scoring his 100th rushing touchdown. But the Eagles would not yield, and after surviving a few scares they took the Bears into overtime. In the extra period, however, the end came quickly. Philadelphia's Charles Crawford fumbled the opening kickoff and Chicago rookie Vestee Jackson recovered possession on the Eagles' 35-yard line. Six rushes by Payton set up Kevin Butler's winning field goal. 'Now we can get back to playing football,' said a relieved Mike Ditka.

Cincinnati was the day's other overtime winner, having had to rally in regulation time to a 33-33 tie against a Jim Kelly-inspired Buffalo club. Earlier, Kelly had passed 84 yards for a touchdown to wide receiver Chris Burkett, but his pass on the first play in overtime was intercepted and returned to the Buffalo 17-yard line, setting up Jim Breech's game-winning 20-yard field goal.

In Washington, Marcus Allen extended his NFL record for consecutive 100-yards-rushing games to eleven, but it was not enough to hold off the Redskins, whose winning score was set up by Jay Schroeder's 59-yard heave to tight end Clint Didier. The Giants intercepted five Dan Fouts passes and used ball control – they held possession for almost 40 minutes – to log their first victory of the campaign at the expense of San Diego.

The Rams beat San Francisco, thanks mainly to cornerback LeRoy Irvin, who returned a fumble 31 yards to set up a Mike Lansford field goal and, later, returned a blocked punt 65 yards for a touchdown.

Elsewhere, Miami, Minnesota and New Orleans opened their accounts, but the day's main stories centred on injuries to key players. A week earlier, San Francisco quarterback Joe Montana had gone out with a back injury, and the subsequent prognosis was that his career might be over. In the Jets' loss to New England, running back Freeman McNeil had suffered a dislocated elbow and would be sidelined for several weeks. The Colts, who didn't need a bit of bad luck, lost starting quarterback Gary Hogeboom with a separated shoulder.

STANDINGS

AFC East	W	L	T	PF	PA
New England	2	0	0	53	9
Miami	1	1	0	58	60
N.Y. Jets	1	1	0	34	44
Buffalo	0	2	0	57	64
Indianapolis	0	2	0	13	63
AFC Central					
Cincinnati	1	1	0	50	57
Cleveland	1	1	0	54	61
Houston	1	1	0	51	26
Pittsburgh	0	2	0	10	51
AFC West					
Denver	2	0	0	59	46
Seattle	2	0	0	53	17
Kansas City	1	1	0	41	37
San Diego	1	1	0	57	48
L.A. Raiders	0	2	0	42	48
NFC East	**W**	**L**	**T**	**PF**	**PA**
Dallas	2	0	0	62	35
Washington	2	0	0	51	20
N.Y. Giants	1	1	0	48	38
Philadelphia	0	2	0	24	54
St Louis	0	2	0	23	49
NFC Central					
Chicago	2	0	0	54	41
Detroit	1	1	0	20	41
Minnesota	1	1	0	33	23
Green Bay	0	2	0	13	55
Tampa Bay	0	2	0	17	54
NFC West					
Atlanta	2	0	0	64	23
L.A. Rams	2	0	0	32	23
New Orleans	1	1	0	34	41
San Francisco	1	1	0	44	23

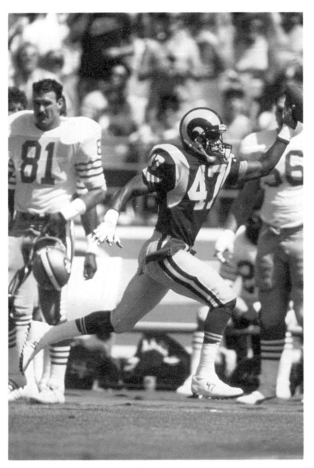

Outstanding Individual Performances

100 Yards Rushing
Walter Payton (Chicago) 34-177-18-1
Tony Dorsett (Dallas) 23-117-33-1
Gerald Riggs (Atlanta) 29-108-10-1
Marcus Allen (L.A. Raiders) 23-104-20-0

100 Yards Pass Receiving
Eric Martin (New Orleans) 3-164-84-1
Jerry Rice (San Francisco) 6-157-66t-1
Reginald Langhorne (Cleveland) 3-115-55t-1
Stanley Morgan (New England) 8-104-22-0
James Lofton (Green Bay) 8-100-21-1

300 Yards Passing
Phil Simms (N.Y. Giants) 37-18-300-1-35-1

LeRoy Irvin completes his 65-yard touchdown return in style.

WEEK THREE

American Football Conference
Cincinnati 30 at Cleveland 13
Houston 13 at Kansas City 27
Miami 45 at New York Jets 51 (OT)
Seattle 38 at New England 31

National Football Conference
Atlanta 37 at Dallas 35
Chicago 25 at Green Bay 12
New Orleans 17 at San Francisco 26
Tampa Bay 24 at Detroit 20

Interconference Games
Denver 33 at Philadelphia 7
Los Angeles Rams 24 at Indianapolis 7
New York Giants 14 at Los Angeles Raiders 9
Pittsburgh 7 at Minnesota 31
St Louis 10 at Buffalo 17
Washington 30 at San Diego 27

Interconference Play
AFC 3 – NFC 7

Above: Jeff Kemp succeeds as the 49ers starter.

Right: Tampa Bay's running back, Nathan Wonsley.

Big plays, comebacks and maybe, just maybe, the emergence of a new contender, were the ingredients which spiced the pot on Week Three.

The big plays, not all of them, but lots of them, came in the Jets-Miami encounter, with the two quarterbacks, the Jets' Ken O'Brien and Miami's Dan Marino, throwing for a combined total of 927 yards and ten touchdowns. Marino tied the Dolphins' club record with six touchdown passes, but it was O'Brien, in combination with wide receiver Wesley Walker, who carried off the honours. With no time remaining in regulation, O'Brien's 21-yard touchdown pass to Walker brought the Jets into a 45-45 tie before, in overtime, he combined with Walker on a 43-yard play for the duo's fourth and game-winning touchdown.

In a game featuring two of the AFC's three unbeaten teams, the Patriots gave up their first touchdown of the year but seemed to have control of the Seahawks, when they went into a 31-21 lead with seven minutes to play. But a Norm Johnson field goal and a touchdown following a blocked punt brought the teams level, and wide receiver Ray Butler finished off the rally with a 67-yard touchdown pass to add to the 54-yarder he'd caught earlier. Washington was another club which had to come from behind after they had trailed San Diego 21-3 halfway through the second quarter. Their victory was sealed when wide receiver Gary Clark completed his personal big-game performance with a 14-yard touchdown reception inside the final two minutes.

Atlanta was the club which had raised a few eyebrows with impressive opening victories over New Orleans and St Louis. But surely they'd been put in their place by Dallas, for whom quarterback Danny White had drilled four touchdown passes as the Cowboys took a 35-27 lead with just over nine minutes remaining. But hold your horses. Gerald Riggs scored from two yards out and then, with only 28 seconds to go, Dave Archer fired a 65-yard pass completion to rookie wide receiver Floyd Dixon, setting up position for a battle-hardened Mick Luckhurst to kick the winning field goal.

In other games, the Giants won a defensive struggle, dropping the Raiders to 0-3, their worst start since 1964. The Raiders' Marcus Allen suffered an ankle injury which would persist. Chicago needed a 15-point, fourth-quarter rally to overcome the winless Green Bay, Cincinnati upset Cleveland, and Tampa Bay gained a welcome victory over Detroit.

STANDINGS

AFC East	W	L	T	PF	PA	NFC East	W	L	T	PF	PA
New England	2	1	0	84	47	Washington	3	0	0	81	47
N.Y. Jets	2	1	0	85	89	Dallas	2	1	0	97	72
Buffalo	1	2	0	74	74	N.Y. Giants	2	1	0	62	47
Miami	1	2	0	103	111	Philadelphia	0	3	0	31	87
Indianapolis	0	3	0	20	87	St Louis	0	3	0	33	66
AFC Central						**NFC Central**					
Cincinnati	2	1	0	80	70	Chicago	3	0	0	79	53
Cleveland	1	2	0	67	91	Minnesota	2	1	0	64	30
Houston	1	2	0	64	53	Detroit	1	2	0	40	65
Pittsburgh	0	3	0	17	82	Tampa Bay	1	2	0	41	74
AFC West						Green Bay	0	3	0	25	80
Denver	3	0	0	92	53	**NFC West**					
Seattle	3	0	0	91	48	Atlanta	3	0	0	101	58
Kansas City	2	1	0	68	50	L.A. Rams	3	0	0	56	30
San Diego	1	2	0	84	78	San Francisco	2	1	0	70	40
L.A. Raiders	0	3	0	51	62	New Orleans	1	2	0	51	67

Outstanding Individual Performances

100 Yards Rushing
Nathan Wonsley (Tampa Bay) 1)-138-55t-2
Eric Dickerson (L.A. Rams) 25-121-14-1
James Brooks (Cincinnati) 14-118-53-0
Joe Morris (N.Y. Giants) 18-110-52-0
Gerald Riggs (Atlanta) 25-109-14-1
Sammy Winder (Denver) 20-104-31-2

100 Yards Pass Receiving
Wesley Walker (N.Y. Jets) 6-194-65t-4
Mark Clayton (Miami) 8-174-42-1
Art Monk (Washington) 7-174-58-0
Stanley Morgan (New England) 7-161-44t-3
Mark Duper (Miami) 7-154-46t-2
Gary Clark (Washington) 6-144-55-1
Hassan Jones (Minnesota) 6-140-55t-2
Ray Butler (Seattle) 3-128-67t-2
Kenny Jackson (Philadelphia) 5-127-38-1
Jerry Rice (San Francisco) 7-120-26-0
Al Toon (N.Y. Jets) 7-111-36-0
Irving Fryar (New England) 6-110-31-0
Mark Bavaro (N.Y. Giants) 6-106-29-0
Jeff Chadwick (Detroit) 5-106-39-0
Tony Hill (Dallas) 4-104-63-1
Dwight Clark (San Francisco) 7-100-29-1

300 Yards Passing
Ken O'Brien (N.Y. Jets) 43-29-479-1-65t-4
Dan Marino (Miami) 50-30-448-2-46t-6
Tony Eason (New England) 45-26-414-0-44t-3
Jay Schroeder (Washington) 36-16-341-0-58-1
Jeff Kemp (San Francisco) 44-29-332-1-29-1
Eric Hipple (Detroit) 46-31-318-2-39-0

WEEK FOUR

American Football Conference
Kansas City 20 at Buffalo 17
New England 20 at Denver 27
New York Jets 26 at Indianapolis 7
Pittsburgh 22 at Houston 16 (OT)
San Diego 13 at Los Angeles Raiders 17

National Football Conference
Atlanta 23 at Tampa Bay 20 (OT)
Dallas 31 at St Louis 7
Green Bay 7 at Minnesota 42
Los Angeles Rams 20 at Philadelphia 34
New Orleans 17 at New York Giants 20

Interconference Games
Chicago 44 at Cincinnati 7
Detroit 21 at Cleveland 24
San Francisco 31 at Miami 16
Seattle 14 at Washington 19

Interconference Play
AFC 4 – NFC 10

Week Four saw both the Rams and Seattle defeated for the first time, while Chicago, Denver and Atlanta remained with Washington as the league's four unbeaten teams.

The Seahawks were outmuscled by a Washington club for whom Steve Cox was at it again, landing a 57-yard field goal which, by now, the reader will have guessed, was the second-shortest of his career – such trivia! Seattle wide receiver Steve Largent caught a pass for the 127th consecutive regular-season game in which he has played (he's missed some along the way), equalling the NFL record held by the retired Harold Carmichael. The Rams were murdered by Philadelphia. After rolling to a 34-0 lead, the Eagles switched off the engine and, to the background of popping corks which celebrated Buddy Ryan's first victory, they freewheeled in by the score of 34-20.

Hitherto, the Bears had been unimpressive, but now, with Jim McMahon returning in fine style after injury – he passed for three touchdowns and ran for another – they hammered Cincinnati by the score of 44-7. Denver used a 24-point second half to get by the Patriots, who'd dominated the opening ex-changes to lead 13-3. The Falcons had an even tougher struggle against Tampa Bay. Trailing the Buccaneers by three points, and at fourth-and-two with little time remaining, Atlanta quarterback Dave Archer completed a desperation 15-yard pass to Sylvester 'Zip Code' Stamps, setting up Mick Luckhurst's game-tying field goal as the clock showed no time left in regulation. In overtime, Luckhurst

obliged with the winning field goal with less than three minutes to go.

If 1985 was the year of the 'Refrigerator', Week Four of 1986 was the day of the 'Ice Cube,' Cleveland's diminutive dual-purpose kick returner, Gerald McNeil. Included in McNeil's 189 total kick return yards was an 84-yard punt return for a touchdown in the Browns' 24-21 win over Detroit.

The Giants were in a little trouble against New Orleans, whom they trailed 17-0 early in the second quarter. But quarterback Phil Simms gradually eased them back and, with the defense putting up the shutters, they ran out 20-17 winners. The Raiders finally won one, beating divisional rival San Diego, despite seeing their quarterback, Marc Wilson, sacked eight times. However, there was no respite for the Dolphins in Miami, where quarterback Dan Marino was intercepted four times, and jeered, in their 31-16 loss to San Francisco.

Below: Bears wide receiver Willie Gault caught seven passes for a career-best 174 yards.

Right: Wide receiver Dokie Williams helped the Raiders to their first win of the campaign.

Outstanding Individual Performances

100 Yards Rushing
Gerald Riggs (Atlanta) 27-129-22-1
George Rogers (Washington) 25-115-24t-2
Curt Warner (Seattle) 16-106-29-1

100 Yards Pass Receiving
Willie Gault (Chicago) 7-174-53t-1
Dokie Williams (L.A. Raiders) 8-143-39-1
Cris Collinsworth (Cincinnati) 6-115-43-0
Steve Jordan (Minnesota) 6-112-30-2
Mark Bavaro (N.Y. Giants) 7-110-26-1
Charlie Brown (Atlanta) 7-110-40-0
Hassan Jones (Minnesota) 6-106-36t-2
Todd Christensen (L.A. Raiders) 8-105-26-0
Art Monk (Washington) 5-103-69-0
Mark Duper (Miami) 7-102-24-0
Tony Nathan (Miami) 10-101-18-0

300 Yards Passing
Marc Wilson (L.A. Raiders) 28-19-314-2-40t-2
Dan Marino (Miami) 46-27-301-4-24-1

STANDINGS

AFC East	W	L	T	PF	PA	NFC East	W	L	T	PF	PA
N.Y. Jets	3	1	0	111	96	Washington	4	0	0	100	61
New England	2	2	0	104	74	Dallas	3	1	0	128	79
Buffalo	1	3	0	91	94	N.Y. Giants	3	1	0	82	64
Miami	1	3	0	119	142	Philadelphia	1	3	0	65	107
Indianapolis	0	4	0	27	113	St Louis	0	4	0	40	97
AFC Central						**NFC Central**					
Cincinnati	2	2	0	87	114	Chicago	4	0	0	123	60
Cleveland	2	2	0	91	112	Minnesota	3	1	0	106	37
Houston	1	3	0	80	75	Detroit	1	3	0	61	89
Pittsburgh	1	3	0	39	98	Tampa Bay	1	3	0	61	97
AFC West						Green Bay	0	4	0	32	122
Denver	4	0	0	119	73	**NFC West**					
Kansas City	3	1	0	88	67	Atlanta	4	0	0	124	78
Seattle	3	1	0	105	67	L.A. Rams	3	1	0	76	64
L.A. Raiders	1	3	0	68	75	San Francisco	3	1	0	101	56
San Diego	1	3	0	97	95	New Orleans	1	3	0	68	87

WEEK FIVE

American Football Conference
Buffalo 13 at New York Jets 14
Cleveland 27 at Pittsburgh 24
Los Angeles Raiders 24 at Kansas City 17
Miami 7 at New England 34
San Diego 7 at Seattle 33

National Football Conference
Minnesota 0 at Chicago 23
New York Giants 13 at St Louis 6
Philadelphia 16 at Atlanta 0
Tampa Bay 20 at Los Angeles Rams 26 (OT)
Washington 14 at New Orleans 6

Interconference Games
Cincinnati 34 v Green Bay 28 (at Milwaukee)
Dallas 14 at Denver 29
Houston 13 at Detroit 24
Indianapolis 14 at San Francisco 35

Interconference Play
AFC 6 – NFC 12

Since taking over from the injured Joe Montana, quarterback Jeff Kemp had done well on caretaker duty, but now he was beginning to spread his wings – the press even had labelled the 49ers' offense, 'Air Kemp'. He combined with wide receiver Jerry Rice for three touchdowns as the 49ers kept the Colts winless on the season. When the Buccaneers meet the Rams, you just know that it will be close, whatever the formline. Their last three encounters had been decided by a total of six points, and though in their Week Five game that cumulative figure was doubled, the six points came in overtime on a touchdown by Eric Dickerson, who became the campaign's first running back to rush for over 200 yards in a game. Wins by both the 49ers and the Rams, coupled with Atlanta's first defeat, produced a three-way tie on top of the NFC West. Atlanta's bubble, though not burst, had developed a slow puncture against Philadelphia, for whom linebacker Garry Cobb registered four quarterback sacks.

Cleveland's Gerald McNeil enjoyed his second big game in consecutive weeks.

Outstanding Individual Performances

100 Yards Rushing
Eric Dickerson (L.A. Rams) 30-207-42t-2
Curt Warner (Seattle) 28-142-21-0
Johnny Hector (N.Y. Jets) 18-117-41-0
George Rogers (Washington) 31-110-11-1
Walter Payton (Chicago) 26-108-41-1
Nathan Wonsley (Tampa Bay) 18-108-59t-1

100 Yards Pass Receiving
Jerry Rice (San Francisco) 6-172-58t-3
Keith Ortego (Chicago) 6-157-58t-1
Ernest Givins (Houston) 5-155-60-0
Floyd Dixon (Atlanta) 8-146-61-0
Stanley Morgan (New England) 6-125-41-1
Byron Franklin (Seattle) 5-118-46t-1
James Lofton (Green Bay) 7-109-24-1
Reginald Langhorne (Cleveland) 4-108-41-0
Mark Duper (Miami) 4-102-45-0
Johnny Hector (N.Y. Jets) 9-100-19-0

300 Yards Passing
Warren Moon (Houston) 38-21-398-3-81t-1

The Raiders were involved in a bad-tempered game with Kansas City – at times it was a brawl. With the Raiders trailing 17-0 and, seemingly, on the way to their fourth loss, hostilities broke out. The after-taste marred what had been yet another heroic re-entry into the fray by veteran quarterback Jim Plunkett, who came on in relief of the injured Marc Wilson and steered the Raiders from 17-7 down to a 24-17 victory. In Seattle's easy win over San Diego, Steve Largent established the new NFL record for consecutive games in which he had caught at least one pass, going one beyond Harold Carmichael's 127. San Diego's Charlie Joiner, who already held the NFL record for career pass receptions, became the all-time leader in career receiving yardage. Denver kept its unbeaten record at the expense of the Cowboys, who struggled in the absence of injured quarterback Danny White.

In the AFC Central, Cleveland broke a sequence when, after sixteen straight losses in Three Rivers Stadium, they came from behind to beat Pittsburgh. Gerald 'Ice Cube' McNeil returned a kickoff 100 yards for a touchdown.

In the AFC East, the Jets needed a touchdown pass from Ken O'Brien to tight end Mickey Shuler, with only 57 seconds remaining, to edge past Buffalo. O'Brien completed fifteen consecutive passes to move alongside the retired Joe Namath in the Jets' record book. However, the Patriots had no trouble at all with Miami, whose lingering demise was a mystery.

The Jets' Johnny Hector gained 100 yards or more in each of rushing and receiving.

STANDINGS					
AFC East	**W**	**L**	**T**	**PF**	**PA**
N.Y. Jets	4	1	0	125	109
New England	3	2	0	138	81
Buffalo	1	4	0	104	108
Miami	1	4	0	126	176
Indianapolis	0	5	0	41	148
AFC Central					
Cincinnati	3	2	0	121	142
Cleveland	3	2	0	118	136
Houston	1	4	0	93	99
Pittsburgh	1	4	0	63	125
AFC West					
Denver	5	0	0	148	87
Seattle	4	1	0	138	74
Kansas City	3	2	0	105	91
L.A. Raiders	2	3	0	92	92
San Diego	1	4	0	104	128
NFC East	**W**	**L**	**T**	**PF**	**PA**
Washington	5	0	0	114	67
N.Y. Giants	4	1	0	95	70
Dallas	3	2	0	142	108
Philadelphia	2	3	0	81	107
St Louis	0	5	0	46	110
NFC Central					
Chicago	5	0	0	146	60
Minnesota	3	2	0	106	60
Detroit	2	3	0	85	102
Tampa Bay	1	4	0	81	123
Green Bay	0	5	0	60	156
NFC West					
Atlanta	4	1	0	124	94
L.A. Rams	4	1	0	102	84
San Francisco	4	1	0	136	70
New Orleans	1	4	0	74	101

WEEK SIX

American Football Conference
Buffalo 14 at Miami 27
Denver 31 at San Diego 14
Kansas City 7 at Cleveland 20
New York Jets 31 at New England 24
Pittsburgh 22 at Cincinnati 24
Seattle 10 at Los Angeles Raiders 14

National Football Conference
Detroit 21 at Green Bay 14
Los Angeles Rams 14 at Atlanta 26
Minnesota 27 at San Francisco 24 (OT)
Philadelphia 3 at New York Giants 35
St Louis 30 at Tampa Bay 19
Washington 6 at Dallas 30

Interconference Games
Chicago 20 at Houston 7
New Orleans 17 at Indianapolis 14

Interconference Play
AFC 6 – NFC 14

With veteran quarterback Danny White out with injury and star running back Tony Dorsett slowed by a sprained knee, the Cowboys used the combination of Steve Pelluer and Herschel Walker to shocking effect against the Redskins. Walker caught six passes for 155 yards and rushed for two touchdowns as Dallas handed Washington its first defeat of the season. With linebacker Lawrence Taylor registering four quarterback sacks, the Giants ended Philadelphia's mini-streak in comprehensive manner and moved into a tie for first place in the NFC East.

The Jets had fast become the AFC team to watch, and reserve running back Johnny Hector was again in prime form as they established a 24-0 halftime lead over New England. But they had to withstand a spirited Patriots comeback before prevailing 31-24. Against Buffalo, Dan Marino quarterbacked the Dolphins out of their slump, though they'd need more than one win to convince their detractors.

Both Chicago and Denver advanced to 6-0, though the manner of the Bears' victory over Houston was less than convincing and head coach Mike Ditka said so – or words to that effect. Denver, on the other hand, dominated the Chargers who, disappointingly after their impressive start to the season, dropped to 1-5. They'd need a miracle now. It was all in a day's work for Raiders quarterback Jim Plunkett, who started in place of the injured Marc Wilson and passed for two touchdowns before the defense took over to protect the lead against Seattle. The Raiders were now at par.

Atlanta running back Gerald Riggs.

Cincinnati used the unorthodox to beat Pittsburgh. Trailing 19-14 in the fourth quarter, on fourth down they lined up in punt formation. But punter Jeff Hayes, who is clearly a frustrated running back, tucked the ball under his arm and ran 61 yards for the go-ahead touchdown. Their win, coupled with Cleveland's third in a row, kept the AFC Central a two-horse race.

There was a turn-up in the NFC West, where the Falcons defied analysis by outrushing the Rams. The combination of 141 yards from running back Gerald Riggs, four field goals from Mick Luckhurst and tough defense against the run, was all too much for the Rams. And the Falcons were helped by the Vikings, who were emerging as possible playoff contenders. Their overtime victory over San Francisco kept them in touch with Chicago in the NFC Central and left Atlanta in control in the West.

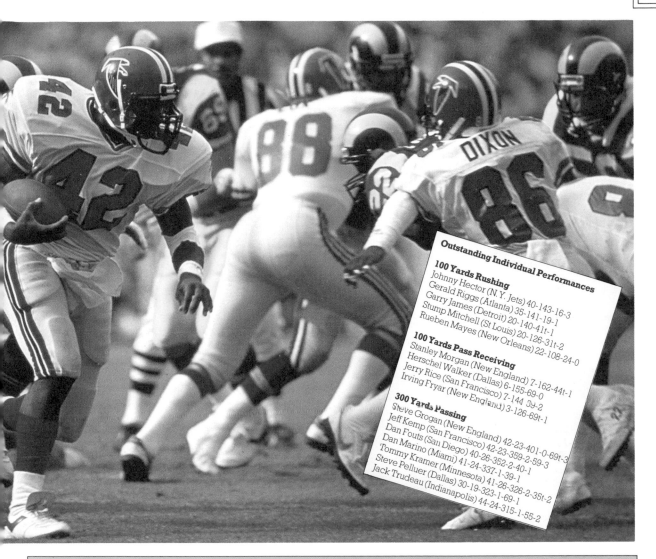

Outstanding Individual Performances

100 Yards Rushing
Johnny Hector (N.Y. Jets) 40-143-16-3
Gerald Riggs (Atlanta) 35-141-19-1
Garry James (Detroit) 20-140-41t-1
Stump Mitchell (St Louis) 20-126-31t-2
Rueben Mayes (New Orleans) 22-108-24-0

100 Yards Pass Receiving
Stanley Morgan (New England) 7-162-44t-1
Herschel Walker (Dallas) 6-155-69-0
Jerry Rice (San Francisco) 7-144-39-2
Irving Fryar (New England) 3-126-69t-1

300 Yards Passing
Steve Grogan (New England) 42-23-401-0-69t-3
Jeff Kemp (San Francisco) 42-23-359-2-59-3
Dan Fouts (San Diego) 40-26-352-2-40-1
Dan Marino (Miami) 41-24-337-1-39-1
Tommy Kramer (Minnesota) 41-26-326-2-35t-2
Steve Pelluer (Dallas) 30-19-323-1-69-1
Jack Trudeau (Indianapolis) 44-24-315-1-55-2

STANDINGS

AFC East	W	L	T	PF	PA	NFC East	W	L	T	PF	PA
N.Y. Jets	5	1	0	156	133	N.Y. Giants	5	1	0	130	73
New England	3	3	0	162	112	Washington	5	1	0	120	97
Miami	2	4	0	153	190	Dallas	4	2	0	172	114
Buffalo	1	5	0	118	135	Philadelphia	2	4	0	84	142
Indianapolis	0	6	0	55	165	St Louis	1	5	0	76	129
AFC Central						**NFC Central**					
Cincinnati	4	2	0	145	164	Chicago	6	0	0	166	67
Cleveland	4	2	0	138	143	Minnesota	4	2	0	133	84
Houston	1	5	0	100	119	Detroit	3	3	0	106	116
Pittsburgh	1	5	0	85	149	Tampa Bay	1	5	0	100	153
AFC West						Green Bay	0	6	0	74	177
Denver	6	0	0	179	101	**NFC West**					
Seattle	4	2	0	148	88	Atlanta	5	1	0	150	108
Kansas City	3	3	0	112	111	L.A. Rams	4	2	0	116	110
L.A. Raiders	3	3	0	106	102	San Francisco	4	2	0	160	97
San Diego	1	5	0	118	159	New Orleans	2	4	0	91	115

WEEK SEVEN

American Football Conference
Denver 10 at New York Jets 22
Houston 28 at Cincinnati 31
Indianapolis 13 at Buffalo 24
Los Angeles Raiders 30 at Miami 28
New England 34 at Pittsburgh 0
San Diego 41 at Kansas City 42

National Football Conference
Chicago 7 at Minnesota 23
Dallas 17 at Philadelphia 14
Detroit 10 at Los Angeles Rams 14
St Louis 21 at Washington 28
San Francisco 10 at Atlanta 10 (OT)
Tampa Bay 7 at New Orleans 38

Interconference Games
Green Bay 17 at Cleveland 14
New York Giants 12 at Seattle 17

Interconference Play
AFC 7 – NFC 15

'And then there was none,' was the final comment at the end of Week Seven, when both Chicago and Denver suffered their first defeats. While the absence of quarterback Jim McMahon was a mitigating factor, there was nothing lucky about Minnesota's victory over Chicago. McMahon's replacement, Steve Fuller, was sacked seven times whereas, for the Vikings, quarterback Tommy Kramer passed sweetly for 239 yards and two touchdowns. Before this game, such had been the Bears' dominance that not since Week Fifteen, 1984, and before then, Week Fourteen, 1983, had they lost to domestic opponents. Phil Simms was another harassed quarterback. He, too, had his collar felt seven times, four times by defensive end Jacob Green, as the Seahawks won a physical battle with the Giants. Eagles quarterbacks Matt Cavanaugh and Randall Cunningham were the object of downright victimisation, going down under sacks a combined total of ten times as the Cowboys won 17-14 and took closer order in the NFC East.

The Jets used two quarterbacks, in turn, Pat Ryan and Ken O'Brien, neither of whom was fully fit, in establishing a game-winning lead over Denver. Before Week Seven, the Broncos had looked home free, at least for some kind of entry qualification for the playoffs. But they could now hear footsteps from Seattle, and both Kansas City and the Raiders had moved within shouting distance following victories over San Diego and Miami respectively. The Chiefs' defense returned four turnovers directly for touchdowns, pride of place going to safety Lloyd Burruss, who returned two of his three interceptions 56 and 47 yards for scores. In the Raiders' win, Marcus Allen rushed for 96 yards and scored three touchdowns.

Cincinnati running back James Brooks rounded off a fine performance, rushing 21 yards for the winning touchdown with 43 seconds remaining, to sink the Oilers. The victory, combined with Cleveland's surprise loss to Green Bay, in what was the Packers' first win of the campaign, took the Bengals one game clear in the AFC Central.

Beating Detroit in a dour affair, the Rams gained half a game on the division-leading Falcons, who battled to a 10-10 tie with San Francisco. The Saints did a number on Tampa Bay and were not, by any means, out of contention. Moreover, in rookie running back Rueben Mayes, who rushed for 172 yards and scored two touchdowns, they could now look to a genuine offensive weapon on which to base their title hopes.

Left: Defensive end Jacob Green was in rampaging form against the Giants.
Right: Rookie running back Rueben Mayes.
Above: Lloyd Burruss, scorer of two touchdowns on interception returns.

STANDINGS

AFC East	W	L	T	PF	PA
N.Y. Jets	6	1	0	178	143
New England	4	3	0	196	112
Buffalo	2	5	0	142	148
Miami	2	5	0	181	220
Indianapolis	0	7	0	68	189
AFC Central					
Cincinnati	5	2	0	176	192
Cleveland	4	3	0	152	160
Houston	1	6	0	128	150
Pittsburgh	1	6	0	85	183
AFC West					
Denver	6	1	0	189	123
Seattle	5	2	0	165	100
Kansas City	4	3	0	154	152
L.A. Raiders	4	3	0	136	130
San Diego	1	6	0	159	201

NFC East	W	L	T	PF	PA
Washington	6	1	0	148	118
Dallas	5	2	0	189	128
N.Y. Giants	5	2	0	142	90
Philadelphia	2	5	0	98	159
St Louis	1	6	0	97	157
NFC Central					
Chicago	6	1	0	173	90
Minnesota	5	2	0	156	91
Detroit	3	4	0	116	130
Green Bay	1	6	0	91	191
Tampa Bay	1	6	0	107	191
NFC West					
Atlanta	5	1	1	160	118
L.A. Rams	5	2	0	130	120
San Francisco	4	2	1	170	107
New Orleans	3	4	0	129	122

Outstanding Individual Performances

100 Yards Rushing
Rueben Mayes (New Orleans) 24-172-34-2
James Brooks (Cincinnati) 18-133-24t-2
Eric Dickerson (L.A. Rams) 24-130-27-1
George Rogers (Washington) 30-118-16-1
Joe Morris (N.Y. Giants) 24-116-16-0

100 Yards Pass Receiving
Mark Clayton (Miami) 4-109-68t-1
Mark Duper (Miami) 5-101-44-0

300 Yards Passing
Eric Hipple (Detroit) 50-31-316-2-27-1

WEEK EIGHT

American Football Conference
Cincinnati 9 at Pittsburgh 30
Los Angeles Raiders 28 at Houston 17
Miami 17 at Indianapolis 13
New England 23 at Buffalo 3
Seattle 13 at Denver 20

National Football Conference
Atlanta 7 at Los Angeles Rams 14
Detroit 7 at Chicago 13
St Louis 6 at Dallas 37
San Francisco 31 v Green Bay 17 (at Milwaukee)
Washington 20 at New York Giants 27

Interconference Games
Cleveland 23 at Minnesota 20
New Orleans 23 at New York Jets 28
San Diego 7 at Philadelphia 23
Tampa Bay 20 at Kansas City 27

Interconference Play
AFC 10 – NFC 16

The Rams used Eric Dickerson's 170 yards rushing and his 15-yard touchdown pass to tight end David Hill to win the showdown in the NFC West. As it turned out, Atlanta's loss would be the first of five in a row as they slid gently out of contention. The 49ers needed three big defensive plays to conquer Green Bay, whom they trailed 14-0 early in the second quarter. Safety Ronnie Lott returned his first interception 18 yards to set up a touchdown, then returned his second interception 55 yards for a score, and cornerback Tory Nixon put the result beyond doubt when he returned an interception 88 yards for a touchdown.

Denver was another club to assert its authority over a close divisional rival, their victory marking the first of a four-game losing streak for Seattle. Seizing the opportunity, the Raiders won their fifth straight game to move into a tie for second place with Seattle and Kansas City, the latter also who won.

'Enough is enough,' the Steelers may have felt before dismissing Cincinnati by the score of 30-9. With running backs Earnest Jackson and Walter Abercrombie rushing for 132 and 109 yards respectively, it was more like the Steelers of old. Cleveland scored thirteen unanswered points in the fourth quarter as they rallied for a good victory over Minnesota. The Browns' reward was a tie with Cincinnati for first place in the AFC Central.

At the end of Week Eight it was all square at the top of the NFC East, with the big three tied at 6-2. The Giants' clash with Washington featured the rushing of Joe Morris against the passing of Washington quarterback Jay Schroeder to wide receiver Gary Clark, the latter who caught eleven passes for a club-record 241 yards. After trailing 20-3, the Redskins pulled back to 20-20, but Morris had the final say, rushing 13 yards for the winning touchdown with 1:38 remaining. With Herschel Walker logging his first 100-yards-rushing day in the NFL, Dallas had no trouble beating St Louis.

The Jets survived a 17-point, fourth-quarter comeback by New Orleans to register their best start in the club's history. New England kept pace by beating Buffalo, and Miami had just too much for the Colts. Even so, their win was preserved only by a crucial tackle by linebacker John Offerdahl on Colts running back Owen Gill at the Miami 14-yard line with 22 seconds remaining.

Chicago laboured against Detroit, but a win is a win, and it re-established their two-game lead in the NFC Central.

Below: 49ers cornerback Tory Nixon settles the issue against Green Bay.
Right: Redskins wide receiver Gary Clark savaged the Giants' defense.

STANDINGS

AFC East	W	L	T	PF	PA
N.Y. Jets	7	1	0	206	166
New England	5	3	0	219	115
Miami	3	5	0	198	233
Buffalo	2	6	0	145	171
Indianapolis	0	8	0	81	206
AFC Central					
Cincinnati	5	3	0	185	222
Cleveland	5	3	0	175	180
Pittsburgh	2	6	0	115	192
Houston	1	7	0	145	178
AFC West					
Denver	7	1	0	209	136
Kansas City	5	3	0	181	172
L.A. Raiders	5	3	0	164	147
Seattle	5	3	0	178	120
San Diego	1	7	0	166	224

NFC East	W	L	T	PF	PA
Dallas	6	2	0	226	134
N.Y. Giants	6	2	0	169	110
Washington	6	2	0	168	145
Philadelphia	3	5	0	121	166
St Louis	1	7	0	103	194
NFC Central					
Chicago	7	1	0	186	97
Minnesota	5	3	0	170	114
Detroit	3	5	0	123	143
Green Bay	1	7	0	108	222
Tampa Bay	1	7	0	127	218
NFC West					
L.A. Rams	6	2	0	144	127
Atlanta	5	2	1	167	132
San Francisco	5	2	1	201	124
New Orleans	3	5	0	152	150

Outstanding Individual Performances

100 Yards Rushing
Joe Morris (N.Y. Giants) 31-181-34-2
Eric Dickerson (L.A. Rams) 30-170-15-0
Curt Warner (Seattle) 21-139-14-0
Earnest Jackson (Pittsburgh) 21-132-31-1
Herschel Walker (Dallas) 26-120-19t-2
Darrin Nelson (Minnesota) 22-118-25-1
James Wilder (Tampa Bay) 25-110-24-1
Walter Abercrombie (Pittsburgh) 22-109-21-0
Curtis Dickey (Cleveland) 19-106-17t-1

100 Yards Pass Receiving
Gary Clark (Washington) 11-241-49-1
Drew Hill (Houston) 7-138-46-0
Mike Sherrard (Dallas) 5-111-40-1
Al Toon (N.Y. Jets) 6-101-62t-3

300 Yards Passing
Jay Schroeder (Washington) 40-22-420-2-71-1
Randy Wright (Green Bay) 54-30-328-3-48-1
John Elway (Denver) 32-18-321-1-47-1
Warren Moon (Houston) 46-18-304-4-46-0

WEEK NINE

American Football Conference
Cleveland 24 at Indianapolis 9
Denver 21 at Los Angeles Raiders 10
Houston 7 at Miami 28
Kansas City 24 at San Diego 23
New York Jets 38 at Seattle 7

National Football Conference
Dallas 14 at New York Giants 17
Los Angeles Rams 20 at Chicago 17
Minnesota 38 at Washington 44 (OT)
Philadelphia 10 at St Louis 13
San Francisco 10 at New Orleans 23

Interconference Games
Atlanta 17 at New England 25
Buffalo 28 at Tampa Bay 34
Cincinnati 24 at Detroit 17
Green Bay 3 at Pittsburgh 27

Interconference Play
AFC 13 – NFC 17

Pride of place on Week Nine went to the Rams, who travelled to Soldier Field and beat the Bears 20-17. Eric Dickerson rushed for 111 yards, as might be expected. It was also in character when the Rams converted two turnovers into points, with Jerry Gray picking off a pass to set up the first field goal and LeRoy Irvin returning a fumble 22 yards for a touchdown. But it was shocking when quarterback Steve Dils whiffed a 65-yard touchdown pass to wide receiver Ron Brown to tie the game at 17-17 in the third quarter. Four seconds remained when Mike Lansford kicked the 50-yard game-winning field goal. The Rams' victory was doubly satisfying follow-ing New Orleans' upset win over San Francisco.

The Jets continued to roll in the most impressive manner, as quarterback Ken O'Brien bombed the Seahawks for 431 yards and four touchdowns in the Kingdome. New England stayed within two games, Tony Franklin kicking four field goals and Irving Fryar returning a punt 59 yards for a touchdown in the Pats' 25-17 win over Atlanta.

In the Los Angeles Coliseum, Denver halted the Raiders' run of five consecutive victories, inter-cepting four Marc Wilson passes and recovering two Raiders fumbles in a 21-10 win. Kansas City stayed in touch after slipping past San Diego and, in so doing, spoiled the debut of Chargers' new head coach Al Saunders, who had taken over from Don Coryell earlier in the week.

In the NFC East, the Giants gained revenge for their Week One loss to Dallas. For the second week in a row, running back Joe Morris rushed for 181 yards, but the Cowboys went down only after an heroic struggle. Starting quarterback Danny White broke his right wrist but his substitute, Steve Pelluer, passed for 339 yards, 148 of them to Herschel Walker, and the Cowboys had every chance to win after, apparently, driving into a possible touchdown-scoring position late in the game. But a series of infringements took them out of sensible range, and Rafael Septien never was likely to succeed with his last-gasp 63-yard field goal attempt. Washington outlasted Minnesota, and their own lapses – Max Zendejas missed three extra point attempts – in a scoring spectacular which was decided when Gary Clark caught a 38-yard touchdown pass, 1:46 into overtime. In a losing cause, Vikings quarterback Tommy Kramer passed for a single-game club-record 490 yards.

STANDINGS

AFC East	W	L	T	PF	PA	NFC East	W	L	T	PF	PA
N.Y. Jets	8	1	0	244	173	N.Y. Giants	7	2	0	186	124
New England	6	3	0	244	132	Washington	7	2	0	212	183
Miami	4	5	0	336	240	Dallas	6	3	0	240	151
Buffalo	2	7	0	173	205	Philadelphia	3	6	0	131	179
Indianapolis	0	9	0	90	230	St Louis	2	7	0	116	204
AFC Central						**NFC Central**					
Cincinnati	6	3	0	209	239	Chicago	7	2	0	203	117
Cleveland	6	3	0	199	189	Minnesota	5	4	0	214	158
Pittsburgh	3	6	0	142	195	Detroit	3	6	0	140	167
Houston	1	8	0	152	206	Tampa Bay	2	7	0	161	246
AFC West						Green Bay	1	8	0	111	249
Denver	8	1	0	230	146	**NFC West**					
Kansas City	6	3	0	205	195	L.A. Rams	7	2	0	164	144
L.A. Raiders	5	4	0	174	168	Atlanta	5	3	1	184	157
Seattle	5	4	0	185	158	San Francisco	5	3	1	211	147
San Diego	1	8	0	189	248	New Orleans	4	5	0	175	160

*Jets quarterback Ken O'Brien, flawless against Seattle.
Right: Vikings quarterback Tommy Kramer was
outstanding in defeat against Washington.*

Outstanding Individual Performances

100 Yards Rushing
Joe Morris (N.Y. Giants) 29-181-28-2
Rueben Mayes (New Orleans) 28-128-27t-2
James Brooks (Cincinnati) 15-120-55-0
Eric Dickerson (L.A. Rams) 29-111-12-0
Gary Anderson (San Diego) 25-100-13-0

100 Yards Pass Receiving
Al Toon (N.Y. Jets) 9-195-50t-2
Steve Jordan (Minnesota) 6-179-68t-1
Wesley Walker (N.Y. Jets) 6-161-83t-1
Leo Lewis (Minnesota) 3-159-76t-2
Todd Christensen (L.A. Raiders) 11-158-35-0
Herschel Walker (Dallas) 9-148-44-0
Gary Clark (Washington) 6-123-38t-1
Pete Metzelaars (Buffalo) 7-113-44t-2
Mark Duper (Miami) 2-110-85t-1
Steve Largent (Seattle) 7-108-30-0
Art Monk (Washington) 6-102-39-1
Jeff Chadwick (Detroit) 6-100-32-0

300 Yards Passing
Tommy Kramer (Minnesota) 35-20-490-1-76t-4
Ken O'Brien (N.Y. Jets) 32-26-431-0-83t-4
Jay Schroeder (Washington) 47-24-378-1-44-2
Marc Wilson (L.A. Raiders) 47-25-367-4-43-1
Jim Kelly (Buffalo) 39-29-342-0-47-3
Steve Pelluer (Dallas) 38-28-339-0-44-1
Mike Moroski (San Francisco) 40-23-332-2-52-1

WEEK TEN

American Football Conference
Cincinnati 28 at Houston 32
Miami 16 at Cleveland 26
New England 30 at Indianapolis 21
Pittsburgh 12 at Buffalo 16
San Diego 9 at Denver 3
Seattle 7 at Kansas City 27

National Football Conference
Chicago 23 at Tampa Bay 3
Los Angeles Rams 0 at New Orleans 6
Minnesota 24 at Detroit 10
New York Giants 17 at Philadelphia 14
St Louis 17 at San Francisco 43
Washington 16 at Green Bay 7

Interconference Games
Los Angeles Raiders 17 at Dallas 13
New York Jets 28 at Atlanta 14

Interconference Play
AFC 15 – NFC 17

The astonishing return of a quarterback whose career was thought to be over, yet another salvage operation by an ageing veteran quarterback, and three shocking upsets, all vied for the spotlight on Week Ten.

Let's give the headline to Joe Montana, who returned from major back surgery following an injury on Week One, to destroy the Cardinals with a fusillade of passes. Completing 13 of 19 attempts, Montana threw touchdown passes of 45, 40 and 44 yards to wide receiver Jerry Rice as the 49ers moved back into the reckoning in the NFC West. They were helped by the Saints, who held the Rams scoreless in a magnificent defensive struggle in New Orleans – upset number one.

You might just expect Denver, an 8-1 team, to hold San Diego to nine points, but who could ever imagine San Diego, a 1-8 team, holding Denver to only three? That was upset number two, and Denver's loss became all the more significant following wins by both Kansas City and the Raiders. Jim Plunkett was the veteran on salvage duty. In their game against Dallas, the Raiders were on the

STANDINGS

AFC East	W	L	T	PF	PA
N.Y. Jets	9	1	0	272	187
New England	7	3	0	274	153
Miami	4	6	0	242	266
Buffalo	3	7	0	189	217
Indianapolis	0	10	0	111	260
AFC Central					
Cleveland	7	3	0	225	205
Cincinnati	6	4	0	237	271
Pittsburgh	3	7	0	154	211
Houston	2	8	0	184	234
AFC West					
Denver	8	2	0	233	155
Kansas City	7	3	0	232	202
L.A. Raiders	6	4	0	191	181
Seattle	5	5	0	192	185
San Diego	2	8	0	198	251
NFC East	**W**	**L**	**T**	**PF**	**PA**
N.Y. Giants	8	2	0	203	138
Washington	8	2	0	228	190
Dallas	6	4	0	253	168
Philadelphia	3	7	0	145	196
St Louis	2	8	0	133	247
NFC Central					
Chicago	8	3	0	220	120
Minnesota	6	4	0	238	168
Detroit	3	7	0	150	191
Tampa Bay	2	8	0	164	269
Green Bay	1	9	0	118	265
NFC West					
L.A. Rams	7	3	0	164	150
San Francisco	6	3	1	254	164
Atlanta	5	4	1	198	185
New Orleans	5	5	0	181	160

point of being overwhelmed several times in the first half alone. But the Cowboys could not capitalise on almost total domination, and when Plunkett began to work his magic, completing touchdown passes of 20 and 40 yards to Dokie Williams, the Cowboys fell away. Steady victories by the Giants and Washington left Dallas trailing by two games in the NFC East.

Despite being without three key defensive players, the Jets machine looked unstoppable as yet another victim was put to the sword. On Week Five, quarterback Ken O'Brien had equalled Joe Namath's club record of fifteen consecutive pass completions, and now, against the sagging Falcons, he went two better and, for good measure, threw three touchdown passes. New England could only keep on winning and hope for the best. In their game against the Colts, they trailed by eleven points before forging ahead with a 27-point burst.

Upset number three saw Houston end an eight-game barren stretch in outgunning Cincinnati. The Bengals' loss opened the door for Cleveland, and they took advantage at the expense of Miami. Cleveland quarterback Bernie Kosar had the curious distinction of becoming the first quarterback in NFL history to pass for 400 or more yards in a game without throwing for a touchdown.

Left: Joe Cribbs on the way to his first 100-yards-rushing game as a 49ers player.
Above: J.T. Smith caught ten passes for a career-best 154 yards.

Outstanding Individual Performances

100 Yards Rushing
Walter Payton (Chicago) 20-139-26-0
Joe Morris (N.Y. Giants) 27-111-19-2
Robb Riddick (Buffalo) 25-108-26-1
Joe Cribbs (San Francisco) 21-105-19-1
Tony Dorsett (Dallas) 22-101-15-1

100 Yards Pass Receiving
Drew Hill (Houston) 10-185-45-0
Jerry Rice (San Francisco) 4-156-45t-3
J.T. Smith (St Louis) 10-154-24t-2
Eddie Brown (Cincinnati) 9-132-26-0
Willie Gault (Chicago) 4-116-50-1
Charlie Brown (Atlanta) 6-112-42-0
Anthony Carter (Minnesota) 5-111-49-1
Arthur Cox (Atlanta) 4-108-49-1
Dokie Williams (L.A. Raiders) 5-107-40t-2

300 Yards Passing
Bernie Kosar (Cleveland) 50-32-401-0-44-0
David Archer (Atlanta) 36-21-350-1-49-2
Ken O'Brien (N.Y. Jets) 33-26-322-0-59t-3
Warren Moon (Houston) 44-25-310-0-45-1

WEEK ELEVEN

American Football Conference
Cleveland 14 at Los Angeles Raiders 27
Houston 10 at Pittsburgh 21
Indianapolis 16 at New York Jets 31
Kansas City 17 at Denver 38
Miami 34 at Buffalo 24
Seattle 7 at Cincinnati 34

National Football Conference
Chicago 13 at Atlanta 10
Detroit 13 at Philadelphia 11
New Orleans 16 at St Louis 7
New York Giants 22 at Minnesota 20
San Francisco 6 at Washington 14
Tampa Bay 7 v Green Bay 31 (at Milwaukee)

Interconference Games
Dallas 24 at San Diego 21
New England 30 at Los Angeles Rams 28

Interconference Play
AFC 16 – NFC 18

At the end of Week Eleven, in four of the NFL's six divisions the front runners had consolidated. In the AFC Central, Cleveland and Cincinnati were locked in a first-place tie for the sixth time in the season, and in the NFC West there was a new threat – maybe.

Quite suddenly, New Orleans, the only club in the NFL which had never had a net winning season, emerged as a contender. Rueben Mayes rushed for 131 yards and Morten Andersen kicked three field goals, while the Saints' defense held the Cardinals to just one touchdown, in the 16-7 victory which left them just one game out of a share of the division lead. Trailing New England 13-0 and with starting quarterback Steve Dils ineffective, the Rams had introduced their new signing, rookie quarterback Jim Everett. And for a time it looked like a master stroke, as he passed for three touchdowns and engineered a fourth to take the Rams into a 28 16 lead. But they were thwarted by two touchdown passes from Patriots quarterback Tony Eason to wide receiver Irving Fryar, the last coming on a 'Hail Mary' pass with no time remaining. Against Washington, San Francisco did everything but win, outgaining the Redskins by 501 yards to 266 and yet contributing mightily to their own downfall with a club-record 15 penalties. Following quickly on the heels of Bernie Kosar, Joe Montana became the second player in NFL history to pass for 400 or more yards without throwing for a touchdown.

Despite allowing eleven quarterback sacks, five by Chargers rookie Leslie O'Neal, Dallas came from behind to beat San Diego 24-21. The Giants, too, were involved in a close one, prevailing over Minnesota on Raul Allegre's fifth field goal of the game with only 12 seconds remaining. Minnesota's loss left the Bears, who won, needing no more than a gentle stroll to retain their NFC Central division title.

In the AFC West, Denver regrouped to bring Kansas City's four-game winning streak to an end, and Jim Plunkett, newly installed as the Raiders' starter, threw three touchdown passes to send the Cleveland Browns home somewhat chastened.

In the AFC East, the Jets moved serenely past the Colts, but their victory was soured by the loss of defensive end Mark Gastineau. Freeman McNeil had rushed for 104 yards and, once again, they'd ridden the golden arm of Ken O'Brien, who had passed to wide receiver Wesley Walker for three touchdowns. Little could anyone have guessed that the Jets would go winless for the remainder of the regular season.

Outstanding Individual Performances

100 Yards Rushing
Rueben Mayes (New Orleans) 25-131-19-0
Randall Cunningham (Philadelphia) 14-113-20-0
Freeman McNeil (N.Y. Jets) 18-104-40-0
George Rogers (Washington) 24-104-18-1
Eric Dickerson (L.A. Rams) 23-102-9-0

100 Yards Pass Receiving
Jerry Rice (San Francisco) 12-204-39-0
Bill Brooks (Indianapolis) 9-177-48t-1
Ernest Givins (Houston) 8-156-33t-1
Gerald Carter (Tampa Bay) 7-143-46-1
Jeff Chadwick (Detroit) 5-139-72t-1
Henry Ellard (L.A. Rams) 8-129-34t-2
Stanley Morgan (New England) 7-118-28-0
Mike Sherrard (Dallas) 4-115-68t-1
Dokie Williams (L.A. Raiders) 3-113-46t-2
Wesley Walker (N.Y. Jets) 5-110-47-3
Mark Duper (Miami) 7-109-27t-1
J.T. Smith (St Louis) 8-106-23-0
Steve Largent (Seattle) 7-102-28-0

300 Yards Passing
Joe Montana (San Francisco) 60-33-441-3-42-0
Dan Marino (Miami) 54-39-404-0-39-4
Tony Eason (New England) 52-36-375-2-28-2
Jack Trudeau (Indianapolis) 57-27-359-4-48t-1
Boomer Esiason (Cincinnati) 33-22-334-1-57-1
Phil Simms (N.Y. Giants) 38-25-310-2-25t-1

STANDINGS

AFC East	W	L	T	PF	PA
N.Y. Jets	10	1	0	303	203
New England	8	3	0	304	181
Miami	5	6	0	276	290
Buffalo	3	8	0	213	251
Indianapolis	0	11	0	127	291
AFC Central					
Cincinnati	7	4	0	271	278
Cleveland	7	4	0	239	232
Pittsburgh	4	7	0	175	221
Houston	2	9	0	194	255
AFC West					
Denver	9	2	0	271	172
Kansas City	7	4	0	249	240
L.A. Raiders	7	4	0	218	195
Seattle	5	6	0	199	219
San Diego	2	9	0	219	275

NFC East	W	L	T	PF	PA
N.Y. Giants	9	2	0	225	158
Washington	9	2	0	242	196
Dallas	7	4	0	377	189
Philadelphia	3	8	0	156	209
St Louis	2	9	0	140	263
NFC Central					
Chicago	9	2	0	239	130
Minnesota	6	5	0	258	190
Detroit	4	7	0	163	202
Green Bay	2	9	0	149	272
Tampa Bay	2	9	0	171	300
NFC West					
L.A. Rams	7	4	0	192	180
San Francisco	6	4	1	260	178
New Orleans	6	5	0	197	167
Atlanta	5	5	1	208	198

Left: Randall Cunningham.
Above: The Colts' Bill Brooks emerged as a big-play wide receiver.

WEEK TWELVE

American Football Conference
Buffalo 19 at New England 22
Indianapolis 17 at Houston 31
Los Angeles Raiders 37 at San Diego 31 (OT)
New York Jets 3 at Miami 45
Pittsburgh 31 at Cleveland 37 (OT)

National Football Conference
Atlanta 0 at San Francisco 20
Dallas 14 at Washington 41
Detroit 38 at Tampa Bay 17
Green Bay 10 at Chicago 12
New Orleans 13 at Los Angeles Rams 26

Interconference Games
Denver 16 at New York Giants 19
Kansas City 14 at St Louis 23
Minnesota 20 at Cincinnati 24
Philadelphia 20 at Seattle 24

Interconference Play
AFC 18 – NFC 20

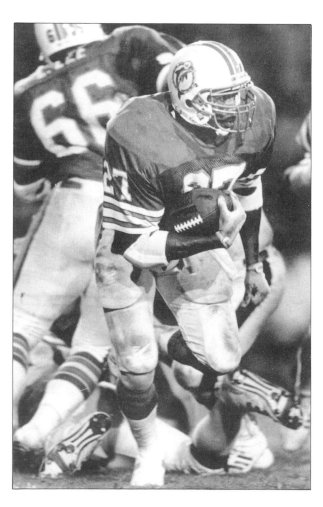

The Giants extended their winning streak to five but they had to fight all the way against a Denver club which gained strength as the game wore on. Denver looked the likely winner when running back Sammy Winder tied the scores with two minutes left. However, quarterback Phil Simms found his touch and swiftly drove the Giants downfield to set up the winning field goal, Raul Allegre's fourth of the game, which came with just six seconds remaining. Washington had no bother with Dallas, against whom they gained revenge for their defeat on Week Six.

The Raiders were involved in a typical shootout with San Diego. Having eased to a 31-10 lead, they were helpless to stop a Mark Herrmann-inspired rally which saw the Chargers draw level with a minute remaining. 8:33 into overtime, Marcus Allen saved their blushes with a 28-yard touchdown run. Unlikely as it may have seemed after Week Three, the Raiders were now only one game off the lead in the AFC West.

New England was another club to draw within one game of the division lead, though they had trouble overcoming the Bills, who rallied for nineteen unanswered points after trailing 15-0, late in the first half. Only just in time did Tony Eason put together a drive, his winning touchdown pass to rookie tight end Greg Baty coming with 1:40 remaining. The Patriots' good news came on Monday evening, when Miami unleashed its pent-up fury in a lambasting of the injury-ridden Jets. For the second time in the campaign against the Jets, Dan Marino went wild, but this time the combined efforts of Ken O'Brien and Pat Ryan could generate only Pat Leahy's field goal in response.

Cleveland was involved in a see-saw battle with Pittsburgh, who drew level at 31-31 on Gary Anderson's 40-yard field goal with seven seconds remaining in regulation time. In the extra period, Browns quarterback Bernie Kosar topped up a career single-game best, taking his passing yardage to 414 with the game-winning 36-yard touchdown throw to wide receiver Webster Slaughter. The Bengals outlasted Minnesota to stay level with Cleveland on top of the AFC Central. So what's new?

In the NFC West, the Rams halted the Saints' charge and San Francisco pushed Atlanta deeper into trouble. Speaking of trouble, Green Bay nose tackle Charles Martin bought plenty of that when he dumped Bears quarterback Jim McMahon, long after the ball had gone. It was a sober reminder of pro football's bad old days and, sadly, though not necessarily because of the late tackle, McMahon went out for the season.

Lorenzo Hampton logged Miami's first 100-yards-rushing performance in their last 42 games.

Todd Christensen.

Below: Cincinnati's Tim McGee.

Outstanding Individual Performances

100 Yards Rushing
Lorenzo Hampton (Miami) 19-148-54t-2
James Wilder (Tampa Bay) 24-130-23-0
Eric Dickerson (L.A. Rams) 27-116-27-1
Kevin Mack (Cleveland) 24-106-17-1
Joe Morris (N.Y. Giants) 23-106-24-0
Roger Craig (San Francisco) 17-101-25-0

100 Yards Pass Receiving
Todd Christensen (L.A. Raiders) 11-173-28-1
Gary Clark (Washington) 8-152-53-1
Webster Slaughter (Cleveland) 6-134-36t-1
Gary Anderson (San Diego) 7-113-26-0
Bill Brooks (Indianapolis) 7-105-37t-2
Ed West (Green Bay) 5-103-46t-1
Ernest Givins (Houston) 7-102-28-0

300 Yards Passing
Bernie Kosar (Cleveland) 46-28-414-1-36t-2
Jim Plunkett (L.A. Raiders) 40-23-348-1-51-2
John Elway (Denver) 47-29-336-2-31-0
Jay Schroeder (Washington) 31-16-325-1-71t-2

STANDINGS

AFC East	W	L	T	PF	PA
N.Y. Jets	10	2	0	306	248
New England	9	3	0	326	200
Miami	6	6	0	321	303
Buffalo	3	9	0	232	273
Indianapolis	0	12	0	144	322
AFC Central					
Cincinnati	8	4	0	295	298
Cleveland	8	4	0	276	263
Pittsburgh	4	8	0	206	258
Houston	3	9	0	225	272
AFC West					
Denver	9	3	0	287	191
L.A. Raiders	8	4	0	255	226
Kansas City	7	5	0	263	263
Seattle	6	6	0	223	239
San Diego	2	10	0	250	312

NFC East	W	L	T	PF	PA
N.Y. Giants	10	2	0	244	174
Washington	10	2	0	283	210
Dallas	7	5	0	291	230
Philadelphia	3	9	0	176	233
St Louis	3	9	0	163	277
NFC Central					
Chicago	10	2	0	251	140
Minnesota	6	6	0	278	214
Detroit	5	7	0	201	219
Green Bay	2	10	0	159	284
Tampa Bay	2	10	0	188	338
NFC West					
L.A. Rams	8	4	0	218	193
San Francisco	7	4	1	280	178
New Orleans	6	6	0	210	193
Atlanta	5	6	1	208	218

WEEK THIRTEEN

American Football Conference
Buffalo 17 at Kansas City 14
Cincinnati 28 at Denver 34
Houston 10 at Cleveland 13 (OT)
San Diego 17 at Indianapolis 3

National Football Conference
Green Bay 44 at Detroit 40
New York Giants 21 at San Francisco 17
Tampa Bay 13 at Minnesota 45
Washington 20 at St Louis 17

Interconference Games
Atlanta 20 at Miami 14
Los Angeles Rams 17 at New York Jets 3
New England 21 at New Orleans 20
Philadelphia 33 at Los Angeles Raiders 27 (OT)
Pittsburgh 10 at Chicago 13 (OT)
Seattle 31 at Dallas 14

Interconference Play
AFC 20 – NFC 24

It's around Week Thirteen when serious projections can be made - who needs to do what to make the playoffs and all that sort of thing. One thing for certain, the Bears clinched the title in the NFC Central, though they were less than convincing in a 13-10 overtime victory against Pittsburgh. Both the Giants and Washington, each of whom had narrow victories, also qualified for at least a wild card spot. Washington survived a few hairy moments against a fired-up St Louis, and they came through on a Max Zendejas 27-yard field goal with only four seconds remaining. Against San Francisco, the Giants had seemed headed for defeat, trailing the 49ers by 17-0 at half time. But Phil Simms engineered a 21-point third quarter, twice passing for touchdowns, to save the day.

San Francisco's loss meant that the Rams, who were helped by key defensive plays in beating the Jets 17-3, moved further ahead in the NFC West. Atlanta rekindled its faint playoff hopes in ending a five-game losing sequence against Miami. The Falcons' Gerald Riggs rushed for 172 yards and a touchdown, while Miami's Dan Marino saw four of his passes intercepted. Sadly, the Saints had flattered to deceive and, after going down bravely in a pulsating game against New England, they were now back in the cellar. For the Patriots, everything was rosy as they moved into a tie for first place in the AFC East.

For the Broncos, who were now well into a win-one-lose-one sequence, quarterback John Elway put on a one-man show against Cincinnati, completing 22 of 34 passes for 228 yards and three touchdowns, and rushing for 41 yards. Also, he was masterly in controlling possession after the Bengals had drawn to within six points on a pair of fourth-quarter touchdown passes from Boomer Esiason to Cris Collinsworth. Cleveland intercepted Houston's Warren Moon and Oliver Luck six times but needed overtime for the victory which took them into first place in the AFC Central.

The Raiders slipped up against the visiting Philadelphia Eagles. In a game of big, big plays, the teams were tied 27-27 at the end of regulation time. In overtime, the Raiders had moved into field goal position when Philadelphia's Andre Waters picked up a fumble and returned 81 yards to set up the game-winning one-yard touchdown run by Randall Cunningham, also who had passed for three touchdowns on his best day as a pro.

On Thanksgiving Day, Green Bay outgunned Detroit, 44-40, and Seattle surprised Dallas, 31-14, reducing the Cowboys' playoff hopes to no more than a long shot.

Left: Minnesota's Wade Wilson.
Above: Mike Quick was at his awesome best against the Raiders.

STANDINGS

AFC East	W	L	T	PF	PA
New England	10	3	0	347	220
N.Y. Jets	10	3	0	309	265
Miami	6	7	0	335	313
Buffalo	4	9	0	249	287
Indianapolis	0	13	0	147	339
AFC Central					
Cleveland	9	4	0	289	273
Cincinnati	8	5	0	323	332
Pittsburgh	4	9	0	216	271
Houston	3	10	0	235	285
AFC West					
Denver	10	3	0	321	219
L.A. Raiders	8	5	0	282	259
Kansas City	7	6	0	277	280
Seattle	7	6	0	254	253
San Diego	3	10	0	267	315

NFC East	W	L	T	PF	PA
*N.Y. Giants	11	2	0	265	191
*Washington	11	2	0	303	227
Dallas	7	6	0	305	261
Philadelphia	4	9	0	209	260
St Louis	3	10	0	180	297
NFC Central					
†Chicago	11	2	0	264	150
Minnesota	7	6	0	323	227
Detroit	5	8	0	241	263
Green Bay	3	10	0	203	324
Tampa Bay	2	11	0	201	383
NFC West					
L.A. Rams	9	4	0	235	196
San Francisco	7	5	1	297	199
Atlanta	6	6	1	228	232
New Orleans	6	7	0	230	214

† Division Champions
* Qualified for playoffs

Outstanding Individual Performances

100 Yards Rushing
Gerald Riggs (Atlanta) 33-172-31-1
Rueben Mayes (New Orleans) 33-157-50-1
Curt Warner (Seattle) 22-122-19-1
Kevin Mack (Cleveland) 28-121-20-0
Robb Riddick (Buffalo) 27-118-13-0
Eric Dickerson (L.A. Rams) 31-107-27-1

100 Yards Pass Receiving
Jessie Hester (L.A. Raiders) 4-193-81t-2
Mike Quick (Philadelphia) 8-145-62t-3
Cris Collinsworth (Cincinnati) 8-138-46t-2
Walter Stanley (Green Bay) 4-124-62-2
Jeff Chadwick (Detroit) 6-121-28-1
Stephone Paige (Kansas City) 9-119-26-1
Stacy Robinson (N.Y. Giants) 5-116-49-1
Mark Duper (Miami) 4-115-54t-1
Wes Chandler (San Diego) 5-110-36-1

300 Yards Passing
Phil Simms (N.Y. Giants) 38-27-388-2-49-2
Jim Plunkett (L.A. Raiders) 42-16-366-2-81t-2
Wade Wilson (Minnesota) 33-22-339-0-36t-3
Boomer Esiason (Cincinnati) 30-21-306-1-46t-2
Dan Marino (Miami) 40-20-303-4-54t-2

WEEK FOURTEEN

American Football Conference
Cincinnati 31 at New England 7
Cleveland 21 at Buffalo 17
Denver 10 at Kansas City 37
Houston 0 at San Diego 27
L.A. Raiders 0 at Seattle 37

National Football Conference
Dallas 10 at L.A. Rams 29
Minnesota 32 at Green Bay 6
New York Giants 24 at Washington 14
St Louis 10 at Philadelphia 10 (OT)
Tampa Bay 14 at Chicago 48

Interconference Games
Detroit 17 at Pittsburgh 27
Indianapolis 28 at Atlanta 23
Miami 31 at New Orleans 27
New York Jets 10 at San Francisco 24

Interconference Play
AFC 23 – NFC 25

On Week Fourteen, Kansas City handed Denver its heaviest loss thus far on the season and yet, even in defeat, the Broncos clinched the AFC Western division title. The Chiefs were particularly tough on Denver quarterbacks John Elway and Gary Kubiak, intercepting five passes and logging five sacks, and safety Lloyd Burruss was again in the spotlight, returning an interception 72 yards for the last of 27 unanswered second-half points. Denver's good news came on Monday evening when the Raiders, who were the only team which could possibly edge Denver, were routed by Seattle in what was the Los Angeles club's worst defeat since 1962.

The race in the AFC Central remained tight as both Cincinnati and Cleveland won. The Bengals amassed a club-record 584 net yards in trouncing New England 31-7. Running back James Brooks became the campaign's third player both to rush for over 100 yards and catch passes for over 100 yards in the same game. If Cleveland's win over Buffalo was less spectacular, it was nonetheless a commanding performance and good enough to keep their one-game lead.

The Jets' loss to San Francisco meant that there would be no change at the top of the AFC East, but Miami's victory kept them in the hunt, albeit as a

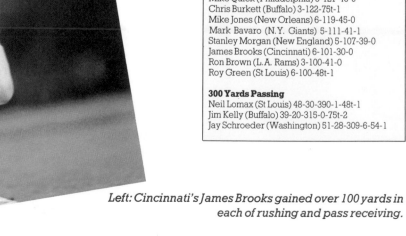

Outstanding Individual Performances

100 Yards Rushing
Rueben Mayes (New Orleans) 28-203-34t-2
James Brooks (Cincinnati) 18-163-56t-1
Earnest Jackson (Pittsburgh) 28-147-23-1
Gerald Riggs (Atlanta) 30-136-19-0
Keith Byars (Philadelphia) 24-127-32-0
Stanley Wilson (Cincinnati) 16-120-58t-1
Curt Warner (Seattle) 23-116-18-2
Eric Dickerson (L.A. Rams) 28-106-12-0

100 Yards Pass Receiving
Louis Lipps (Pittsburgh) 8-150-48-2
Calvin Magee (Tampa Bay) 8-143-40-1
J.T. Smith (St Louis) 10-131-24-0
Kelvin Bryant (Washington) 13-130-23-1
Mike Quick (Philadelphia) 5-127-46-0
Chris Burkett (Buffalo) 3-122-75t-1
Mike Jones (New Orleans) 6-119-45-0
Mark Bavaro (N.Y. Giants) 5-111-41-1
Stanley Morgan (New England) 5-107-39-0
James Brooks (Cincinnati) 6-101-30-0
Ron Brown (L.A. Rams) 3-100-41-0
Roy Green (St Louis) 6-100-48t-1

300 Yards Passing
Neil Lomax (St Louis) 48-30-390-1-48t-1
Jim Kelly (Buffalo) 39-20-315-0-75t-2
Jay Schroeder (Washington) 51-28-309-6-54-1

Left: Cincinnati's James Brooks gained over 100 yards in each of rushing and pass receiving.

rank outsider. Against New Orleans, Dan Marino passed for three touchdowns as the Dolphins went out to a 31-10 halftime lead. But with rookie running back Rueben Mayes rushing for 203 yards, the Saints came back and even appeared to have completed the job with a minute to go, only to see a Mayes touchdown run called back for an obscure technical infringement, an illegal shift.

As one might expect, there was high drama in Los Angeles, where the Rams entertained Dallas. But the excitement was on the sideline, where Dallas head coach Tom Landry was obliged to don a bullet-proof vest after a crank caller had threatened his life. On the field, the Cowboys were sluggish and went down tamely by the score of 29-10. The Cowboys still held out slender playoff hopes but, in all common sense, their main goal was simply to avoid their first net-losing season since 1964.

Ever since Week Eight, the Giants had been tied with Washington for at least a share of the lead in the NFC East, but they finally broke the deadlock, controlling the Redskins 24-14 to become the outright leader for the first time. Needing only one win from the remaining two games, both of which were against modest opponents, they looked to be home free.

STANDINGS

AFC East	W	L	T	PF	PA
New England	10	4	0	354	251
N.Y. Jets	10	4	0	319	289
Miami	7	7	0	366	340
Buffalo	4	10	0	266	308
Indianapolis	1	13	0	175	362
AFC Central					
Cleveland	10	4	0	310	290
Cincinnati	9	5	0	354	339
Pittsburgh	5	9	0	243	288
Houston	3	11	0	235	312
AFC West					
†Denver	10	4	0	331	256
Kansas City	8	6	0	314	290
L.A. Raiders	8	6	0	282	296
Seattle	8	6	0	291	253
San Diego	4	10	0	294	315

NFC East	W	L	T	PF	PA
*N.Y. Giants	12	2	0	289	205
*Washington	11	3	0	317	251
Dallas	7	7	0	315	290
Philadelphia	4	9	1	219	270
St Louis	3	10	1	190	307
NFC Central					
†Chicago	12	2	0	312	104
Minnesota	8	6	0	355	233
Detroit	5	9	0	258	290
Green Bay	3	11	0	209	356
Tampa Bay	2	12	0	215	431
NFC West					
L.A. Rams	10	4	0	264	206
San Francisco	8	5	1	321	209
Atlanta	6	7	1	251	260
New Orleans	6	8	0	257	245

† Division Champions
* Qualified for playoffs

Right: Pittsburgh wide receiver Louis Lipps had his most productive game of the season.

WEEK FIFTEEN

American Football Conference
Buffalo 14 at Indianapolis 24
Cleveland 34 at Cincinnati 3
Kansas City 20 at L.A. Raiders 17
Pittsburgh 45 at New York Jets 24
Seattle 34 at San Diego 24

National Football Conference
Chicago 16 at Detroit 13
Green Bay 21 at Tampa Bay 7
New Orleans 14 at Atlanta 9
Philadelphia 23 at Dallas 21
St Louis 7 at New York Giants 27

Interconference Games
Miami 37 at L.A. Rams 31 (OT)
Minnesota 10 at Houston 23
San Francisco 29 at New England 24
Washington 30 at Denver 31

Interconference Play
AFC 26 – NFC 26

On Week Fifteen, two more division races were settled and three teams became assured of playoff spots.

In one of the two Saturday games, Denver played host to Washington and fell behind 13-0, before quarterback John Elway brought them back into a winning position. For the one-point difference we had to look back to an extra-point failure by the Redskins' Max Zendejas, following Ricky Sanders' opening touchdown. Denver's victory handed the NFC Eastern division title to the Giants but on Sunday the New Yorkers won anyway, easing comfortably past St Louis. As a warmup for the playoffs, Joe Morris rushed for 179 yards and three touchdowns.

In the other Saturday game, Pittsburgh became the latest team to torment the Jets as they ran up 45 points. But even in defeat, the Jets became assured of at least the senior wild card spot in the playoffs, following the Raiders' loss to Kansas City. Also, the Jets still held out hopes for the outright title in the AFC East after seeing the Patriots lose their second game in a row. The Patriots were now in a tricky

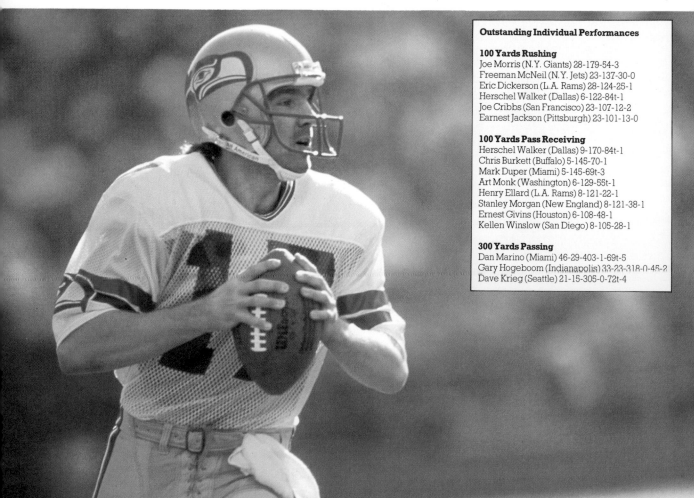

Outstanding Individual Performances

100 Yards Rushing
Joe Morris (N.Y. Giants) 28-179-54-3
Freeman McNeil (N.Y. Jets) 23-137-30-0
Eric Dickerson (L.A. Rams) 28-124-25-1
Herschel Walker (Dallas) 6-122-84t-1
Joe Cribbs (San Francisco) 23-107-12-2
Earnest Jackson (Pittsburgh) 23-101-13-0

100 Yards Pass Receiving
Herschel Walker (Dallas) 9-170-84t-1
Chris Burkett (Buffalo) 5-145-70-1
Mark Duper (Miami) 5-145-69t-3
Art Monk (Washington) 6-129-55t-1
Henry Ellard (L.A. Rams) 8-121-22-1
Stanley Morgan (New England) 8-121-38-1
Ernest Givins (Houston) 6-108-48-1
Kellen Winslow (San Diego) 8-105-28-1

300 Yards Passing
Dan Marino (Miami) 46-29-403-1-69t-5
Gary Hogeboom (Indianapolis) 33-23-318-0-45-2
Dave Krieg (Seattle) 21-15-305-0-72t-4

STANDINGS

AFC East	W	L	T	PF	PA	NFC East	W	L	T	PF	PA
New England	10	5	0	378	280	†N.Y. Giants	13	2	0	316	212
*N.Y. Jets	10	5	0	343	334	*Washington	11	4	0	347	282
Miami	8	7	0	403	371	Dallas	7	8	0	336	313
Buffalo	4	11	0	280	332	Philadelphia	5	9	1	242	291
Indianapolis	2	13	0	199	376	St Louis	3	11	1	197	334
AFC Central						**NFC Central**					
†Cleveland	11	4	0	344	293	†Chicago	13	2	0	328	177
Cincinnati	9	6	0	357	373	Minnesota	8	7	0	365	256
Pittsburgh	6	9	0	288	312	Detroit	5	10	0	271	306
Houston	4	11	0	258	322	Green Bay	4	11	0	230	363
AFC West						Tampa Bay	2	13	0	222	452
†Denver	11	4	0	362	286	**NFC West**					
Kansas City	9	6	0	334	307	*L.A. Rams	10	5	0	295	243
Seattle	9	6	0	325	277	*San Francisco	9	5	1	350	233
L.A. Raiders	8	7	0	299	316	New Orleans	7	8	0	271	254
San Diego	4	11	0	318	349	Atlanta	6	8	1	260	274

† Division Champions
* Qualified for playoffs

position. The vagaries of the tie-breaking system, combined with probable wins by contenders from other divisions within the AFC, meant that their only serious chance of making the playoffs lay in winning the AFC Eastern division title outright. And they would be facing a Miami Dolphins club which had confirmed its return to competitiveness in a titanic struggle with the Rams. Dan Marino passed for 403 yards and threw his fifth touchdown pass of the game, 3:04 into overtime, to break a 31-31 deadlock. Minnesota's upset loss against Houston assured the Rams of a playoff spot but the destination of the title in the NFC West would be decided on the final weekend, when they would meet San Francisco, also who were now assured of a berth in the playoffs.

Cleveland finally settled its running battle with Cincinnati, winning the AFC Central title in the most impressive manner, scoring 34 points while holding the Bengals to just three. The Bengals were now in what, sensibly, was a four-team race with New England, Kansas City and Seattle for a playoff spot. Neither the Raiders nor the Dolphins were yet eliminated, but their chances were remote, resting as they did on losses by at least three of the front runners.

Elsewhere, an astonishing dual-purpose performance by Herschel Walker, who gained a combined 292 yards and scored two touchdowns, went for nought as the Philadelphia Eagles prevailed to give Dallas its fourth consecutive loss.

Left: Seattle's Dave Krieg looks for gaps in the Chargers' defense.

Herschel Walker – a one-man assault on the Eagles.

WEEK SIXTEEN

American Football Conference
Buffalo 7 at Houston 16
Denver 16 at Seattle 41
Indianapolis 30 at L.A. Raiders 24
Kansas City 24 at Pittsburgh 19
New England 34 at Miami 27
New York Jets 21 at Cincinnati 52
San Diego 17 at Cleveland 47

National Football Conference
Atlanta 20 at Detroit 6
Chicago 24 at Dallas 10
Green Bay 24 at New York Giants 55
L.A. Rams 14 at San Francisco 24
New Orleans 17 at Minnesota 33
Tampa Bay 17 at St Louis 21
Washington 21 at Philadelphia 14

Interconference Play
AFC 26 – NFC 26

The first issue was settled on the Friday evening of Week Sixteen, when the 49ers closed down on Eric Dickerson and exposed the inexperience of rookie quarterback Jim Everett in a commanding victory over the Rams. The title in the NFC West thus went to San Francisco while the Rams were relegated to the rank of away-team wild card.

Saturday saw the Giants crush Green Bay to secure home-field advantage throughout the play-offs. In the National Football Conference, everything was now resolved. Over on the west coast later in the day, Seattle running back Curt Warner battered a Denver defense which isn't used to that kind of thing, as he rampaged for 192 yards and three touchdowns. The Seahawks' victory kept them in the hunt but they'd need a loss by Kansas City the next day.

It may become a trivia question, 'Which club was outgained by 515 yards to 171 but still won 24-19?' Answer, 'The Kansas City Chiefs, who scored touchdowns on a blocked punt recovered by Deron Cherry, a 97-yard kickoff return by Boyce Green, and Lloyd Burruss' 78-yard return of a blocked field goal.' The Chiefs' victory took them into the playoffs for the first time since 1971 and slammed the door on Seattle. Cincinnati, however, stayed in contention after mauling the hapless Jets by the score of 52-21. Cincinnati quarterback Boomer Esiason passed for 425 yards and five touchdowns as the Bengals rolled to a club-record 621 yards offense. For Cincinnati it was now a matter of sweating through the Monday Night Game, which would provide the final piece for the AFC jigsaw. A Miami victory would eliminate New England and allow Cincinnati to squeeze in.

Boomer Esiason kept alive the Bengals' playoff hopes.

Right: Kansas City's Boyce Green on his 97-yard touchdown return.

The final game of the 1986 regular season came down to the final minute. It was decided when veteran quarterback Steve Grogan, who had replaced the injured Tony Eason early in the second quarter, fired a 31-yard touchdown pass to wide receiver Stanley Morgan. Cincinnati was eliminated and New England won the title in the AFC East.

A race of a different kind also was resolved. It concerned the destination of the first pick in the 1987 collegiate draft. With three weeks remaining in the regular season, it seemed certain to go to the winless Indianapolis Colts. But under new head coach Ron Meyer, they reeled off three straight victories, relegating themselves to second place in the pecking order and placing Tampa Bay in prime position for the sixth time in their twelve-year history.

Outstanding Individual Performances

100 Yards Rushing
Curt Warner (Seattle) 24-192-60t-3
Albert Bentley (Indianapolis) 25-162-70t-1
Joe Morris (N.Y. Giants) 22-115-19-1
Lorenzo Hampton (Miami) 13-109-47-0
Freeman McNeil (N.Y. Jets) 17-106-19-2

100 Yards Pass Receiving
Rod Barksdale (L.A. Raiders) 6-179-54-0
Brian Brennan (Cleveland) 7-176-57t-1
Stanley Morgan (New England) 8-148-31t-2
Rodney Holman (Cincinnati) 6-129-34t-1
Drew Hill (Houston) 5-114-35-0
Wes Chandler (San Diego) 6-113-25-1
Todd Christensen (L.A. Raiders) 9-104-25-2
Steve Largent (Seattle) 6-101-27-0
Hassan Jones (Minnesota) 5-100-39-0

300 Yards Passing
Boomer Esiason (Cincinnati) 30-23-425-1-49-5
Wade Wilson (Minnesota) 39-24-361-0-39-3
Mark Malone (Pittsburgh) 43-22-351-1-38-0

STANDINGS

AFC East	W	L	T	PF	PA	NFC East	W	L	T	PF	PA
†New England	11	5	0	412	307	†N.Y. Giants	14	2	0	371	236
*N.Y. Jets	10	6	0	364	386	*Washington	12	4	0	368	296
Miami	8	8	0	430	405	Dallas	7	9	0	346	337
Buffalo	4	12	0	287	348	Philadelphia	5	10	1	256	312
Indianapolis	3	13	0	229	400	St Louis	4	11	1	218	351
AFC Central						**NFC Central**					
†Cleveland	12	4	0	391	310	†Chicago	14	2	0	352	187
Cincinnati	10	6	0	409	394	Minnesota	9	7	0	398	273
Pittsburgh	6	10	0	307	336	Detroit	5	11	0	277	326
Houston	5	11	0	274	329	Green Bay	4	12	0	254	418
AFC West						Tampa Bay	2	14	0	239	473
†Denver	11	5	0	378	327	**NFC West**					
*Kansas City	10	6	0	358	326	†San Francisco	10	5	1	374	247
Seattle	10	6	0	366	293	*L.A. Rams	10	6	0	309	267
L.A. Raiders	8	8	0	323	346	Atlanta	7	8	1	280	280
San Diego	4	12	0	335	396	New Orleans	7	9	0	288	287

† Division Champions
* Wild Card

WEEK SEVENTEEN – WILD CARD WEEKEND

AFC   Kansas City 15 at New York Jets 35

Who could have imagined after Week Eleven, when they'd beaten the Colts 31-16 to record their ninth victory in a row, that the Jets would end the regular season with the AFC's longest losing streak – they lost their last five games? Outscored 183-61 over that period, they'd only just squeezed into the playoffs, and for their opening bid they had Pat Ryan at quarterback in place of Ken O'Brien, whose late-season form had been disappointing. The Chiefs were not expected to dominate offensively, even against a Jets defense weakened by the absences of Joe Klecko and Lance Mehl, but they marched unhindered to a touchdown, nine plays after stopping the Jets cold on their opening possession. Chiefs kicker Nick Lowery failed with the PAT after 123 consecutive successes, and maybe it sparked

the Jets. Certainly, a 24-yard bootleg by Ryan on the return drive did. That play, which came on fourth-and-six from the Kansas City 33, kept alive a drive which ended with Freeman McNeil's four-yard touchdown run. McNeil went on to rush for a game total of 135 yards, pausing to catch the first of three Ryan touchdown passes early in the second quarter. The Chiefs scored what was almost the mandatory touchdown by the special team, when Albert Lewis recovered a blocked punt in the end zone. But the Jets still held a 15-point cushion and never were in danger of being caught.

NFC   L.A. Rams 7 at Washington 19

With George Rogers rushing for 115 yards, the Redskins played ball-control, error-free football, while the Rams lost possession on four fumbles and saw two passes intercepted. The result was inevitable, though for the brief period before the Rams' first act of profligacy, the first of three Eric Dickerson fumbles, they'd looked good, moving smoothly to the

Above: Running back Freeman McNeil helped the Jets to victory over Kansas City.
Right: Jets quarterback Pat Ryan (10) called the signals.
Far right: George Rogers (38).

Washington 35-yard line and threatening more. Washington's replacement kicker, Jess Atkinson, who only two weeks before the game had been working in a local bank, punished the error with the first of his four field goals (it equalled the club's single-game playoff record.) Trailing 10-0, the Rams marched to the Washington 17-yard line, only to lose possession on Dickerson's second fumble. The Redskins didn't capitalise on that unexpected bonus but they did after the next gift when, again, the Rams had looked dangerous, having moved to the Washington 28-yard line. A fumble by tight end David Hill was recovered by Neal Olkewicz and, with that possession, Atkinson obliged with his second field goal. Dickerson did break free for one big gain, a 65-yard run, only to be caught from behind by Washington cornerback Darrell Green. Said victorious head coach Joe Gibbs after the game, 'The good news is that we won. The bad news is that we have to go play the Bears!'

WEEK EIGHTEEN – DIVISIONAL PLAYOFFS

American Football Conference

New England 17 at Denver 22

In Denver, the combination of vintage John Elway, solid running by Sammy Winder, and stout defense, was just too good for the Patriots who, nonetheless, were far from disgraced in defeat. Elway opened in whirlwind style, going for broke, it seemed, on every play. He'd calmed down a little by the time he put together the drive on which he almost rushed for a touchdown but had to settle for Rich Karlis's 27-yard field goal. Later, he did score a touchdown, rushing 22 yards to take Denver into a 10-7 lead. But the Patriots came back, and they were in with every chance of victory when wide receiver Stanley Morgan caught a 45-yard touchdown pass to make the score 17-13. By now, Elway had been hobbling for some time with an injured ankle and Winder had been on extended duty, keeping the offense moving. But Elway returned to the air, completing a 20-yard pass to tight end Bobby Micho on the drive

which he finished off with a 48-yard touchdown pass to wide receiver Vance Johnson. With solid defense, the Broncos kept control throughout the third quarter and the Patriots' last hopes disappeared when quarterback Tony Eason was sacked for a safety by Denver defensive end Rulon Jones.

New York Jets 20 at Cleveland 23 (OT)

In what was the third-longest game in AFL-NFL history, Cleveland quarterback Bernie Kosar set new playoff records for passes attempted (64) and yards (489), and tied the record for completions (33). Yet despite his efforts, the Jets went out into a 20-10 lead with just 4:14 remaining in regulation time. However, helped by a roughing-the-passer penalty, Kosar quickly took the Browns 67 yards to set up Kevin Mack's one-yard touchdown run. And following another Jets penalty, a 25-yarder for pass interference, he drove the Browns into position for Mark Moseley's 22-yard game-tying field goal, which came with only seven seconds remaining in regulation time. In overtime, the Browns assumed almost total dominance, and even though Moseley missed a 23-yard 'sitter', he hit the winner from 27 yards, 2:02 into the second period of overtime.

National Football Conference

Washington 27 at Chicago 13

Quarterback Jay Schroeder foiled the famed Chicago Bears blitz to throw for a pair of touchdown passes to wide receiver Art Monk, and the Redskins' defense held the fearsome Bears rushing offense to just 93 net yards, as the reigning Super Bowl Champions were eliminated. But it was a sub-par Chicago club which failed in its attempt to emulate Pittsburgh, which was the last team to retain its Super Bowl title. Quite simply, the Bears didn't take advantage of their opportunities and the Redskins did. The Bears failed to capitalise on Dennis Gentry's opening 60-yard kickoff return. Later, a 43-yard interception return by Mike Richardson, down to the Washington four-yard line, led to just a field goal. With the Bears trailing 13-14, Gentry's second big return of the game, a 47-yarder, gave them an excellent springboard. However, Walter Payton fumbled and, with the ensuing possession, the Redskins drove 83 yards for the George Rogers touchdown which put the result beyond doubt.

San Francisco 3 at New York Giants 49

The 49ers had bitter memories of their defeat at the hands of the Giants in the 1985 NFC Wild Card Game. They'd vowed to return and here they were, winners of the title in the NFC West, once more doing battle with the Giants in East Rutherford. And they couldn't have wished for a better start, closing down on the Giants' first possession and easing into a drive of their own. Joe Montana back to pass; it's in the air; wide receiver Jerry Rice catches the ball and he's off to the races on a certain 50-yard touchdown play. But wait a minute. Inexplicably, Rice drops the ball and, in his clumsy attempt to recover possession, bats it into the Giants' end zone. The Giants recover and the threat is over. Giants tight end Mark Bavaro completed the return drive with the opening touchdown, and though the 49ers replied with a field goal it was their first and last statement of the day. The Giants were awesomely efficient, rushing, passing and in stifling the best efforts of Montana who, sadly, went out with concussion. The result was the equal third-most lopsided victory in playoff history and set up the third meeting of the season between the Giants and their great rivals from the NFC East, the Redskins.

Above: Cleveland veteran Mark Moseley kicking the winning field goal.
Right: Joe Morris on his 45-yard touchdown run.
Left: Jay Schroeder checks his options.

WEEK NINETEEN – CONFERENCE CHAMPIONSHIPS

American Football Conference

Denver 23 at Cleveland 20 (OT)

It had been a good regular season for the Browns, who established a team record with twelve victories to enter postseason play as the AFC's senior club. In the 1985 playoffs, they had almost beaten Miami, but the pressures of the occasion had been a little too much for their young quarterback, Bernie Kosar. Now, however, Kosar was a player of stature, and never was that more evident than in the gripping struggle with the Jets the previous weekend. That victory, the Browns' sixth in a row, had applied an extra layer of hardness to a teak-tough outfit, and they had to be favoured to beat the Broncos. That meant, of course, beating John Elway, in all his guises of passer, runner, leader and the rest. The Broncos were entering the tenth week of a sequence which had seen them alternate wins with losses. They'd beaten a solid New England club in the divisional playoffs but the Browns presented much tougher opposition. Even Elway's brilliance might not be enough, one felt.

In the end, Elway's brilliance proved to be too much. After trailing to a first quarter touchdown catch by Cleveland running back Herman Fontenot, Denver led 10-7 and 13-10, but the Browns appeared to be on the way to Super Bowl XXI when Kosar passed 48 yards for a touchdown to wide receiver Brian Brennan to break a 13-13 tie with just 5:43 remaining in regulation time. What followed has been described as the greatest drive in playoff history, as Elway engineered a 15-play, 98-yard drive to tie the game on Mark Jackson's five-yard touchdown reception. In overtime he struck quickly, completing passes of 22 and 28 yards to tight end Orson Mobley and wide receiver Steve Watson respectively, to set up Rich Karlis's winning 33-yard field goal.

National Football Conference

Washington 0 at New York Giants 17

The Giants were on a roll, having established a club all-time best with fourteen wins in the regular season before crushing San Francisco in the divisional playoffs. They had a few doubts but no serious weaknesses, and they held a small but distinct edge over the Redskins, not least for having beaten them twice during the regular season. But the Redskins had not been blown out and they had just cleared pro football's most difficult hurdle, having beaten the Bears in their own lair.

Curiously, the game may have been decided by the wind and a good punter. The Giants, who won the toss and opted for the choice of direction – they selected the wind – chose well. And when, for the Redskins, it was time to punt, their punter did poorly. Following Steve Cox efforts of 27 and 23 yards, the Giants drove for Raul Allegre's 11-yard field goal and Lionel Manuel's 11-yard touchdown reception from Phil Simms. Still in the first half, a 51-yard field goal attempt by Washington went wrong when the ball was badly snapped, and Giants linebacker Carl Banks recovered. Six plays later, the Giants led 17-0 on Joe Morris's one-yard touchdown run. For the third year in a row, the NFC Championship Game was a shutout – and each time the victorious team had gone on to win the Super Bowl. This Giants team was a little different though. They'd won, one felt, without ever bringing out the big guns.

Left: Redskins players leap in the vain attempt to block a kick.
Above: Denver quarterback John Elway and his 'minders' Keith Bishop (# 54) and Sammy Winder (# 23).

SUPER BOWL XXI

New York Giants 39 – Denver Broncos 20
The Rose Bowl, Pasadena, California
January 25th, 1987

Settling down to write the big-game preview for the Giants, it's tempting to begin as last year, replacing 'Chicago' by 'New York', for the last time either team had been in the Championship Game was in 1963, the year the Bears beat the Giants 14-10. And just as had the Bears in 1985, the Giants arrived here in style, winning fourteen games (one fewer than the 1985 Bears) during the regular season and conceding only three points in their two playoff games (the Bears conceded none). Looking back to the year 1963, a young man by the name of Bill Parcells was taking on his first coaching job, as an assistant in college. It's by no means certain that he watched that 1963 NFL Championship Game on TV, but now he was the head coach of the favourites, the overpowering Giants, who, like most title winners, had gathered momentum as the season wore on. They had a great running back, Joe Morris, who was ranked the second-best rusher in the NFL but was perhaps more dangerous than the man who'd won the individual title, Eric Dickerson. You knew how Dickerson would go about his job, but Morris had more ways to beat you than you dared think. Quarterback Phil Simms would not figure in anybody's lists for style, productivity and the like. His passer rating was usually something like the price of a pint, 72-75, depending upon the pub. But he'd developed a kind of presence – dare one say a Terry Bradshaw kind of presence? Here was a quarterback who could complete the passes which mattered. He had wide receivers whose strength was perhaps their anonymity. They'd make a great reception and then disappear before you could catch their names. The Giants' defense was the best in pro football – give or take a yard or two – and they weren't expected to give an inch.

The Broncos had started out the season in the way one has come to expect of a club well-drilled by head coach Dan Reeves. But this was no collection of robots – there was red blood running in 'them there' veins of a squad which, after Week Nine, stood at 8-1. After then, they'd looked human, a little too human for those who questioned the playoff credentials of a club which alternated wins with losses over

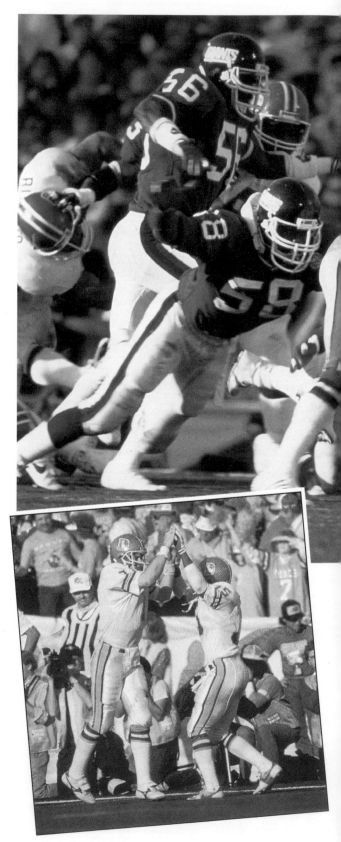

Above: Denver running back Steve Sewell (# 30) stopped by Giants cornerback Elvis Patterson (# 34).
Right: John Elway and Ken Bell celebrate the Broncos' opening score.
Far right: Phil Simms protected by his offensive line.

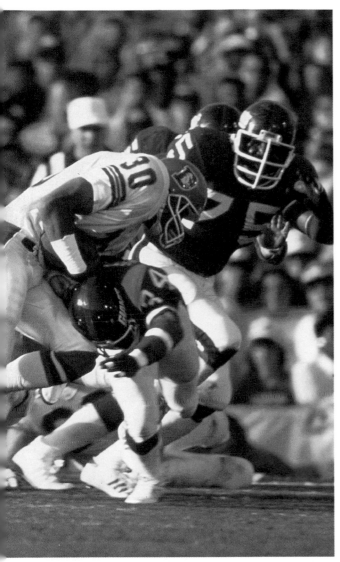

THE GAME

Scoring By Quarters

1st Quarter
Denver: Karlis, 48-yard field goal (4:09)
Denver 3 – New York 0
New York: Mowatt, 6-yard pass from Simms; Allegre kick (9:33)
Denver 3 – New York 7
Denver: Elway, 4-yard run; Karlis kick (12:54)
Denver 10 – New York 7

2nd Quarter
New York: Martin safety (12:14)
Denver 10 – New York 9

3rd Quarter
New York: Bavaro, 13-yard pass from Simms; Allegre kick (4:52)
Denver 10 – New York 16
New York: Allegre, 21-yard field goal (11:06)
Denver 10 – New York 19
New York: Morris, 1-yard run; Allegre kick (14:36)
Denver 10 – New York 26

4th Quarter
New York: McConkey, 6-yard pass from Simms; Allegre kick (4:04)
Denver 10 – New York 33
Denver: Karlis, 28-yard field goal (8:59)
Denver 13 – New York 33
New York: Anderson, 2-yard run; kick failed (10:42)
Denver 13 – New York 39
Denver: Johnson, 47-yard pass from Elway; Karlis kick (12:54)
Denver 20 – New York 39

the rest of the regular season, culminating in an embarrassing 41-16 loss to Seattle. In the playoffs, though, they'd looked sharp. And increasingly, quarterback John Elway had become the focus of attention. With every game, his became the responsibility to make something happen. And he'd made it happen, both against New England and in that tense AFC Championship Game when the Cleveland Browns had done most of the things needed for victory. If Elway was the star, the supporting cast on offense was modest. There was pace at wide receiver in the likes of Steve Watson and Vance Johnson, but running backs Sammy Winder and Gerald Willhite struck no fear. However, on defense, it was a different story. They were tough, fast and there were lots of them, starters and backups of high quality, itching to ring a few bells, preferably the Giant variety.

Left: Super Bowl MVP Phil Simms.
Above: Giants head coach Bill Parcells enjoys the traditional 'Gatorade' celebration.

For three quarters it was one of the best Super Bowls in the twenty-one game series. Entering the final quarter, Denver trailed by sixteen points but they were not out of it by any means. They were, however, in a spot of bother, facing a 2nd-and-21 from their own nine-yard line. And they dug a deeper hole for themselves when tackle Ken Lanier was guilty of a false start. That made it 2nd-and-26, and in attempting to bomb his way out of trouble, Elway was intercepted by Giants cornerback Elvis Patterson. Seven plays later, the Giants went into a 33-10 lead when wide receiver Phil McConkey caught a pass which had deflected off the hands of tight end Mark Bavaro. Now it really was over bar the shouting.

In the early going, both teams had been surprisingly reluctant to commit themselves to the big pass rush, and the quarterbacks had a field day. Elway completed his first six passes and Simms was good on his first seven. The Broncos had slightly the

better of the first half but even though they led by one point, they suffered the disappointment of seeing two Rich Karlis field goal attempts drift wide of the target. The first failure, a 23-yarder, was a major setback after the Broncos had driven from their own 20-yard line·down to the New York one-yard line. The second came just before the halftime gun and could have lifted the Broncos, who had seen Elway sacked for a safety but had stopped the Giants on their subsequent possession and then driven down to the New York 16-yard line.

In the second half, Simms connected on all ten of his passes to establish a Super Bowl record for consecutive completions, and he ended up with the new single-game playoff record for completion percentage, a remarkable 88%. Walking into the locker room as the game's Most Valuable Player, his thoughts may have drifted back to 1979, the year he'd been picked in the first round by the Giants. Coming off a modest senior-year performance, and at that while playing small college football, he was not a popular choice – the Giants fans sniggered, 'Phil Who?' and booed him roundly. There'd be no more of that.

ANATOMY OF SUPER BOWL XXI
– QUARTER BY QUARTER –

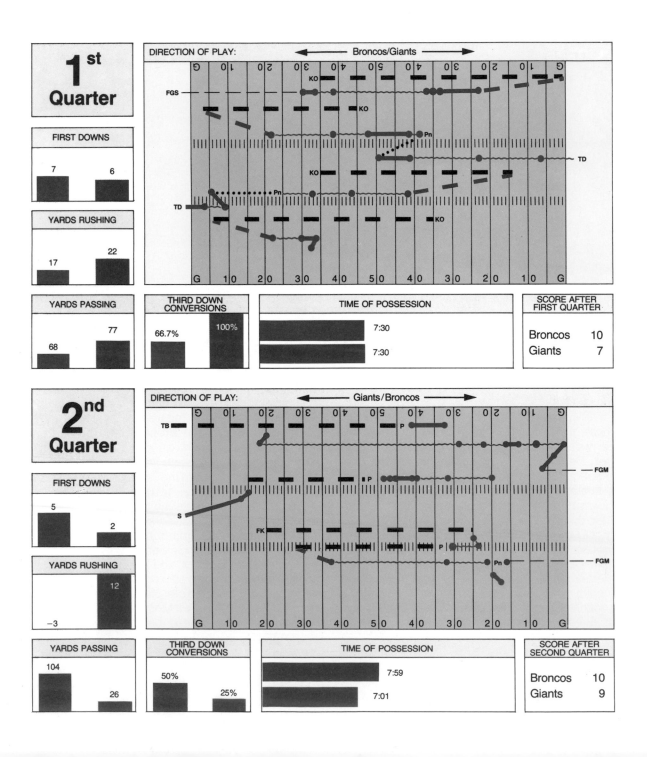

1st Quarter

FIRST DOWNS
7   6

YARDS RUSHING
17   22

YARDS PASSING
68   77

THIRD DOWN CONVERSIONS
66.7%   100%

TIME OF POSSESSION
7:30
7:30

SCORE AFTER FIRST QUARTER
Broncos   10
Giants   7

DIRECTION OF PLAY: ← Broncos/Giants →

2nd Quarter

FIRST DOWNS
5   2

YARDS RUSHING
−3   12

YARDS PASSING
104   26

THIRD DOWN CONVERSIONS
50%   25%

TIME OF POSSESSION
7:59
7:01

SCORE AFTER SECOND QUARTER
Broncos   10
Giants   9

DIRECTION OF PLAY: ← Giants/Broncos →

KEY

Kickoff/Punt/Interception/Fumble/Free Kick Return

Broncos

Giants

Running play

Passing play

Downs ● ●

Penalty yardage ● ● ● ● ● ●

Kickoff/Punt/Free Kick — Field Goal

KO – Kickoff
P – Punt
FGS – Field Goal Scored
FGM – Field Goal Missed
TD – Touchdown
S – Safety
Pn – Penalty
TB – Touchback
I – Interception
FK – Free Kick

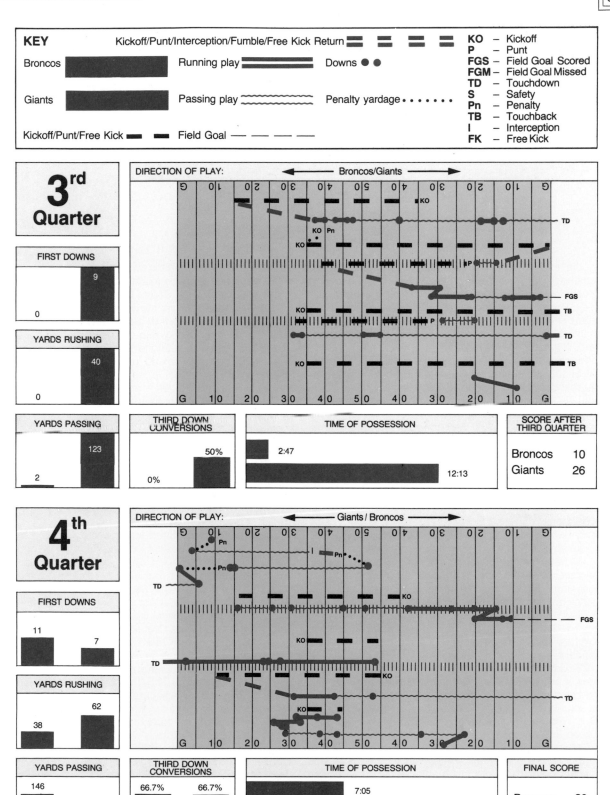

3rd Quarter

DIRECTION OF PLAY: ← Broncos/Giants →

FIRST DOWNS — 9 / 0
YARDS RUSHING — 40 / 0
YARDS PASSING — 123 / 2
THIRD DOWN CONVERSIONS — 0% / 50%
TIME OF POSSESSION — 2:47 / 12:13

SCORE AFTER THIRD QUARTER
Broncos 10
Giants 26

4th Quarter

DIRECTION OF PLAY: ← Giants / Broncos →

FIRST DOWNS — 11 / 7
YARDS RUSHING — 38 / 62
YARDS PASSING — 146 / 37
THIRD DOWN CONVERSIONS — 66.7% / 66.7%
TIME OF POSSESSION — 7:05 / 7:55

FINAL SCORE
Broncos 20
Giants 39

CHAPTER TWO

A HISTORY OF THE NEW YORK GIANTS

By the end of 1924, the National Football League had somehow survived the first five years of its existence. Teams still came and went with a frequency which meant that only rarely was it possible to make an accurate list of member clubs. As for where they played, franchises were shunted around like goods wagons in the marshalling yard. But unlike for the marshalling yard, there was no master plan. Three teams, the Bears, the Cardinals and Green Bay, were well established and would endure, but the rest would not. There were others which were competitive, such as the Bulldogs, who had won the last three league titles, and the Yellow Jackets, who would win the title in 1926. But by 1932, they, together with the thirteen clubs which made up the 1924 membership, had gone out of business.

In 1924, the New York City newspapers would carry only the occasional report on pro football, for which the centre of interest, such as it was, lay in the Mid-west. On the East coast, the sports headlines were reserved for the great personalities of the day, such as Bill Tilden, Babe Ruth, Bobby Jones and Jack Dempsey.

Timothy J. Mara was a sports personality of one kind – he earned a comfortable living as a bookmaker down at the race track. Also, he had a nose for a good business deal, and it was on such a mission, in the summer of 1925, that he met with Billy Gibson, hoping to acquire an interest in Gene Tunney. The substance of the meeting is not recorded but, by its conclusion, Mara had agreed to purchase not a piece of a boxer but, rather, an NFL franchise for the city of New York.

The down payment was $500 and led to one of the great lines of pro football lore, as Mara asserted, 'A New York franchise in anything is worth $500 – including a franchise for shining shoes'. (According to the Giants, the full price, often overlooked by historians, was $2,500 – but why spoil a good line just for historical accuracy?)

Only in retrospect would the full implications of Mara's purchase be recognised. He was about to give the NFL its first firm foothold in America's media capital, and if the pro game could succeed in New York City, its future was assured.

Back in 1925, however, very quickly for the Giants it became a matter of sheer financial survival, and that meant packing in the fans on Sunday. 'One of the most vivid memories of my boyhood,' reflects Wellington Mara, Tim's son and current Giants President, 'was the sight of my father on Saturday nights during the season. Pop kept walking to the front window, peering out into the darkness to see if there were any rain clouds obscuring the stars. Weather meant everything to us in the old days. It was the difference between losing money, breaking even, or maybe making a little.

The Giants were given a good start when 20,000 fans paid to watch the first home game at the Polo Grounds, a stadium which they shared with the baseball team of the same nickname. The fans would see the legendary Jim Thorpe, a Sac and Fox Indian who, at the age of thirty-seven, was way past his prime but had been signed to supply veteran savvy to what otherwise was a young squad. Amongst the rookies were Century Milstead, Lynn Bomar, Art Carney, Jack McBride and a nifty little back-field player who would become a particular favourite with the fans, Henry 'Hinkey' Haines.

The Giants disappointed in their home opener, a 14-0 loss to the Frankford Yellow Jackets which left them at 0-3, but they promptly ripped off seven straight wins. The show was 'on the road'. But the attendances diminished and, by December, Mara was in the red to the tune of $40,000 with little prospect of turning things around. Fortunately, another show, which really was on the road, stopped off at the Polo Grounds and saved the day.

Earlier in the year, Mara had been one of several owners who tried to sign Harold 'Red' Grange, the University of Illinois running back, who had been nick-named the 'Galloping Ghost' and was the most famous collegian of his day, perhaps of all time. However, Grange signed for George Halas's Chicago Bears, joining the pro ranks immediately on completion of the college football season in late November. There still remained two already-scheduled games and Halas hastily arranged five more league games (NFL rules allowed for this in those days) which would be fitted into a seventeen-game barn-storming tour of the nation.

Jim Thorpe with Giants' first head coach, Bob Folwell. Inset: Tim Mara, founder of the New York Giants.

It was on 6 December that the Bears came to the Polo Grounds, and such was the magnetism of Grange that 73,000 people poured through the turnstiles. Said Mara, 'I felt sure pro football was about to go, but it wasn't going any too fast. It wasn't going as fast as my money was. Then we met the Bears with 'Red' Grange. I would have been glad to see 25,000 in the stands. Instead, the house was swamped. I knew that pro football had arrived and my worries were over.'

In fact, pro football hadn't yet arrived – there were difficult days ahead – and, in company with the other club owners, Mara would face financial problems for several more years.

The Giants didn't have to wait long for their first NFL Championship which, at that time and until the 1933 season, was decided purely on regular-season play. In 1927, Mara had signed Joe Guyon, a versatile backfield player who had been a teammate of Thorpe at Carlisle Indian School, and Cal Hubbard, a 6-5, 250-pound tackle. Hubbard, a future Hall-of-Famer, couldn't displace the incumbents, Steve Owen and Milstead, right away and was instead used as the league's biggest end while doubling as an outstanding linebacker on defense.

The crunch game came on 27 November, when the Giants met the Bears. Entering the game, the Giants were 8-1-1 and the Bears 7-1-2. The season was not yet over but this encounter would almost certainly produce the league champion. Later, Owen, who was not the most gentle of players, would describe the confrontation as 'the toughest, roughest game' he'd ever been in. Chicago's Halas suffered two broken ribs in an encounter with Guyon and, as he left the field, was given the piece of advice, 'George, let that be a lesson to you. Never try to sneak up on an Indian'. With the score tied at 7-7, Owen and Hubbard spearheaded a goal-line stand which kept the Bears out. Shortly afterwards, Haines, standing in his own end zone, faked a punt before combining with Charlie Corgan on a 58-yard pass play to set up the deciding score, giving the Giants a 13-7 victory. They rounded off their championship season with two shutouts over their New York City rival, the Yankees. Remarkably, the Giants had allowed only 20 points over the entire thirteen-game season.

The championship win could have marked the beginning of a dynasty, but the combination of complacency and squabbling among the players meant that the Giants never challenged in 1928, when they dropped to sixth place in the ten-team league. Instant action was required and Mara knew it. He'd lost $40,000 in 1926 and a similar bundle in 1928, but there was no stopping him now.

In their championship season, the Giants had suffered only one loss and one tie, both coming in games against the Cleveland Bulldogs, who had a second-year player by the name of Benny Friedman at quarterback. Subsequently, Friedman had moved to the Detroit Wolverines where he had been named All-Pro. He was one of the first quarterbacks to adopt the role we know today – he would drop back and pass, occasionally even on first down. In the 1920s, such style was considered little short of reckless but there was no doubting the player's outstanding skills and drawing power.

Mara wanted Friedman but, try as he might, he couldn't

work out a trade. So he did what seemed to him to be the sensible thing – he bought the entire Detroit club. 'Imagine it,' said Mara, 'a Jewish boy playing for an Irishman in New York. How wonderful.'

In addition to picking out the best of the Wolverines' players, Mara also appointed their former head coach, LeRoy Andrews, as head coach of the Giants. Andrews put together a 26-5-1 record in guiding the Giants to two consecutive second-place finishes (they were 13-1-1 in 1929 but Green Bay was 12-0-1), before being fired after failing to sign a player whom Mara coveted. The player was Ken Strong, who had been outstanding in the backfield at New York University and currently was playing for the Stapletons. Not only would he have helped the club, Mara reasoned, but he could also have been a crowd-puller. But Andrews wasn't of the same opinion and made only a half-hearted attempt to get him. Strong eventually re-signed for the Staten Island club.

As Andrews' replacement, in 1931, Mara chose Steve Owen, who would coach the Giants for 23 years, during which the Giants would win eight Eastern Division and two NFL Championships in the span of just fourteen seasons.

the 1932 season, one year before the NFL began keeping official statistics, McBride threw six touchdown passes to rank second in the league behind Green Bay's Arnie Herber, who threw nine. Catching five touchdown passes, Flaherty led the league and, with 21 pass receptions for 350 yards on the season, came second to the Bears' Luke Johnsos, who caught 24 passes for 321 yards.

But the quantum leap which took the Giants to the Eastern division title and a championship game encounter with the Chicago Bears, came with the signings of Harry Newman, a highly-talented tailback from the University of Michigan, and Ken Strong, who had become available when the Staten Island club folded. Newman led the league in passing and Strong tied for the lead in scoring (he scored 64 points), as the Giants won the division title with six victories more than the second-placed Dodgers.

The Championship Game, which was the first under the league's new two-division format, was exciting from start to finish. The lead had changed hands five times before Chicago's 'Bronko' Nagurski threw a jump pass to Bill Hewitt, who gained 14 yards before lateralling to Bill Karr, who ran the remaining 19 yards into the end zone to give Chicago a 23-21 victory.

The following year, the Giants were less impressive but they finished comfortably ahead of the Redskins to retain their division title. Again, they would meet the Bears for the championship and they gained revenge for their 1933 loss in what became known as the 'Sneakers Game'.

It was clear that the playing surface was going to be frozen solid but overnight rain had coated the pitch with a sheet of ice. Recognising that traction would be a

Left: Steve Owen, former Giants player seen here as head coach.

Above: Cal Hubbard, Hall of Fame tackle-end.

Right: Hall of Fame center Mel Hein.

In the first two years under Owen, the Giants were less than spectacular, but they were building steadily. In 1930, they had acquired a future Hall-of-Famer in end Morris 'Red' Badgro, a punishing blocker who would develop into a solid receiver. But perhaps the key signing was that of the former Washington State University star, center Mel Hein, who would anchor the Giants' offensive line for fifteen years, beginning in his rookie year, 1931. In eight consecutive years he was selected All-Pro. When it comes to picking the all-time NFL team, Hein's name is one of the first to come up and, in the eyes of the professional scouts, he has no serious challenger at his position. He never missed a game, despite doubling on defense as a superb linebacker. Hein, who had the unique distinction of being the NFL's first official Most Valuable Player (1938), was a charter member of the Hall of Fame in 1963.

Ray Flaherty, who had been with the Giants in 1928 and 1929, returned and had matured into a first-class pass-receiving end. Benny Friedman had left to become the player-coach of the Brooklyn Dodgers, but Jack McBride, who had been a rookie with the Giants in 1925, came the other way after being released by the same Dodgers. In

problem, head coach Owen and his captain, Flaherty, put their heads together and, with the aid of the equipment man, Abe Cohen, they begged and borrowed enough 'sneakers' (tennis shoes, basketball shoes and the like) to kit out the team. But the Giants didn't get around to wearing them until the beginning of the second half, by which time they trailed 10-3. When Bears head coach George Halas was informed of the Giants' change of footwear, he said, 'Good; step on their toes.' The Giants would fall further behind on Jack 'Automatic' Manders' second field goal, but then the rubber soles began to work their magic.

Rookie tailback Ed Danowski, who had replaced the injured Newman halfway through the regular season, threw a 28-yard touchdown pass to left end Ike Frankian. On their next possession, Strong ran 42 yards for the first of his two quick touchdowns, and Danowski put the final touches to a 27-point fourth-quarter rout when he rambled nine yards for the final score.

1935 saw the Giants win the Eastern division title for the third year in a row, and it came with some ease. Entering the season, Danowski displaced Newman as the starting quarterback and confirmed his status by leading the league in passing. Another player to come to prominence was Tod Goodwin, who had taken over from Flaherty as the starting right end. Goodwin, who was a rookie, led the NFL with 26 pass receptions. The passing game had become the Giants' strength, even though the offensive backfield still featured running back Strong, who had been joined by the fast emerging Elvin 'Kink' Richards.

Their NFL Championship Game opponents, the Detroit Lions, relied heavily on the rushing game and had three players, Ernie Caddel, Bill Shepherd and Earl 'Dutch' Clark amongst the NFL's top five rushers. Clark led the league in scoring with 55 points.

Again, as in the previous year, the playing conditions were far from ideal, with the heavy rains having transformed the pitch into a swamp which rapidly became a quagmire. While the Giants' passing game never got off the ground – an early injury to Goodwin did not help – Detroit sprung a surprise, completing two long passes on the opening drive which culminated in Leroy 'Ace' Gutowsky's two-yard touchdown run. The Lions were never seriously challenged and won easily by the score of 26-7.

There followed two quiet seasons, with the Giants just missing out on the division title in 1936, when they lost the final regular-season game to the Redskins. Newman, Badgro and Strong defected to a rival pro football organization, the American Football League. But there was new talent in the form of tackle Art Lewis and fullback Alphonse 'Tuffy' Leemans. The latter led the league in rushing with 830 yards, a Giants club record.

The following year, the Giants had a major shake-out with rookies filling 17 places on the 25-man squad. Also, they had new colours, blue jerseys and silver pants, and even a new offensive system, the 'A-formation', designed by head coach Owen. It had a line strong to one side while the backfield was strong to the other side. The ball was put

'Tuffy' Leemans (# 4), fullback, 1936-43.

in play by a direct snap to the left halfback instead of the T-formation quarterback. For the second year in a row, the Giants could have won the division title by beating the Redskins in the final game. But they were simply brushed aside 49-14 by the eventual NFL Champion Redskins, who were led by the sensational rookie quarterback, Sammy Baugh.

For the third year in a row, in 1938, it came down to a Giants-Redskins matchup to decide the destination of the Eastern division title. Once again, the Redskins fans came to the Polo Grounds in their thousands and in a manner befitting the expressive showman style of the Redskins' club owner, George Preston Marshall. In other words, they marched up Broadway behind their club band making lots of noise. But they weren't making much noise as they slipped out of town after seeing their heroes shut out 36-0. In the Championship Game, against the Green Bay Packers, the Giants were outgained by some way and trailed 17-16 in the third quarter. But victory, and their third NFL title came when Hank Soar leapt to catch a Danowski pass, despite being well covered by two defenders, before crashing into the end zone.

Not until 1956 would the Giants win their next NFL Championship, though over the intervening seventeen years they contested the Championship Game four times. Twice they lost to Green Bay and twice to the Chicago Bears. The closest they came to winning was against Green Bay in 1944. Four weeks earlier, the Giants had beaten the Packers 24-0 on the way to establishing the NFL's best regular-season record of 8-1-1 (Green Bay was 8-2-0). But for most of the Championship Game they were missing their top running back, the NFL's leading rusher, Bill Paschal, who had injured his ankle in the final regular-season game against Washington.

The Packers went into a second-quarter lead when fullback Ted Fritsch plunged one yard for a touchdown on a fourth-down play after the offense had been held for no gain in three downs. In the same quarter, with the Giants' defense keying on Green Bay's peerless wide receiver, Don Hutson, Fritsch drifted unmarked out of the backfield and caught a 23-yard pass from Irv Comp, before strolling unmolested the remaining five yards for a touchdown. The Giants scored a touchdown on the opening play of the fourth quarter but made no further inroads and lost 14-7.

Their 24-14 Championship Game loss to the Bears in 1946 ushered in a three-year period of mediocrity. And when they did put together a solid team for three years in a row they were thwarted by the Cleveland Browns, who had completely dominated in the four-year lifetime of the All-America Football Conference before joining the NFL in 1950. Over the three years, the Giants actually held a 4-2 edge in regular-season play but always were edged out of first place. In 1950, they were tied with the Browns at 10-2-0 but lost 8-3 in a specially-arranged playoff to decide the conference champion.

The big moment, when it came in 1956, was worth

Quarterback Charlie Conerly (1948-61).

Inset: Frank Gifford.

waiting for. The Giants buried the Bears 47-7 to win their fourth NFL Championship. The victory came under a new head coach, Jim Lee Howell, who had played nine seasons at end for the Giants, either side of his service in the Second World War. Howell, promoted from assistant coach with the Giants, applied the finishing touches to a rebuilding programme initiated in the later years of former head coach Owen, whom he replaced in 1954.

Perhaps Howell's smartest move was in hiring two assistant coaches, a little-known Vince Lombardi and a young Tom Landry, the latter who had played at defensive back for the Giants since 1950 and would remain active for two more seasons. Lombardi, whose special expertise lay in coaching the offense, was a rigid disciplinarian who placed great emphasis on football's basic principles. Landry was more the innovator and, following the lead given by coach Owen, who had introduced his famous 'Umbrella' defense in 1950 as one of his attempts to handle the Cleveland Browns, Landry came up with a defensive formation which would find wide acceptance throughout the league.

In the 'Umbrella' defense, the two defensive ends, on what formally was a six-man defensive line, would sometimes rush the passer and sometimes drop back into pass coverage, much in the manner of the modern-day outside linebackers. At that time, there would be only one player at linebacker, stationed in a central position to defend against the run, and four defensive backs. Extending this system, Landry produced the so-called 4-3 defense, which features four down-linemen and three linebackers. It is still in use by several NFL clubs, though the majority uses a further refinement, the 3-4 defense, which features three down-linemen and four linebackers.

Howell's new players included ends Ken MacAfee and Bob Schnelker, the latter who came in a trade with Philadelphia. Other newcomers were Dick Nolan, a defensive back who too would go on to a career in the coaching ranks; Don Heinrich, the former University of Washington quarterback who was signed as a backup to the incumbent, Charlie Conerly, and another quarterback, Bobby Clatterbuck. Conerly, an underrated passer who had played for the Giants since 1948, considered retirement but was talked out of it by Howell.

Already, the Giants had a stock of first-class veterans, numbering amongst them running backs Kyle Rote and Frank Gifford, defensive back Emlen Tunnell and tackle Roosevelt Brown. In 1955, Alex Webster would bring his power to the offensive backfield and Roosevelt Grier was acquired for the defensive line. A year later, the defense was further strengthened by the addition of linebacker Sam Huff, defensive ends Andy Robustelli and Jim Katcavage, and defensive tackle Dick Modzelewski.

It was a squad which would rate with the best of the modern-day clubs, though the nature of the game at that time meant that the statistics of individuals would appear very modest by comparison with the numbers logged by superstars of the present day.

Gifford was a beautiful athlete. Intelligent, silky-smooth, cultivated, with good speed and great hands, he was amongst the best in an era of outstanding dual-purpose backfield players.

Tunnell was one of the finest defensive backs in the history of the game. On his retirement in 1961 (he spent his last three years with Green Bay) he held the NFL records for both pass interceptions (79), interception yardage (1,282) and punt return yardage (2,209). The interception return yardage record still stands.

The Giants had finished strongly in 1955 and now, in 1956, they were ready. 1956 was the year they moved to Yankee Stadium. A sequence of five straight victories in mid-season enabled them to survive a modest final stretch in which they went 2-2-1. Their losses were to Washington and Cleveland, and the tie was against the Bears, to whom they would play host in the Championship Game. The pattern of the Giants' play in that season was that Heinrich would start at quarterback, probing for weaknesses, before Conerly came on to complete the execution. With Heinrich at the controls, the Giants took a 13-0 first-quarter lead and then Conerly directed a 21-point second-quarter scoring orgy. Third-stringer Clatterbuck was on at the end of the 47-7 rout.

The win marked the beginning of the second period of great success enjoyed by the Giants. Over the seven years beyond 1956, they won five more Eastern Conference Championships but, sadly, were defeated in all five NFL Championship Games.

Below: Del Shofner, split end, 1961-67.

Right: Quarterback Y.A. Tittle in pensive mood.

It was of little consolation to the Giants, but they did play in the game which, more than any other, is credited with bringing the excitement and spectacle of pro football to the American public. Their 1958 NFL Championship Game against the Baltimore Colts later was called 'The Greatest Game Ever Played', which, of course, it wasn't. But it was a thriller and held the attention of a national television audience for the full sixty minutes of regulation time and into overtime – the first ever.

The rosters were those one might expect of all-star teams. The Colts fielded Raymond Berry, Art Donovan, Gino Marchetti, Lenny Moore, Jim Parker, and had the fabled Johnny Unitas at quarterback. The Giants could point to Gifford, Huff, Robustelli, Brown and Tunnell. All eleven men are now enshrined in the Pro Football Hall of Fame. Pat Summerall, the highly respected CBS TV commentator, was the Giants' kicker.

The Giants took a 3-0 lead on Summerall's 36-yard field goal, and came from behind to lead 17-14 on a one-yard touchdown run by Mel Triplett and a 15-yard touchdown pass from Conerly to Gifford. Only seven seconds remained in regulation time when the Colts drew level on a 20-yard field goal by Steve Myhra. In overtime, the Colts took over after the Giants had been forced to punt and Unitas directed an 80-yard drive, culminating in fullback Alan Ameche's one-yard touchdown run which settled it.

The Giants had the opportunity to take revenge the following year when, again, they faced the Colts in the championship game. The Giants held the whip-hand entering the final quarter, as they led 9-7, but Unitas sparked a 24-point scoring burst to take the Colts to 31-16.

Before the start of the 1959 season, Lombardi left to become the head coach of the Green Bay Packers. In early 1960, Landry was named the head coach of the newly-formed Dallas Cowboys and at the end of that year, Howell relinquished his post as head coach of the Giants. The club's first choice as Howell's replacement was Lombardi but, after their approaches had been rejected, they promoted Allie Sherman, who had been a Giants assistant coach for the period 1949-53 and since 1959 (between times, he had been coaching in the Canadian Football League).

In each of Sherman's first three seasons, the Giants won the Eastern Conference title. They failed in all three league championship games but that period will be remembered more for the sheer exhuberance and brightness which they injected into the pro game.

In one of the master trades in pro football history, the Giants acquired the San Francisco quarterback, Y.A. Tittle, in exchange for a little known offensive guard, Lou Cordileone. Tittle took over at quarterback from Conerly in the second game of the season. In that year, 1961, the Giants also traded with the Rams for Del Shofner, a spectacular wide receiver. Another end, Joe Walton (he is now the head coach of the Jets), was obtained from Philadelphia, and cornerback Erich Barnes arrived from the Bears. On the season, Alex Webster came third in rushing behind Cleveland's Jim Brown and Green Bay's Jim Taylor, Shofner was the third-leading receiver with 68 catches, Dick Lynch led the league with nine pass interceptions and Barnes returned an interception 102 yards against Dallas, equalling an NFL record which still stands.

They came up short against Lombardi's Green Bay in the NFL Championship Game, when they were held scoreless while the Packers rolled up 37 points.

The following season was much the same, now with Tittle in full flow directing an offense which reached even greater heights of expression. Tittle set an NFL record with 33 touchdown passes and though no one else finished high in the league rankings, it seemed that everybody did something of note. Tittle threw seven touchdown passes against Washington to equal the NFL single-game record. On that day, Shofner caught eleven passes for 269 yards. Gifford, who had made a comeback after a year's absence, played mostly as a flanker, catching 39 passes for 796 yards and seven touchdowns. Once again, however, they fell to Green Bay in the championship game, though this time, they went down 16-7 with honour.

The final fling under Sherman came the following year. Tittle won the league passing title as the Giants maintained their grip on the Eastern Conference by the margin of one win ahead of Cleveland. But in the second quarter of the NFL title game against the Bears, he suffered a leg injury. The Giants fought all the way, even leading 7-0 and 10-7, but they couldn't quite hold off the Bears, who won by the score of 14-10.

A couple of surprising trades, Huff to Washington and Modzelewski to Cleveland, and the steady retirement of former star players over the next few years, left gaps which could not adequately be filled. The Giants eased into the period during which they were mostly mediocre and occasionally very poor.

Giants Personnel in the Pro Football Hall of Fame

Tim Mara, Owner (1925-59) 1963*
Jim Thorpe, Halfback (1925) 1963*
Joe Guyon, Halfback (1927) 1966*
Steve Owen, Tackle-Coach (1926-30, 1931-53) 1966*
Wilbur 'Pete' Henry, Tackle (1927) 1963*
Cal Hubbard, Tackle-End (1927-28, 1936) 1963*
Ray Flaherty, End (1928-29, 1931-35) 1976*
Morris 'Red' Badgro, End (1930-35) 1981*
Mel Hein, Center (1931-45) 1963*
Ken Strong, Halfback (1933-35, 1939, 1944-47) 1971*
Alphonse 'Tuffy' Leemans, Fullback (1937-43) 1978*
Arnie Herber, Quarterback (1944-45) 1966*
Emlen Tunnell, Safety (1948-58) 1967*
Frank Gifford, Halfback (1952-60, 1962-64) 1977*
Arnie Weinmeister, Defensive Tackle (1950-53) 1984*
Roosevelt Brown, Offensive Tackle (1953-65) 1975*
Sam Huff, Linebacker (1956-63) 1982*
Andy Robustelli, Defensive End (1956-64) 1971*
Don Maynard, Wide Receiver (1958) 1987*
Y.A. Tittle, Quarterback (1961-64) 1971*
Hugh McElhenny, Halfback (1963) 1970*
Fran Tarkenton, Quarterback (1967-71) 1986*
Larry Csonka, Running Back (1976-78) 1987*

*Indicates year of induction

Below: Ron Johnson (# 30), the Giants' first 1,000-yard rusher.
Right: Head coach Bill Parcells.
Far right: All-Pro linebacker Lawrence Taylor.

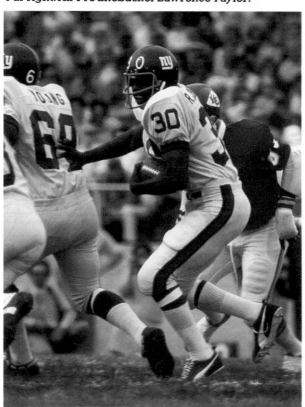

Giants Head Coaches

Coach	Years	Record (incl. playoffs)		
		W	L	T
Bob Folwell	1925	8	4	0
Joe Alexander	1926	8	4	1
Earl Potteiger	1927-28	15	8	3
LeRoy Andrews	1929-30	26	5	1
Steve Owen	1931-53	153	108	17
Jim Lee Howell	1954-60	54	29	4
Allie Sherman	1961-68	57	54	4
Alex Webster	1969-73	29	40	1
Bill Arnsparger*	1974-76	7	28	0
John McVay	1976-78	14	23	0
Ray Perkins	1979-82	24	35	0
Bill Parcells	1983-86	41	29	·1

*Replaced after seven games in 1976

They did sign several outstanding individuals, especially for the offense, but only rarely did they challenge for a title. The prolific but unpredictable and crazy-scrambling quarterback, Fran Tarkenton, who had frustrated the Vikings into letting him go, came in a trade in 1967. In combination with wide receiver Homer Jones, or anybody else for that matter, he was always dangerous. Jones was one of the league's most-feared deep threats even before the arrival of Tarkenton. Jones caught passes for more than 1,000 yards in each of 1966, 1967 and 1968, always at an average better than 20 yards per reception. In a change of emphasis, in 1970 Jones was traded to Cleveland in exchange for running back Ron Johnson, who became the first Giants player to rush for more than 1,000 yards in a single season (he gained 1,027 yards in 1970 and 1,182 yards in 1972). But the magic formula would not emerge, despite the efforts of head coach Sherman and his successors, Alex Webster, Bill Arnsparger and John McVay.

Ray Perkins, who became the head coach in 1979, fared no better initially, but in 1981, he took the Giants to the playoffs for the first time after seventeen fruitless years. It is to his tenure, which began shortly after the appointment of George Young as the club's vice president and general manager, that the true origins of the Giants' return to the top can be traced.

Quarterback Phil Simms was their prime pick in the 1979 draft. The Giants fans said, 'Phil who?' and booed the selection. But he proved them wrong, coming through adversity to give the finest performance in the history of the Super Bowl. No one argued with the selection of linebacker Lawrence Taylor in 1981. He was the best then and has been ever since. The diminutive running back, Joe Morris, came in the second round of the 1982 draft. He turned out to be lightning in a bottle and is on the way to rewriting the Giants' record book in all categories connected with rushing.

The process of wise selection and sound management continued when Bill Parcells filled the spot vacated by Perkins who, in December 1982, left to become the head coach at the University of Alabama. Perkins guided the Giants to a wild card spot in the playoffs in 1981 and, after two troubled seasons, Parcells' squads made the same trip in both 1984 and 1985. The story of their triumphant 1986 season has been told in Chapter One. The Giants are at the top, and when that happens they usually stick around.

GIANTS RECORD 1925-86

Year	Won	Lost	Tied	PF	PA						
1925	8	4	0	122	67	1959 (c)	10	2	0	284	170
1926	8	4	1	147	51	1960	6	4	2	271	261
1927 (a)	11	1	1	197	20	1961 (c)	10	3	1	368	220
1928	4	7	2	79	136	1962 (c)	12	2	0	398	283
1929	13	1	1	312	86	1963 (c)	11	3	0	448	280
1930	13	4	0	308	98	1964	2	10	2	241	399
1931	7	6	1	164	100	1965	7	7	0	270	338
1932	4	6	2	93	113	1966	1	12	1	263	501
1933 (b)	11	3	0	244	101	1967	7	7	0	369	379
1934 (b) (a)	8	5	0	147	107	1968	7	7	0	294	325
1935 (b)	9	3	0	180	96	1969	6	8	0	264	298
1936	5	6	1	115	163	1970	9	5	0	301	270
1937	6	3	2	128	109	1971	4	10	0	228	362
1938 (b) (a)	8	2	1	194	79	1972	8	6	0	331	247
1939 (b)	9	1	1	168	85	1973	2	11	1	226	362
1940	6	4	1	131	133	1974	2	12	0	195	299
1941 (b)	8	3	0	238	114	1975	5	9	0	216	306
1942	5	5	1	155	139	1976	3	11	0	170	250
1943	6	3	1	197	170	1977	5	9	0	181	265
1944 (b)	8	1	1	206	75	1978	6	10	0	264	298
1945	3	6	1	179	198	1979	6	10	0	237	323
1946 (b)	7	3	1	236	162	1980	4	12	0	249	425
1947	2	8	2	190	309	1981 (d)	9	7	0	295	257
1948	4	8	0	297	388	1982	4	5	0	164	160
1949	6	6	0	287	298	1983	3	12	1	267	347
1950	10	2	0	268	150	1984 (d)	9	7	0	299	301
1951	9	2	1	254	161	1985 (d)	10	6	0	399	283
1952	7	5	0	234	231	1986 (e) (f)	14	2	0	371	236
1953	3	9	0	179	277	(a) NFL Champion					
1954	7	5	0	293	184	(b) NFL Eastern Division Champion					
1955	6	5	1	267	223	(c) NFL Eastern Conference Champion					
1956 (c) (a)	8	3	1	264	197	(d) NFC Wild Card					
1957	7	5	0	254	211	(e) NFC Eastern Division Champion					
1958 (c)	9	3	0	246	183	(f) Super Bowl (NFL) Champion					

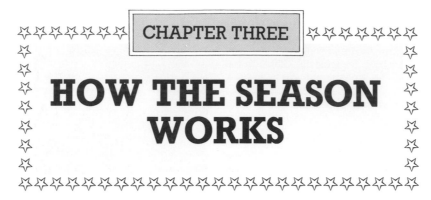

CHAPTER THREE

HOW THE SEASON WORKS

The National Football League consists of twenty-eight teams divided into two **Conferences,** the American Football Conference (AFC) and the National Football Conference (NFC). Each conference has fourteen teams, and is subdivided into two five-team **Divisions** and one four-team **Division.** These are essentially based on sensible geographical considerations but also take into account the traditional rivalries which were in existence when the expanded NFL was restructured in 1970. The teams are listed below in order of their final 1986 division standings since this is of importance in arriving at a team's schedule (fixture list) for 1987.

THE SCHEDULE

When considering a team's schedule, it's best to set aside the four teams who each finished the 1986 season in fifth place in their divisions. Looking at the remaining twenty-four, every team plays twelve games against others from its own conference. Again, excluding the four fifth-placed teams, every team will play four games against teams from the rival conference (known as Interconference games), specifically to allow fans in the cities of one conference the opportunity of seeing the star players and teams of the other conference. The structure of a team's schedule depends on whether it plays in a four-team or a five-team division.

AMERICAN FOOTBALL CONFERENCE

Eastern Division

	W	L	T
New England	11	5	0
New York Jets	10	6	0
Miami	8	8	0
Buffalo	4	12	0
Indianapolis	3	13	0

Central Division

	W	L	T
Cleveland	12	4	0
Cincinnati	10	6	0
Pittsburgh	6	10	0
Houston	5	11	0

Western Division

	W	L	T
Denver	11	5	0
Kansas City	10	6	0
Seattle	10	6	0
Los Angeles Raiders	8	8	0
San Diego	4	12	0

NATIONAL FOOTBALL CONFERENCE

Eastern Division

	W	L	T
New York Giants	14	2	0
Washington	12	4	0
Dallas	7	9	0
Philadelphia	5	10	1
St Louis	4	11	1

Central Division

	W	L	T
Chicago	14	2	0
Minnesota	9	7	0
Detroit	5	11	0
Green Bay	4	12	0
Tampa Bay	2	14	0

Western Division

	W	L	T
San Francisco	10	5	1
Los Angeles Rams	10	6	0
Atlanta	7	8	1
New Orleans	7	9	0

Four-Team Division

A typical schedule, e.g., for the Los Angeles Rams, appears below. It is set out, deliberately not in chronological order, but to emphasise that the schedule has a quite definite structure.

LOS ANGELES RAMS (NFC West)

Atlanta Falcons	NFC West	Home
Atlanta Falcons	NFC West	Away
New Orleans Saints	NFC West	Home
New Orleans Saints	NFC West	Away
San Francisco 49ers	NFC West	Home
San Francisco 49ers	NFC West	Away
Minnesota Vikings	NFC Central	Home
Tampa Bay Buccaneers	NFC Central	Home
Detroit Lions	NFC Central	Away
Dallas Cowboys	NFC East	Home
St Louis Cardinals	NFC East	Away
Washington Redskins	NFC East	Away
Cincinnati Bengals	AFC Central	Home
Cleveland Browns	AFC Central	Away
Houston Oilers	AFC Central	Away
Pittsburgh Steelers	AFC Central	Home

The Rams will always play their division rivals, Atlanta, New Orleans and San Francisco, both home and away. The flavour of intra-conference competition is maintained by six games, every year, against teams from outside their division but within their conference. There will always be three games against the NFC East and three against the NFC West. Again, every year, there will be four games against teams from a particular division of the rival conference, based on a three-year cycle. In 1987, they play against the AFC Central; in 1988 they will play teams from the AFC West and in 1989, the AFC East. For every team in the NFL, a complete list of opponents, other than those within a team's own division, is arrived at by applying the following formula. The letters and numbers refer to Conference, Division and final standing in that division. Thus the New York Giants, who are in the National Conference Eastern Division and finished first in that division, are identified as NE-1. Equally, the Houston Oilers, who are in the American Conference Central Division and finished fourth in that division, are labelled AC-4.

AFC EAST-AE

AE-1		AE-2		AE-3		AE-4		AE-5	
H	**A**	**H**	**A**	**H**	**A**	**H**	**A**	**H**	**A**
AC-1	AC-4	AC-2	AC-3	AC-3	AC-2	AC-4	AC-1	AC-2	AC-1
AW-4	AW-1	AW-3	AW-2	AW-2	AW-3	AW-1	AW-4	AC-4	AC-3
NE-3	NE-1	NE-3	NE-1	NE-1	NE-3	NE-1	NE-3	AW-5	AW-5
NE-4	NE-2	NE-4	NE-2	NE-2	NE-4	NE-2	NE-4	NC-5	NE-5

AFC CENTRAL-AC

AC-1		AC-2		AC-3		AC-4	
H	**A**	**H**	**A**	**H**	**A**	**H**	**A**
AE-4	AE-1	AE-3	AE-2	AE-2	AE-3	AE-1	AE-4
AE-5	AW-4	AW-2	AW-3	AE-5	AW-2	AW-4	AE-5
AW-1	AW-5	AW-5	AE-5	AW-3	AW-5	AW-5	AW-1
NW-2	NW-1	NW-1	NW-2	NW-1	NW-2	NW-2	NW-1
NW-3	NW-4	NW-4	NW-3	NW-4	NW-3	NW-3	NW-4

AFC WEST-AW

AW-1		AW-2		AW-3		AW-4		AW-5	
H	**A**	**H**	**A**	**H**	**A**	**H**	**A**	**H**	**A**
AC-4	AC-1	AC-3	AC-2	AC-2	AC-3	AC-1	AC-4	AC-1	AC-2
AE-1	AE-4	AE-2	AE-3	AE-3	AE-2	AE-4	AE-1	AC-3	AC-4
NC-1	NC-2	NC-2	NC-1	NC-2	NC-1	NC-1	NC-2	AE-5	AE-5
NC-3	NC-4	NC-4	NC-3	NC-4	NC-3	NC-3	NC-4	NE-5	NC-5

NFC EAST-NE

NE-1		NE-2		NE-3		NE-4		NE-5	
H	**A**	**H**	**A**	**H**	**A**	**H**	**A**	**H**	**A**
NC-4	NC-1	NC-3	NC-2	NC-2	NC-3	NC-1	NC-4	NC-5	NC-5
NW-1	NW-4	NW-2	NW-3	NW-3	NW-2	NW-4	NW-1	NW-2	NW-1
AE-1	AE-3	AE-1	AE-3	AE-3	AE-1	AE-3	AE-1	NW-4	NW-3
AE-2	AE-4	AE-2	AE-4	AE-4	AE-2	AE-4	AE-2	AE-5	AW-5

NFC CENTRAL-NC

NC-1		NC-2		NC-3		NC-4		NC-5	
H	**A**	**H**	**A**	**H**	**A**	**H**	**A**	**H**	**A**
NE-1	NE-4	NE-2	NE-3	NE-3	NE-2	NE-4	NE-1	NE-5	NE-5
NW-4	NW-1	NW-3	NW-2	NW-2	NW-3	NW-1	NW-4	NW-1	NW-2
AW-2	AW-1	AW-1	AW-2	AW-2	AW-1	AW-1	AW-2	NW-3	NW-4
AW-3	AW-4	AW-4	AW-3	AW-3	AW-4	AW-4	AW-3	AW-5	AE-5

NFC WEST-NW

NW-1		NW-2		NW-3		NW-4	
H	**A**	**H**	**A**	**H**	**A**	**H**	**A**
NC-1	NC-4	NC-2	NC-3	NC-3	NC-2	NC-4	NC-1
NE-4	NC-5	NC-5	NE-2	NE-2	NC-5	NC-5	NE-4
NE-5	NE-1	NE-3	NE-5	NE-5	NE-3	NE-1	NE-5
AC-1	AC-2	AC-2	AC-1	AC-2	AC-1	AC-1	AC-2
AC-4	AC-3	AC-3	AC-4	AC-3	AC-4	AC-4	AC-3

Five-Team Division (Top Four Teams Only)

In the AFC East the schedules for the top four teams have identical structure and include home and away games against the other four teams in the division. Each of the top four teams plays two games against AFC Central teams and two against the AFC West. Also, they play the top four teams in the NFC East as part of their three-year cycle of interconference games. In 1988, they will play teams from the NFC Central and, in 1989, the NFC West. Below is the schedule structure for the New England Patriots.

NEW ENGLAND PATRIOTS (AFC East)

Buffalo Bills	AFC East	Home
Buffalo Bills	AFC East	Away
Indianapolis Colts	AFC East	Home
Indianapolis Colts	AFC East	Away
Miami Dolphins	AFC East	Home
Miami Dolphins	AFC East	Away
New York Jets	AFC East	Home
New York Jets	AFC East	Away
Cleveland Browns	AFC Central	Home
Houston Oilers	AFC Central	Away
Los Angeles Raiders	AFC West	Home
Denver Broncos	AFC West	Away
Dallas Cowboys	NFC East	Home
New York Giants	NFC East	Away
Philadelphia Eagles	NFC East	Home
Washington Redskins	NFC East	Away

Fifth-Placed Teams

In the AFC, the two fifth-placed teams will each play eight games against teams from their own division and will always play single games against each of the four AFC Central division teams. In the NFC, the two fifth-placed teams each play eight games against teams within their own division and will always play single games against the four NFC West teams. Each of the four fifth-placed teams is guaranteed home and away games against the other fifth-placed team in its own conference, and single games against the two fifth-placed teams from the rival conference. The schedule structures for all four teams are set out as follows:

Indianapolis (AFC East)

AFC East		8 games
AFC Central		4 games
San Diego	(AFC)	Home
San Diego	(AFC)	Away
St Louis	(NFC)	Away
Tampa Bay	(NFC)	Home

San Diego (AFC West)

AFC West		8 games
AFC Central		4 games
Indianapolis	(AFC)	Home
Indianapolis	(AFC)	Away
St Louis	(NFC)	Home
Tampa Bay	(NFC)	Away

St Louis (NFC East)

NFC East		8 games
NFC West		4 games
Tampa Bay	(NFC)	Home
Tampa Bay	(NFC)	Away
Indianapolis	(AFC)	Home
San Diego	(AFC)	Away

Tampa Bay (NFC Central)

NFC Central		8 games
NFC West		4 games
St Louis	(NFC)	Home
St Louis	(NFC)	Away
Indianapolis	(AFC)	Away
San Diego	(AFC)	Home

THE PLAYOFFS

On completion of the regular season, each conference holds an elimination competition known as the Playoffs. The teams involved are the three division winners and two Wild Card teams, namely those two, other than the division winners, who have the best won-lost-tied records. The two Wild Card teams play each other to decide which one advances to join the three division winners in the Divisional Playoffs (conference semi-final games). The results of the 1986 National Football Conference playoffs are set out as follows:

Wild Card Game
Los Angeles Rams 7 at Washington 19

Divisional Playoffs
San Francisco 3 at New York Giants 49
Washington 27 at Chicago 13

NFC Championship Game
Washington 0 at New York Giants 17
New York advanced to Super Bowl XXI as NFC Champions.

Home-Field Advantage in the Playoffs
For the Wild Card game, the team with the better regular-season record is given the home-field advantage. Again, in the Divisional Playoffs, the home-field advantage goes to the team with the better regular-season record except in so far as the Wild Card winner can never play at home. For the NFC playoffs then, the pecking order was as follows:

	W	L	T
New York Giants*	14	2	0
Chicago*	14	2	0
San Francisco*	10	5	1
Washington†	12	4	0
Los Angeles Rams†	10	6	0

* Division Champions
† Wild Card teams

TIE-BREAKING PROCEDURES

Ties are broken by the following list of criteria:

Teams in the same division
A: Two teams
1. Head-to-head (best record in games played between the two teams)
2. Best record in games played within the division
3. Best record in games played within the conference
4. Best record in common games
5. Best net points scored in division games (just like goal difference in soccer)
6. Best net points in all games

B: Three or More Teams (if two teams remain tied after all other teams are eliminated, the tie-breaking procedure reverts to A:1.)
1. Head-to-head (best record in games played between the teams)
2. Best record in games played within the division
3. Best record in games played within the conference
4. Best record in common games
5. Best net points in division games
6. Best net points in all games

Tie-Breakers for the Wild Card places
(a) If the teams are from the same division, the division tie-breaker is applied.
(b) If the teams are from different divisions, the following procedure is adopted:
C: Two Teams
1. Head-to-head (if they have played each other)
2. Best record in games played within the conference
3. Best record in common games (minimum of four)
4. Best average net points in conference games
5. Best net points in all games

D: Three or More Teams (If two teams remain tied after all other teams are eliminated, the tie-breaking procedure reverts to A:1, or C:1, whichever is applicable.)
1. Head-to-head sweep (this applies only if one team has either beaten or lost to all the others)
2. Best record in games played within the conference
3. Best record in common games (minimum of four)
4. Best average net points in conference games
5. Best net points in all games

1986 Tie-Breakers
Giants-Bears (Home-field advantage):
C:2; Giants (11-1), Bears (10-2)
Broncos-Patriots (Home-field advantage):
C:1; Broncos 27 – Patriots 20
Jets-Chiefs-Bengals-Seahawks (Wild Cards):
D:2; Jets (8-4), Chiefs (9-5), Bengals (7-5), Seahawks (7-5)
The Bengals and the Seahawks were eliminated.
Jets-Chiefs (Home-field advantage):
C:2; Jets (8-4), Chiefs (9-5)

1987 Pro Bowl MVP Reggie White.

THE SUPER BOWL

Though the obvious comparison is with the FA Cup Final, the Super Bowl is best seen as the culmination of an end-of-season knockout competition, involving the champions of six mini leagues together with the Wild Card teams, the latter being considered, perhaps, as potential giant killers. (Only one team, the Oakland Raiders, has won the Super Bowl Championship starting out as a Wild Card.) Unlike for the FA Cup Final, the Super Bowl venue changes from year to year and, since the site is chosen some three years in advance, it is possible for one team to be playing 'at home'. This has never occurred, though both the Los Angeles Rams and the San Francisco 49ers were close to home when they played in Super Bowls XIV and XIX respectively. In selecting the venue, great importance is placed on good weather. Consequently, with the exception of the Pontiac Silverdome (this is a domed stadium), all past Super Bowl stadia have been in the 'sunshine belt', stretching from Florida to California. Super Bowl XXII will be played at San Diego's Jack Murphy Stadium and XXIII at Robbie Stadium, Miami.

THE PRO BOWL

At the end of the season, the best players from each conference fly off to Hawaii to give the fans out there a treat. The teams are selected by a ballot of head coaches and players in each conference. Each team has two equal votes, those being the head coach's and a consensus of the players' selections. Coaches and players vote only for players in their own conference and may not vote for players from their own teams. Last year, in the lowest-scoring AFC-NFC Pro Bowl thus far, the AFC held on to win 10-6.

AFC-NFC Pro Bowl Results – NFC leads series 10-7

YEAR	DATE	WINNER	LOSER	SITE	ATTENDANCE
1987	Feb 1	AFC 10	NFC 6	Honolulu	50,101
1986	Feb. 2	NFC 28	AFC 24	Honolulu	50,101
1985	Jan. 27	AFC 22	NFC 14	Honolulu	50,385
1984	Jan. 29	NFC 45	AFC 3	Honolulu	50,445
1983	Feb. 6	NFC 20	AFC 19	Honolulu	49,883
1982	Jan. 31	AFC 16	NFC 13	Honolulu	50,402
1981	Feb. 1	NFC 21	AFC 7	Honolulu	50,360
1980	Jan. 27	NFC 37	AFC 27	Los Angeles	49,800
1979	Jan. 29	NFC 13	AFC 7	Tampa	46,281
1978	Jan. 23	NFC 14	AFC 13	Seattle	51,337
1977	Jan. 17	AFC 24	NFC 14	New Orleans	64,752
1976	Jan. 26	NFC 23	AFC 20	Miami	30,546
1975	Jan. 20	NFC 17	AFC 10	Kansas City	26,484
1974	Jan. 20	AFC 15	NFC 13	Dallas	66,918
1973	Jan. 21	AFC 33	NFC 28	Los Angeles	37,091
1972	Jan. 23	AFC 26	NFC 13	Los Angeles	53,647
1971	Jan. 24	NFC 27	AFC 6		48,222

PRO BOWL ROSTERS
(Original selections – starters in Capitals)

OFFENSE	AMERICAN FOOTBALL CONFERENCE		NATIONAL FOOTBALL CONFERENCE	
Wide Receivers	AL TOON	N.Y. Jets	JERRY RICE	San Francisco
	STEVE LARGENT	Seattle	GARY CLARK	Washington
	Stanley Morgan	New England	Mike Quick	Philadelphia
	Mark Duper	Miami	Art Monk	Washington
Tight Ends	TODD CHRISTENSEN	L.A. Raiders	MARK BAVARO	N.Y. Giants
	Ozzie Newsome	Cleveland	Steve Jordan	Minnesota
Tackles	ANTHONY MUNOZ	Cincinnati	JIM COVERT	Chicago
	CODY RISIEN	Cleveland	JACKIE SLATER	L.A. Rams
	Chris Hinton	Indianapolis	Brad Benson	N.Y. Giants
			Joe Jacoby*	Washington
Guards	MAX MONTOYA	Cincinnati	DENNIS HARRAH	L.A. Rams
	KEITH BISHOP	Denver	BILL FRALIC	Atlanta
	Roy Foster	Miami	Russ Grimm	Washington
Centers	DWIGHT STEPHENSON	Miami	JAY HILGENBERG	Chicago
	Ray Donaldson	Indianapolis	Doug Smith	L.A. Rams
Quarterbacks	DAN MARINO	Miami	TOMMY KRAMER	Minnesota
	John Elway	Denver	Jay Schroeder	Washington
Running Backs	CURT WARNER	Seattle	ERIC DICKERSON	L.A. Rams
	JAMES BROOKS	Cincinnati	WALTER PAYTON	Chicago
	Marcus Allen	L.A. Raiders	Rueben Mayes	New Orleans
	Gary Anderson	San Diego	Joe Morris	N.Y. Giants

DEFENSE

Defensive Ends	RULON JONES	Denver	DEXTER MANLEY	Washington
	HOWIE LONG	L.A. Raiders	REGGIE WHITE	Philadelphia
	Jacob Green	Seattle	Leonard Marshall	N.Y. Giants
Nose Tackles	BILL MAAS	Kansas City	STEVE McMICHAEL	Chicago
	Bob Golic	Cleveland	Jim Burt	N.Y. Giants
Outside Linebackers	ANDRE TIPPETT	New England	LAWRENCE TAYLOR	N.Y. Giants
	CHIP BANKS	Cleveland	WILBER MARSHALL	Chicago
	Mike Merriweather	Pittsburgh	Rickey Jackson	New Orleans
Inside Linebackers	KARL MECKLENBURG	Denver	MIKE SINGLETARY	Chicago
	JOHN OFFERDAHL	Miami	HARRY CARSON	N.Y. Giants
	Fredd Young	Seattle	Carl Ekern	L.A. Rams
Cornerbacks	MIKE HAYNES	L.A. Raiders	DARRELL GREEN	Washington
	HANFORD DIXON	Cleveland	LeROY IRVIN	L.A. Rams
	Ray Clayborn	New England	Jerry Gray	L.A. Rams
	Frank Minnifield*	Cleveland		
Safeties	DERON CHERRY	Kansas City	DAVE DUERSON	Chicago
	DENNIS SMITH	Denver	RONNIE LOTT	San Francisco
	Lloyd Burruss	Kansas City	Joey Browner	Minnesota

SPECIAL TEAMS

Placekicker	TONY FRANKLIN	New England	MORTEN ANDERSEN	New Orleans
Punter	ROHN STARK	Indianapolis	SEAN LANDETA	N.Y. Giants
Kick Returner	BOBBY JOE EDMONDS	Seattle	VAI SIKAHEMA	St Louis
Specialist	MOSI TATUPU	New England	RON WOLFLEY	St Louis
Head Coach	MARTY SCHOTTENHEIMER	Cleveland	JOE GIBBS	Washington

*Special selection made by head coach

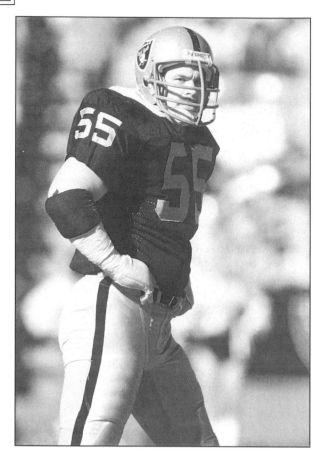

Above: Matt Millen.

Below: Eric Dickerson blocks for Walter Payton (# 34) in the 1987 Pro Bowl.

AN ALL-PRO TEAM

Anyone can pick his or her own All-Pro team and just about everyone does. Here's the list of my heroes.

Wide Receivers	Stanley Morgan	New England
	Mike Quick	Philadelphia
Tight End	Mark Bavaro	N.Y. Giants
Tackles	Gary Zimmerman	Minnesota
	Chris Hinton	Indianapolis
Guards	Mike Munchak	Houston
	Bill Fralic	Atlanta
Center	Dwight Stephenson	Miami
Quarterback	Dan Marino	Miami
Running Backs	Eric Dickerson	L.A. Rams
	Walter Payton	Chicago
Defensive Ends	Howie Long	L.A. Raiders
	Reggie White	Philadelphia
Defensive Tackles	Dan Hampton	Chicago
	Joe Klecko	N.Y. Jets
Outside Linebackers	Lawrence Taylor	N.Y. Giants
	Andre Tippett	New England
Inside Linebackers	Mike Singletary	Chicago
	Matt Millen	L.A. Raiders
Safeties	Kenny Easley	Seattle
	Ronnie Lott	San Francisco
Cornerbacks	Mike Haynes	L.A. Raiders
	Hanford Dixon	Cleveland
Placekicker	Morten Andersen	New Orleans
Punter	Rohn Stark	Indianapolis
Punt Returner	Darrell Green	Washington
Kickoff Returner	Dennis Gentry	Chicago
Special-team Specialist	Fredd Young	Seattle
Head Coach	Dan Reeves	Denver

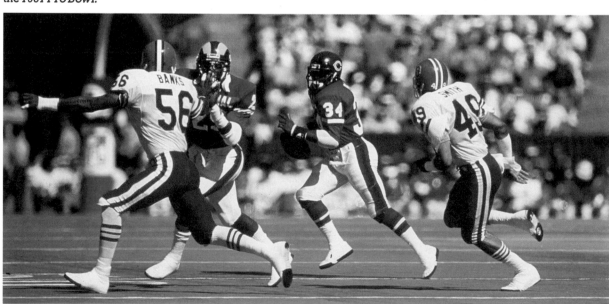

CHAPTER FOUR

ALL-TIME RECORDS

CHAMPIONS 1920-1986

National Football League 1920-1969
(Until 1933 based solely on regular-season play)

1920 Akron Pros
1921 Chicago Staleys
1922 Canton Bulldogs
1923 Canton Bulldogs
1924 Cleveland Bulldogs
1925 Chicago Cardinals
1926 Frankford Yellow Jackets
1927 New York Giants
1928 Providence Steam Roller
1929 Green Bay Packers
1930 Green Bay Packers
1931 Green Bay Packers
1932 Chicago Bears 9 – Portsmouth Spartans 0
     (Championship Playoff)

NFL Championship Games 1933-69

1933 Chicago Bears 23 – New York Giants 21
1934 New York Giants 30 – Chicago Bears 13
1935 Detroit Lions 26 – New York Giants 7
1936 Green Bay Packers 21 – Boston Redskins 6
1937 Washington Redskins 28 – Chicago Bears 21
1938 New York Giants 23 – Green Bay Packers 17
1939 Green Bay Packers 27 – New York Giants 0
1940 Chicago Bears 73 – Washington Redskins 0
1941 Chicago Bears 37 – New York Giants 9
1942 Washington Redskins 14 – Chicago Bears 6
1943 Chicago Bears 41 – Washington Redskins 21
1944 Green Bay Packers 14 – New York Giants 7
1945 Cleveland Rams 15 – Washington Redskins 14
1946 Chicago Bears 24 – New York Giants 14
1947 Chicago Cardinals 28 – Philadelphia Eagles 21
1948 Philadelphia Eagles 7 – Chicago Cardinals 0
1949 Philadelphia Eagles 14 – Los Angeles Rams 0
1950 Cleveland Browns 30 – Los Angeles Rams 28
1951 Los Angeles Rams 24 – Cleveland Browns 17
1952 Detroit Lions 17 – Cleveland Browns 7
1953 Detroit Lions 17 – Cleveland Browns 16
1954 Cleveland Browns 56 – Detroit Lions 10
1955 Cleveland Browns 38 – Los Angeles Rams 14
1956 New York Giants 47 – Chicago Bears 7
1957 Detroit Lions 59 – Cleveland Browns 14
1958 Baltimore Colts 23 – New York Giants 17 (OT)
1959 Baltimore Colts 31 – New York Giants 16
1960 Philadelphia Eagles 17 – Green Bay Packers 13
1961 Green Bay Packers 37 – New York Giants 0
1962 Green Bay Packers 16 – New York Giants 7
1963 Chicago Bears 14 – New York Giants 10
1964 Cleveland Browns 27 – Baltimore Colts 0
1965 Green Bay Packers 23 – Cleveland Browns 12
1966 Green Bay Packers 34 – Dallas Cowboys 27
1967 Green Bay Packers 21 – Dallas Cowboys 17
1968 Baltimore Colts 34 – Cleveland Browns 0
1969 Minnesota Vikings 27 – Cleveland Browns 7

American Football League Championship Games 1960-1969

1960 Houston Oilers 24 – Los Angeles Chargers 16
1961 Houston Oilers 10 – San Diego Chargers 3
1962 Dallas Texans 20 – Houston Oilers 17 (OT)
1963 San Diego Chargers 51 – Boston Patriots 10
1964 Buffalo Bills 20 – San Diego Chargers 7
1965 Buffalo Bills 23 – San Diego Chargers 0
1966 Kansas City Chiefs 31 – Buffalo Bills 7
1967 Oakland Raiders 40 – Houston Oilers 7
1968 New York Jets 27 – Oakland Raiders 23
1969 Kansas City Chiefs 17 – Oakland Raiders 7

CONFERENCE CHAMPIONSHIP GAMES 1970-1986
NFC

1970 Dallas Cowboys 17 – San Francisco 49ers 10
1971 Dallas Cowboys 14 – San Francisco 49ers 3
1972 Washington Redskins 26 – Dallas Cowboys 3
1973 Minnesota Vikings 27 – Dallas Cowboys 10
1974 Minnesota Vikings 14 – Los Angeles Rams 10
1975 Dallas Cowboys 37 – Los Angeles Rams 7
1976 Minnesota Vikings 24 – Los Angeles Rams 13
1977 Dallas Cowboys 23 – Minnesota Vikings 6
1978 Dallas Cowboys 28 – Los Angeles Rams 0
1979 Los Angeles Rams 9 – Tampa Bay Buccaneers 0
1980 Philadelphia Eagles 20 – Dallas Cowboys 7
1981 San Francisco 49ers 28 – Dallas Cowboys 27
1982 Washington Redskins 31 – Dallas Cowboys 17
1983 Washington Redskins 24 – San Francisco 49ers 21
1984 San Francisco 49ers 23 – Chicago Bears 0
1985 Chicago Bears 24 – Los Angeles Rams 0
1986 New York Giants 17 – Washington Redskins 0

AFC

1970 Baltimore Colts 27 – Oakland Raiders 17
1971 Miami Dolphins 21 – Baltimore Colts 0
1972 Miami Dolphins 21 – Pittsburgh Steelers 17
1973 Miami Dolphins 27 – Oakland Raiders 10
1974 Pittsburgh Steelers 24 – Oakland Raiders 13
1975 Pittsburgh Steelers 16 – Oakland Raiders 10
1976 Oakland Raiders 24 – Pittsburgh Steelers 7
1977 Denver Broncos 20 – Oakland Raiders 17
1978 Pittsburgh Steelers 34 – Houston Oilers 5
1979 Pittsburgh Steelers 27 – Houston Oilers 13
1980 Oakland Raiders 34 – San Diego Chargers 27
1981 Cincinnati Bengals 27 – San Diego Chargers 7
1982 Miami Dolphins 14 – New York Jets 0
1983 Los Angeles Raiders 30 – Seattle Seahawks 14
1984 Miami Dolphins 45 – Pittsburgh Steelers 28
1985 New England Patriots 31 – Miami Dolphins 14
1986 Denver Broncos 23 – Cleveland Browns 20 (OT)

Above: The Orange Bowl, scene of five Super Bowls.

Left: The Chicago Bears' Super Bowl Championship ring.

Super Bowl 1966-1986

Season	SB	Winner		Loser		Stadium	Attendance
1966	I	Green Bay	35	Kansas City	10	Los Angeles Coliseum	61,946
1967	II	Green Bay	33	Oakland	14	Miami Orange Bowl	75,546
1968	III	N.Y. Jets	16	Baltimore	7	Miami Orange Bowl	75,389
1969	IV	Kansas City	23	Minnesota	7	New Orleans Tulane Stadium	80,562
1970	V	Baltimore	16	Dallas	13	Miami Orange Bowl	79,204
1971	VI	Dallas	24	Miami	3	New Orleans Tulane Stadium	81,023
1972	VII	Miami	14	Washington	7	Los Angeles Coliseum	90,182
1973	VIII	Miami	24	Minnesota	7	Houston Rice Stadium	71,882
1974	IX	Pittsburgh	16	Minnesota	6	New Orleans Tulane Stadium	80,997
1975	X	Pittsburgh	21	Dallas	17	Miami Orange Bowl	80,187
1976	XI	Oakland	32	Minnesota	14	Pasadena Rose Bowl	103,438
1977	XII	Dallas	27	Denver	10	New Orleans Superdome	75,583
1978	XIII	Pittsburgh	35	Dallas	31	Miami Orange Bowl	79,484
1979	XIV	Pittsburgh	31	L.A. Rams	19	Pasadena Rose Bowl	103,985
1980	XV	Oakland	27	Philadelphia	10	New Orleans Superdome	76,135
1981	XVI	San Francisco	26	Cincinnati	21	Pontiac Silverdome	81,270
1982	XVII	Washington	27	Miami	17	Pasadena Rose Bowl	103,667
1983	XVIII	L.A. Raiders	38	Washington	9	Tampa Stadium	72,920
1984	XIX	San Francisco	38	Miami	16	Stanford Stadium	84,059
1985	XX	Chicago	46	New England	10	New Orleans Superdome	73,818
1986	XXI	N.Y. Giants	39	Denver	20	Pasadena Rose Bowl	101,643

ALL-TIME INDIVIDUAL RECORDS
(Regular Season only – New Records and Records tied are in bold type)

CAREER BEST

SEASONS PLAYED	26	George Blanda
GAMES PLAYED	340	George Blanda
POINTS	2,002	George Blanda (9-TD, 943-EP, 335-FG)
EXTRA POINTS	943	George Blanda
FIELD GOALS	373	Jan Stenerud
TOUCHDOWNS		
Rushing and Pass Receiving	126	Jim Brown (106-R, 20-P)
Rushing	106	Jim Brown
		Walter Payton
Pass Receiving	99	Don Hutson
Passes Thrown	342	Fran Tarkenton
By Interception Return	9	Ken Houston
By Punt Return	8	Jack Christiansen
		Rick Upchurch
By Kickoff Return	6	Ollie Matson
		Gale Sayers
		Travis Williams
By Fumble Recovery Return	4	Billy Thompson
YARDAGE		
Rushing	**16,193**	**Walter Payton**
Pass Receiving	**12,146**	**Charlie Joiner**
Passing	47,003	Fran Tarkenton
HOW MANY TIMES		
Pass Receptions	**750**	**Charlie Joiner**
Passes Completed	3,686	Fran Tarkenton
Interceptions	81	Paul Krause
100-Yard Rushing Games	**77**	**Walter Payton**
100-Yard Pass Receiving Games	50	Don Maynard
1,000-Yard Rushing Seasons	**10**	**Walter Payton**
MOST SEASONS LEADING LEAGUE		
Points	5	Don Hutson, Green Bay 1940-44
		Gino Cappelletti, Boston 1961, 1963-66
Extra Points	8	George Blanda, Chicago Bears 1956, Houston 1961-62,
		Oakland 1967-69, 1972, 1974
Field Goals	5	Lou Groza, Cleveland Browns 1950, 1952-54, 1957
Touchdowns	8	Don Hutson, Green Bay 1935-38, 1941-44
Touchdowns, Rushing	5	Jim Brown, Cleveland Browns 1957-59, 1963, 1965
Touchdowns, Pass Receiving	9	Don Hutson, Green Bay 1935-38, 1940-44
Touchdowns, Passes Thrown	4	Johnny Unitas, Baltimore 1957-60
		Len Dawson, Dallas Texans 1962, Kansas City 1963, 1965-66
Yards, Rushing	8	Jim Brown, Cleveland Browns 1957-61, 1963-65
Yards, Pass Receiving	7	Don Hutson, Green Bay 1936, 1938-39, 1941-44
Yards, Passing	5	Sonny Jurgensen, Philadelphia 1961-62, Washington 1966-67, 1969
Pass Receptions	8	Don Hutson, Green Bay 1936-37, 1939, 1941-45
Passes Completed	5	Sammy Baugh, Washington 1937, 1943, 1945, 1947-48
Pass Interceptions	3	Everson Walls, Dallas 1981-82, 1985

Walter Payton (# 34), whose name continues to be written in bold.

SEASON BEST

POINTS	176	Paul Hornung, Green Bay 1960 (15-TD, 41-EP, 15-FG)
EXTRA POINTS	66	Uwe von Schamann, Miami 1984
FIELD GOALS	35	Ali Haji-Sheikh, N.Y. Giants 1983
TOUCHDOWNS		
Rushing and Pass Receiving	24	John Riggins, Washington 1983 (24-R)
Rushing	24	John Riggins, Washington 1983
Pass Receiving	18	Mark Clayton, Miami 1984

Passes Thrown	48	Dan Marino, Miami 1984
By Interception Return	4	Ken Houston, Houston 1971
		Jim Kearney, Kansas City 1972
By Punt Return	4	Jack Christiansen, Detroit 1951
		Rick Upchurch, Denver 1976
By Kickoff Return	4	Travis Williams, Green Bay 1967
		Cecil Turner, Chicago 1970
By Fumble Recovery Return	2	By many players
YARDAGE		
Rushing	2,105	Eric Dickerson, L.A. Rams 1984
Pass Receiving	1,746	Charley Hennigan, Houston 1961
Passing	5,084	Dan Marino, Miami 1984
HOW MANY TIMES		
Pass Receptions	106	Art Monk, Washington 1984
Passes Completed	**378**	**Dan Marino, Miami 1986**
Interceptions	14	Dick 'Night Train' Lane, L.A. Rams 1952

GAME BEST

POINTS	40	Ernie Nevers (6-TD, 4-EP), Chicago Cardinals v Chicago Bears 1929
EXTRA POINTS	9	Pat Harder, Chicago Cardinals v N.Y. Giants 1948
		Bob Waterfield, L.A. Rams v Baltimore 1950
		Charlie Gogolak, Washington v N.Y. Giants 1966
FIELD GOALS	7	Jim Bakken, St Louis v Pittsburgh 1967
TOUCHDOWNS		
All methods of scoring	6	Ernie Nevers (6-R), Chicago Cardinals v Chicago Bears 1929
		Dub Jones (4-R, 2-P), Cleveland v Chicago Bears 1951
		Gale Sayers (4-R, 1-P, 1-Ret) Chicago Bears v San Francisco 1965
Rushing	6	Ernie Nevers, Chicago Cardinals v Chicago Bears 1929
Pass Receiving	5	Bob Shaw, Chicago Cardinals v Baltimore 1950
		Kellen Winslow, San Diego v Oakland 1981
Passes Thrown	7	Sid Luckman, Chicago Bears v N.Y. Giants 1943
		Adrian Burk, Philadelphia v Washington 1954
		George Blanda, Houston v N.Y. Titans 1961
		Y.A. Tittle, N.Y. Giants v Washington 1962
		Joe Kapp, Minnesota v Baltimore 1969
YARDAGE		
Rushing	275	Walter Payton, Chicago Bears v Minnesota 1977
Pass Receiving	309	Stephone Paige, Kansas City v San Diego 1985
Passing	554	Norm Van Brocklin, L.A. Rams v N.Y. Yanks 1951
HOW MANY TIMES		
Rushing Attempts	43	Butch Woolfolk, N.Y. Giants v Philadelphia 1983
		James Wilder, Tampa Bay v Green Bay 1984 (OT)
Pass Receptions	18	Tom Fears, L.A. Rams v Green Bay 1950
Passes Completed	42	Richard Todd, N.Y. Jets v San Francisco 1980
Interceptions	4	By many players
LONGEST		
Touchdown Rushing	99 yds	Tony Dorsett, Dallas v Minnesota 1982
Touchdown Pass Receiving	99 yds	Andy Farkas (from Filchock), Washington v Pittsburgh 1939
		Bobby Mitchell (from Izo), Washington v Cleveland 1963
		Pat Studstill (from Sweetan), Detroit v Baltimore 1966
		Gerry Allen (from Jurgensen), Washington v Chicago 1968
		Cliff Branch (from Plunkett), L.A. Raiders v Washington 1983
		Mike Quick (from Jaworski), Philadelphia v Atlanta 1985
Field Goal	63 yds	Tom Dempsey, New Orleans v Detroit 1970
Punt Return (All TDs)	98 yds	Gil LeFebvre, Cincinnati v Brooklyn 1933
		Charlie West, Minnesota v Washington 1968
		Dennis Morgan, Dallas v St Louis 1974

Kickoff Return (All TDs)	106 yds	Al Carmichael, Green Bay v Chicago Bears 1956
		Noland Smith, Kansas City v Denver 1967
		Roy Green, St Louis v Dallas 1979
Interception Return (All TDs)	102 yds	Bob Smith, Detroit v Chicago Bears 1949
		Erich Barnes, N.Y. Giants v Dallas 1961
		Gary Barbaro, Kansas City v Seattle 1977
		Louis Breeden, Cincinnati v San Diego 1981
Fumble Recovery Return (TD)	104 yds	Jack Tatum, Oakland v Green Bay 1972

TEAM RECORDS

Most Championships	11	Green Bay, 1929-31, 1936, 1939, 1944, 1961-62, 1965-67
	9	Chicago Bears, 1921, 1932-33, 1940-41, 1943, 1946, 1963, 1985
	5	**N.Y. Giants, 1927, 1934, 1938, 1956, 1986**
	4	Detroit, 1935, 1952-53, 1957
		Cleveland Browns, 1950, 1954-55, 1964
		Baltimore, 1958-59, 1968, 1970
		Pittsburgh, 1974-75, 1978-79
		Oakland/L.A. Raiders, 1967, 1976, 1980, 1983
Most Consecutive Games Won (inc. playoffs)	18	Chicago Bears, 1933-34 and 1941-42; Miami, 1972-73
Most Consecutive Games Won (exc. playoffs)	17	Chicago Bears, 1933-34
Most Consecutive Games Lost	26	Tampa Bay, 1976-77
Most Points in a Season	541	Washington, 1983
Fewest Points in a Season (Since 1932)	37	Cincinnati-St Louis, 1934
Most Points in a Game	72	Washington v N.Y. Giants, 1966
Most Points (Both Teams) in a Game	113	Washington v N.Y. Giants, 1966
Fewest Points (Both Teams) in a Game	0	Many teams; last time N.Y. Giants v Detroit, 1943

ALL-TIME TOP TWENTY
(1986 Active players in capitals)

All-Time Leading Rushers

		Yrs.	Att.	Yards	Ave.	TDs
1.	WALTER PAYTON	12	3,692	16,193	4.4	106
2.	Jim Brown	9	2,359	12,312	5.2	106
3.	Franco Harris	13	2,949	12,120	4.1	91
4.	TONY DORSETT	10	2,625	11,580	4.4	71
5.	John Riggins	14	2,916	11,352	3.9	104
6.	O.J. Simpson	11	2,404	11,236	4.7	61
7.	Earl Campbell	8	2,187	9,407	4.3	74
8.	Jim Taylor	10	1,941	8,597	4.4	83
9.	Joe Perry	14	1,737	8,378	4.8	53
10.	Larry Csonka	11	1,891	8,081	4.3	64
11.	OTTIS ANDERSON	8	1,882	8,080	4.3	47
12.	MIKE PRUITT	11	1,844	7,378	4.0	51
13.	Leroy Kelly	10	1,727	7,274	4.2	74
14.	ERIC DICKERSON	4	1,465	6,968	4.8	55
15.	John Henry Johnson	13	1,571	6,803	4.3	48
16.	Wilbert Montgomery	9	1,540	6,789	4.4	45
17.	Chuck Muncie	9	1,561	6,702	4.3	71
18.	Mark Van Eeghen	10	1,652	6,650	4.0	37
19.	Lawrence McCutcheon	10	1,521	6,578	4.3	26
20.	GEORGE ROGERS	6	1,529	6,563	4.3	48

All-Time Leading Receivers

		Yrs.	No.	Yards	Ave.	TDs
1.	CHARLIE JOINER	18	750	12,146	16.2	65
2.	STEVE LARGENT	11	694	11,129	16.0	87
3.	Charley Taylor	13	649	9,110	14.0	79
4.	Don Maynard	15	633	11,834	18.7	88
5.	Raymond Berry	13	631	9,275	14.7	68
6.	Harold Carmichael	14	590	8,985	15.2	79
7.	Fred Biletnikoff	14	589	8,974	15.2	76
8.	Harold Jackson	15	579	10,372	17.9	76
9.	Lionel Taylor	10	567	7,195	12.7	45
10.	Lance Alworth	11	542	10,266	18.9	85
11.	OZZIE NEWSOME	9	541	6,698	12.4	42
12.	JAMES LOFTON	9	530	9,656	18.2	49
13.	Bobby Mitchell	11	521	7,954	15.3	65
14.	WES CHANDLER	9	516	8,316	16.1	54
15.	NAT MOORE	13	510	7,546	14.8	74
16.	Billy Howton	12	503	8,459	16.8	61
17.	CLIFF BRANCH	14	501	8,685	17.3	67
18.	JOHN STALLWORTH	13	496	8,202	16.5	61
19.	Tommy McDonald	12	495	8,410	17.0	84
	Ahmad Rashad	10	495	6,831	13.8	44

Below: San Diego's Dan Fouts became the third man in league history to pass for over 40,000 yards in a career.

All-Time Leading Scorers

		Yrs.	TDs	EPs	FGs	Total
1.	George Blanda	26	9	943	335	2,002
2.	Jan Stenerud	19	0	580	373	1,699
3.	Jim Turner	16	1	521	304	1,439
4.	MARK MOSELEY	16	0	482	300	1,382
5.	Jim Bakken	17	0	534	282	1,380
6.	Fred Cox	15	0	519	282	1,365
7.	Lou Groza	17	1	641	234	1,349
8.	Gino Cappelletti*	11	42	350	176	1,130
9.	Don Cockroft	13	0	432	216	1,080
10.	Garo Yepremian	14	0	444	210	1,074
11.	RAY WERSCHING	14	0	412	209	1,039
12.	Bruce Gossett	11	0	374	219	1,031
13.	PAT LEAHY	13	0	393	200	993
14.	Sam Baker	15	2	428	179	977
15.	RAFAEL SEPTIEN	10	0	420	180	960
16.	CHRIS BAHR	11	0	397	187	958
17.	Lou Michaels**	13	1	386	187	955
18.	Roy Gerela	11	0	351	184	903
19.	Bobby Walston	12	46	365	80	881
20.	Pete Gogolak	10	0	344	173	863

* Includes four two-point conversions
** Includes a safety recorded in 1965 when Michaels played as a defensive end.

All-Time Passer Ratings (Minimum 1,500 attempts)

		Yrs.	Att.	Comp.	Yards	TDs	Int.	Rating
1.	DAN MARINO	4	2,050	1,249	16,177	142	67	95.2
2.	JOE MONTANA	8	2,878	1,818	21,498	141	76	91.2
3.	DAVE KRIEG	7	1,822	1,046	13,677	107	73	84.1
4.	Roger Staubach	11	2,958	1,685	22,700	153	109	83.4
5.	DANNY WHITE	11	2,546	1,517	19,068	142	112	83.2
6.	Len Dawson	19	3,741	2,136	28,711	239	183	82.6
	Sonny Jurgensen	18	4,262	2,433	32,224	255	189	82.6

Seattle's Steve Largent could become the all-time leading receiver in 1987.

8.	KEN ANDERSON	10	4,176	2,654	32,838	197	160	81.9
9.	DAN FOUTS	14	5,240	3,091	40,523	244	227	80.0
10.	NEIL LOMAX	6	2,247	1,287	15,989	92	67	80.7
11.	Bart Starr	16	3,149	1,808	24,718	152	138	80.5
12.	Fran Tarkenton	18	6,467	3,686	47,003	342	266	80.4
13.	Otto Graham	6	1,565	872	13,499	88	94	78.2
	Bert Jones	10	2,551	1,430	18,190	124	101	78.2
	Johnny Unitas	18	5,186	2,830	40,239	290	253	78.2
16.	Frank Ryan	13	2,133	1,090	16,042	149	111	77.6
17.	BILL KENNEY	7	2,043	1,118	14,621	90	72	77.5
18.	Joe Theismann	12	3,602	2,044	25,206	160	138	77.4
19.	Bob Griese	14	3,429	1,926	25,092	192	172	77.1
20.	GARY DANIELSON	9	1,847	1,049	13,159	77	77	75.6

PASSES COMPLETED	No.	YARDS PASSING	Yards	TOUCHDOWN PASSES	No.
1. Fran Tarkenton	3,686	1. Fran Tarkenton	47,003	1. Fran Tarkenton	342
2. DAN FOUTS	3,091	2. DAN FOUTS	40,523	2. Johnny Unitas	290
3. Johnny Unitas	2,830	3. Johnny Unitas	40,239	3. Sonny Jurgensen	255
4. KEN ANDERSON	2,654	4. Jim Hart	34,665	4. DAN FOUTS	244
5. Jim Hart	2,593	5. John Hadl	33,503	John Hadl	244
6. John Brodie	2,469	6. KEN ANDERSON	32,838	6. Len Dawson	239
7. Sonny Jurgensen	2,433	7. Sonny Jurgensen	32,224	7. George Blanda	236
8. Roman Gabriel	2,366	8. John Brodie	31,548	8. John Brodie	214
9. John Hadl	2,363	9. Norm Snead	30,797	9. Terry Bradshaw	212
10. JOE FERGUSON	2,292	10. Roman Gabriel	29,444	Y.A. Tittle	212
11. Norm Snead	2,276	11. JOE FERGUSON	28,895	11. Jim Hart	209
12. Ken Stabler	2,270	12. Len Dawson	28,711	12. Roman Gabriel	201
13. RON JAWORSKI	2,142	13. Y.A. Tittle	28,339	13. KEN ANDERSON	197
14. Len Dawson	2,136	14. Terry Bradshaw	27,989	14. Norm Snead	196
15. Y.A. Tittle	2,118	15. Ken Stabler	27,938	Bobby Layne	196
16. Craig Morton	2,053	16. Craig Morton	27,908	16. Ken Stabler	194
17. Joe Theismann	2,044	17. RON JAWORSKI	27,682	17. Bob Griese	192
18. Terry Bradshaw	2,025	18. Joe Namath	27,663	18. JOE FERGUSON	190
19. Archie Manning	2,011	19. George Blanda	26,920	19. Sammy Baugh	187
20. Brian Sipe	1,944	20. Bobby Layne	26,768	20. Craig Morton	183

INDEX OF RETIRED PLAYERS
LISTED IN THE ALL-TIME STATISTICS

KELLY Leroy, Cleveland (1964-73)

KRAUSE Paul, Washington (1964-67), Minnesota (1968-79)

LANE Dick 'Night Train', L.A. Rams (1952-53), Chicago Cardinals (1954-59), Detroit (1960-65)

LAYNE Bobby, Chicago Bears (1948), N.Y. Bulldogs (1949), Detroit (1950-58), Pittsburgh (1958-62)

LeFEBVRE Gil, Cincinnati Reds (1933-34), Detroit (1935)

LUCKMAN Sid, Chicago Bears (1939-50)

MANNING Archie, New Orleans (1971-75 and 1977-82), Houston (1982-83), Minnesota (1983-84)

MATSON Ollie, Chicago Cardinals (1952 and 1954-58), L.A. Rams (1959-62), Detroit (1963), Philadelphia (1964-66)

MAYNARD Don, N.Y. Giants (1958), N.Y. Titans/Jets (1960-72), St Louis (1973)

McCUTCHEON Lawrence, L.A. Rams (1972-79), Denver (1980), Seattle (1980), Buffalo (1981)

McDONALD Tommy, Philadelphia (1957-63), Dallas (1964), L.A. Rams (1965-66), Atlanta (1967), Cleveland (1968)

MICHAELS Lou, L.A. Rams (1958-60), Pittsburgh (1961-63), Baltimore (1964-69), Green Bay (1971)

MITCHELL Bobby, Cleveland (1958-61), Washington (1962-68)

MONTGOMERY Wilbert, Philadelphia (1977-84), Detroit (1985)

MORGAN Dennis, Dallas (1974), Philadelphia (1975)

MORTON Craig, Dallas (1965-74), N.Y. Giants (1974-76), Denver (1977-82)

MUNCIE Chuck, New Orleans (1976-80), San Diego (1980-84)

NAMATH Joe, N.Y. Jets (1965-76), L.A. Rams (1977)

NEVERS Ernie, Duluth Eskimos (1926-27), Chicago Cardinals (1929-31)

PERRY Joe, San Francisco (1948-60 and 1963), Baltimore (1961-62)

RASHAD Ahmad, St Louis (1972-73), Buffalo (1974), Minnesota (1976-82)

RIGGINS John, N.Y. Jets (1971-75), Washington (1976-79 and 1981-85)

RYAN Frank, L.A. Rams (1958-61), Cleveland (1962-68), Washington (1969-70)

SAYERS Gale, Chicago (1965-71)

SHAW Bob, Cleveland/L.A. Rams (1945-46 and 1949), Chicago Cardinals (1950)

SIMPSON O.J., Buffalo (1969-77), San Francisco (1978-79)

SIPE Brian, Cleveland (1974-83)

SMITH Bob, Buffalo (AAFC) (1948), Brooklyn (AAFC) (1948), Chicago Hornets (AAFC) (1949), Detroit (1949-53)

SMITH Noland, Kansas City (1967-69), San Francisco (1969)

SNEAD Norm, Washington (1961-63), Philadelphia (1964-70), Minnesota (1971), N.Y. Giants (1972-74 and 1976), San Francisco (1974-75)

STABLER Ken, Oakland (1970-79), Houston (1980-81), New Orleans (1982-84)

STARR Bart, Green Bay (1956-71)

STAUBACH Roger, Dallas (1969-79)

STENERUD Jan, Kansas City (1967-79), Green Bay (1980-83), Minnesota (1984-85)

STUDSTILL Pat, Detroit (1961-62 and 1964-67), L.A. Rams (1968-71), New England (1972)

SWEETAN Karl, Detroit (1966-67), New Orleans (1968), L.A. Rams (1969-70)

TARKENTON Fran, Minnesota (1961-66 and 1972-78), N.Y. Giants (1967-71)

TATUM Jack, Oakland (1971-79), Houston (1980)

TAYLOR Charley, Washington (1964-75, 1977)

TAYLOR Jim, Green Bay (1958-66), New Orleans (1967)

TAYLOR Lionel, Chicago Bears (1959), Denver (1960-66), Houston (1967-68)

THEISMANN Joe, Washington (1974-85)

THOMPSON Billy, Denver (1969-81)

TITTLE Y.A., Baltimore (1948-50), San Francisco (1951-60), N.Y. Giants (1961-64)

TODD Richard, N.Y. Jets (1976-83), New Orleans (1984-85)

TURNER Cecil, Chicago (1968-73)

TURNER Jim, N.Y. Jets (1964-70), Denver (1971-79)

UNITAS Johnny, Baltimore (1956-72), San Diego (1973)

UPCHURCH Rick, Denver (1975-83)

VAN BROCKLIN Norm, L.A. Rams (1949-57), Philadelphia (1958-60)

van EEGHEN Mark, Oakland (1974-81), New England (1982-83)

von SCHAMANN Uwe, Miami (1979-84)

WALSTON Bobby, Philadelphia (1951-62)

WATERFIELD Bob, Cleveland/L.A. Rams (1945-52)

WEST Charlie, Minnesota (1968-73), Detroit (1974-77), Denver (1978-79)

WILLIAMS Travis, Green Bay (1967-70), L.A. Rams (1971)

YEPREMIAN Garo, Detroit (1966-67), Miami (1970-78), New Orleans (1979), Tampa Bay (1980-81)

Game by Game – 1986

Opponent	Att	Comp	Passing Yds	Lg	Int	TD
Detroit	38	21	223	34	1	1
at Tampa Bay	21	9	130	26	0	1
Pittsburgh	27	19	257	55t	0	3
Green Bay	25	16	241	36t	0	6
at Chicago	30	11	163	45	2	0
at San Francisco	41	26	326	35t	2	2
Chicago	18	12	239	60t	0	2
Cleveland	35	18	261	32	1	1
at Washington	35	20	490	76t	1	4
at Detroit	39	24	283	49	2	1
N.Y. Giants	25	16	187	24	0	1
at Cincinnati	Injured – did not play					
Tampa Bay	Injured – did not play					
at Green Bay	25	13	153	26	1	1
at Houston	13	3	47	32t	0	1
New Orleans	Injured – did not play					
Totals	**372**	**208**	**3,000**	**76t**	**10**	**24**

TOMMY KRAMER

Ever since taking over as the Vikings' starter in 1979, Tommy Kramer had been the kind of quarterback which one might describe as 'good but not great'. He could come out and take the opposition apart, but on other days he would appear ordinary, and it was reflected in his career passer rating which stood at 71.3 entering the 1986 campaign. But there was another side to the story. His 1983 season was restricted to just three games with a knee injury which threatened his career. The following year, he suffered the kind of injury which every quarterback dreads, when he dislocated his throwing shoulder and was forced to miss three games. Bravely, he returned on Week Twelve, but he re-injured the shoulder and went out for the season. Despite the setbacks, and playing for a Vikings club which had few stars on its roster, over the years he established some highly-impressive figures, most notably passing for over 400 yards in a game three times and throwing four or more touchdown passes in a game seven times. But in 1986, it all came together as he won the NFC passing title by the huge margin of 11.9 rating points, and he even pipped the AFC's Dan Marino for the NFL passing title. Passing for 490 yards against Washington, he had the best single-game total in the NFL, and that performance made him the first quarterback in league history to pass for more than 450 yards in a game twice. In the Vikings' Week-Seven victory over Chicago, he was outstanding, both as a passer and as a field general. If there is an NFC Central club which can challenge the Bears in the 1987 season, it is Minnesota with Kramer at the controls.

STANLEY MORGAN

Stanley Morgan's fall from prominence was one of the most inexplicable and disappointing features of recent seasons. And it took an orthopaedic surgeon to discover the cause. It turned out that the middle joint of his little finger was worn beyond repair from the thousands of times it had taken the impact in Morgan's style of catching the ball. For every pass reception, and even for many of those which he didn't make, he paid the price with severe pain. It had reached the point where he dreaded a passing down. There was no problem with his speed – he averaged over 20 yards per reception in each of his first six years in the league and averaged 19.5 yards in 1985 – but rather, he simply wasn't making the number of receptions which might be expected of a top-class receiver. Surgery was performed in the offseason and the transformation was remarkable. Quite suddenly, the ball began to stick. Arguably, the 1986 season was the finest of his career. It is true that his average per reception (17.8 yards) was the second-lowest of his ten-year career, and he did catch a greater number of touchdown passes (12) in 1979. But he caught more passes for more yards than ever before; ten touchdown receptions would be good enough for anybody, and not many wide receivers would even think of averaging 17.8 yards. The new Stanley Morgan has emerged. He's always been a burner and now he's prolific. He led the AFC in reception yardage, logging nine 100-yards-receiving games on the way (the NFL single-season record is ten). Without doubt, he now is heading for the all-time top twenty and one more campaign might see him there.

Stanley Morgan Game by Game – 1986				
		Receiving		
Opponent	No	Yds	Lg	TD
Indianapolis	7	116	43t	1
at N.Y. Jets	8	104	22	0
Seattle	7	161	44t	3
at Denver	2	14	9	1
Miami	6	125	41	1
N.Y. Jets	7	162	44t	1
at Pittsburgh	2	45	27	0
at Buffalo	3	49	19	0
Atlanta	3	36	21	0
at Indianapolis	5	89	26	0
at L.A. Rams	7	118	28	0
Buffalo	3	45	24	0
at New Orleans	3	51	20	0
Cincinnati	5	107	39	0
San Francisco	8	121	38	1
at Miami	8	148	31t	2
Totals	**84**	**1,491**	**44t**	**10**

Left: Tommy Kramer won his first league passing title. Right: Stanley Morgan, ten years as a pro and still improving.

JOE MORRIS

If there is one player who might challenge the Rams' Eric Dickerson for the title of most valuable running back, it would be the Giants' Joe Morris. In 1985 he emerged from obscurity to rush for 1,336 yards, a total which was the fourth-best in the NFL. Confirming that it was no fluke, in 1986 he really set about the league's defenses, rushing for a regular-season total of 1,516 yards, despite missing one game through illness and suffering from the lingering effects for two further games. In postseason play, he was a major factor in the Giants' march to the Super Bowl Championship, as he rushed for 313 yards and four touchdowns in three games. Morris has now joined that elite group of players for whom opponents must make special plans. And even when they do, only rarely can he be contained. He'll knife through the slightest gap in the line of scrimmage, or accelerate into that smooth, curving outside run which has become his trademark. His 1986 performance established Giants single-season records for rushing, rushing attempts (341) and 100-yards-rushing games (8), and Giants career records for 100-yards-rushing games (15), rushing average (4.35) and rushing touchdowns (40). His mere presence ensures the continued effectiveness of the Giants' offense, and he is crucial to their chances of retaining the league title.

Game by Game – 1986		Rushing		
Opponent	Att	Yds	Lg	TD
at Dallas	20	87	34	1
San Diego	30	83	20	1
at L.A. Raiders	18	110	52	0
New Orleans	Illness – did not play			
at St Louis	17	53	12	1
Philadelphia	19	69	30t	1
at Seattle	24	116	16	0
Washington	31	181	34	2
Dallas	29	181	28	2
at Philadelphia	27	111	19	2
at Minnesota	18	49	15	0
Denver	23	106	24	0
at San Francisco	13	14	17	0
at Washington	22	62	11	0
St Louis	28	179	54	3
Green Bay	22	115	19	1
Totals	**341**	**1,516**	**54**	**14**

Left: Joe Morris has joined the ranks of the superstars.

Right: Jerry Rice's 1,570 yards receiving was the third-best single-season total in league history.

JERRY RICE

Of the many options available for judging the value of a wide receiver, three are obvious. They are his number of receptions, his yardage and his touchdowns. Jerry Rice beat every wide receiver in the NFL in all three categories, with 86, 1,570 and 15 respectively. Of the top ten pass receivers in the league (the official method for listing receivers is in terms of passes caught), he had the highest average per reception (18.3). There is no official grading for the elegance of the art, but if there were he'd score maximum points. He's said not to be the fastest wide receiver in the league, but it doesn't show, as he disguises any lack of pace with an impressive array of subtle moves, tremendous strength and stamina. Also, it should be borne in mind that his incredible performance came in a season when the 49ers used three different quarterbacks, two of whom, Jeff Kemp and Mike Moroski, were new to the 49ers' system. With Kemp installed as the replacement for the injured Joe Montana, Rice prospered to the extent of four big games in a spell of five weeks (Weeks Two to Six). By contrast, with Moroski installed on Weeks Eight and Nine, he was out in the cold and caught only eight passes for 93 yards and one touchdown in the two games. When Joe Montana returned, on Week Ten, so did Rice's form. One wonders just what this young man might achieve over a full season with Montana at quarterback.

Game by Game – 1986

Opponent	No	Yds	Lg	TD
at Tampa Bay	5	54	14	0
at L.A. Rams	6	157	66t	1
New Orleans	7	120	26	0
at Miami	3	76	50t	2
Indianapolis	6	172	58t	3
Minnesota	7	144	59	2
at Atlanta	3	58	27	0
v Green Bay*	4	49	16	1
at New Orleans	4	44	21	0
St Louis	4	156	45t	3
at Washington	12	204	39	0
Atlanta	4	47	17	1
N.Y. Giants	9	86	15	1
N.Y. Jets	5	97	42	0
at New England	4	35	22	0
L.A. Rams	3	71	44t	1
Totals	**86**	**1,570**	**66t**	**15**

*Played at Milwaukee

CHAPTER SIX

AMERICAN FOOTBALL CONFERENCE

TEAM RANKINGS

	OFFENSE						DEFENSE					
	Total Yds.	Rushing	Passing	Points For	%Intercepted	%Sacked	Total Yds.	Rushing	Passing	Points Against	%Interceptions	%Sacks
Buffalo	11	8	10	12	7	11 =	11	4	13	9	14	12
Cincinnati	1	1	2	3	9	4	8	12	4	11	7	6
Cleveland	4	9	5	4	1	6	7	10	6	3	6	9 =
Denver	9	7	7	5	3	5	3	1	7	5	9	4
Houston	10	6	9	13	14	10	4	11	2	6	10	11
Indianapolis	13	12	11	14	10 =	11 =	12	9	12	13	11	13
Kansas City	14	13	13	8	5	13	2	6	5	4	1	8
L.A. Raiders	8	4	8	10	12	14	1	5	3	8	2	1
Miami	2	11	1	1	6	1	13 =	14	9	14	13	9 =
New England	7	14	3	2	2	7 =	5	13	1	2	3	3
N.Y. Jets	5	5	6	7	8	7 =	13 =	2	14	10	8	14
Pittsburgh	12	3	14	11	10 =	2	6	8	8	7	5	7
San Diego	6	10	4	9	13	3	10	3	11	12	12	2
Seattle	3	2	12	6	4	9	9	7	10	1	4	5

AFC PASSERS

	Att	Comp	% Comp	Yards	Ave Gain	TD	% TD	Long	Int	% Int	Rating Points
Marino, Dan, *Mia.*	623	378	60.7	4746	7.62	44	7.1	t85	23	3.7	92.5
Krieg, Dave, *Sea.*	375	225	60.0	2921	7.79	21	5.6	t72	11	2.9	91.0
Eason, Tony, *N.E.*	448	276	61.6	3328	7.43	19	4.2	49	10	2.2	89.2
Esiason, Boomer, *Cin.*	469	273	58.2	3959	8.44	24	5.1	57	17	3.6	87.7
O'Brien, Ken, *Jets*	482	300	62.2	3690	7.66	25	5.2	t83	20	4.1	85.8
Kosar, Bernie, *Clev.*	531	310	58.4	3854	7.26	17	3.2	t72	10	1.9	83.8
Kelly, Jim, *Buff.*	480	285	59.4	3593	7.49	22	4.6	t84	17	3.5	83.3
Plunkett, Jim, *Raiders*	252	133	52.8	1000	7.88	14	5.6	t81	9	3.6	82.5
Elway, John, *Den.*	504	280	55.6	3485	6.91	19	3.8	53	13	2.6	79.0
Fouts, Dan, *S.D.*	430	252	58.6	3031	7.05	16	3.7	t65	22	5.1	71.4
Kenney, Bill, *K.C.*	308	161	52.3	1922	6.24	13	4.2	53	11	3.6	70.8
Wilson, Marc, *Raiders*	240	129	53.8	1721	7.17	12	5.0	t57	15	6.3	67.4
Malone, Mark, *Pitt.*	425	216	50.8	2444	5.75	15	3.5	48	18	4.2	62.5
Moon, Warren, *Hou.*	488	256	52.5	3489	7.15	13	2.7	t81	26	5.3	62.3
Trudeau, Jack, *Ind.*	417	204	48.9	2225	5.34	8	1.9	t84	18	4.3	53.5
Non-qualifiers											
Grogan, Steve, *N.E.*	102	62	60.8	976	9.57	9	8.8	t69	2	2.0	113.8
Ryan, Pat, *Jets*	55	34	61.8	342	6.22	2	3.6	36	1	1.8	84.1
Hogeboom, Gary, *Ind.*	144	85	59.0	1154	8.01	6	4.2	60	6	4.2	81.2
Gilbert, Gale, *Sea.*	76	42	55.3	485	6.38	3	3.9	t38	3	3.9	71.4
Blackledge, Todd, *K.C.*	211	96	45.5	1200	5.69	10	4.7	t70	6	2.8	67.6
Herrmann, Mark, *S.D.*	97	51	52.6	627	6.46	2	2.1	28	3	3.1	66.8
Luck, Oliver, *Hou.*	60	31	51.7	341	5.68	1	1.7	27	5	8.3	39.7
Brister, Bubby, *Pitt.*	60	21	35.0	291	4.85	0	0.0	58	2	3.3	37.6
Flick, Tom, *S.D.*	73	33	45.2	361	4.95	2	2.7	26	8	11.0	29.9

t = Touchdown
Leader based on rating points, minimum 224 attempts

Wesley Walker led all AFC receivers with 12 touchdowns.

AFC RECEIVERS – Most Receptions

	No	Yards	Ave	Long	TD
Christensen, Todd, *Raiders*	95	1153	12.1	35	8
Toon, Al, *Jets*	85	1176	13.8	t62	8
Morgan, Stanley, *N.E.*	84	1491	17.8	t44	10
Anderson, Gary, *S.D.*	80	871	10.9	t65	8
Collins, Tony, *N.E.*	77	684	8.9	49	5
Bouza, Matt, *Ind.*	71	830	11.7	33	5
Largent, Steve, *Sea.*	70	1070	15.3	t38	9
Shuler, Mickey, *Jets*	69	675	9.8	t36	4
Duper, Mark, *Mia.*	67	1313	19.6	t85	11
Brooks, Bill, *Ind.*	65	1131	17.4	t84	8
Hill, Drew, *Hou.*	65	1112	17.1	t81	5
Winslow, Kellen, *S.D.*	64	728	11.4	t28	5
Willhite, Gerald, *Den.*	64	529	8.3	31	3
Collinsworth, Cris, *Cin.*	62	1024	16.5	t46	10
Givins, Ernest, *Hou.*	61	1062	17.4	60	3
Hampton, Lorenzo, *Mia.*	61	446	7.3	19	3
Clayton, Mark, *Mia.*	60	1150	19.2	t68	10
Brown, Eddie, *Cin.*	58	964	16.6	57	4
Chandler, Wes, *S.D.*	56	874	15.6	40	4
Brennan, Brian, *Clev.*	55	838	15.2	t57	6
Brooks, James, *Cin.*	54	686	12.7	54	4
Hardy, Bruce, *Mia.*	54	430	8.0	t18	5
Reed, Andre, *Buff.*	53	739	13.9	t55	7
Paige, Stephone, *K.C.*	52	829	15.9	51	11
Walker, Wesley, *Jets*	49	1016	20.7	t83	12
Metzelaars, Pete, *Buff.*	49	485	9.9	t44	3
Riddick, Robb, *Buff.*	49	468	9.6	t31	1
McNeil, Freeman, *Jets*	49	410	8.4	26	1
Nathan, Tony, *Mia.*	48	457	9.5	t23	2
Fontenot, Herman, *Clev.*	47	559	11.9	t72	1
Abercrombie, Walter, *Pitt.*	47	395	8.4	27	2
Marshall, Henry, *K.C.*	46	652	14.2	31	1
Allen, Marcus, *Raiders*	46	453	9.8	36	2
Watson, Steve, *Den.*	45	699	15.5	46	3
Williams, Dokie, *Raiders*	43	843	19.6	53	8

t = Touchdown

AFC RECEIVERS – Most Yards

	Yards	No	Ave	Long	TD
Morgan, Stanley, *N.E.*	1491	84	17.8	t44	10
Duper, Mark, *Mia.*	1313	67	19.6	t85	11
Toon, Al, *Jets*	1176	85	13.8	t62	8
Christensen, Todd, *Raiders*	1153	95	12.1	35	8
Clayton, Mark, *Mia.*	1150	60	19.2	t68	10
Brooks, Bill, *Ind.*	1131	65	17.4	t84	8
Hill, Drew, *Hou.*	1112	65	17.1	t81	5
Largent, Steve, *Sea.*	1070	70	15.3	t38	9
Givins, Ernest, *Hou.*	1062	61	17.4	60	3
Collinsworth, Cris, *Cin.*	1024	62	16.5	t46	10
Walker, Wesley, *Jets*	1016	49	20.7	t83	12
Brown, Eddie, *Cin.*	964	58	16.6	57	4
Chandler, Wes, *S.D.*	874	56	15.6	40	4
Anderson, Gary, *S.D.*	871	80	10.9	t65	8
Williams, Dokie, *Raiders*	843	43	19.6	53	8
Brennan, Brian, *Clev.*	838	55	15.2	t57	6
Bouza, Matt, *Ind.*	830	71	11.7	33	5
Paige, Stephone, *K.C.*	829	52	15.9	51	11
Burkett, Chris, *Buff.*	778	34	22.9	t84	4
Reed, Andre, *Buff.*	739	53	13.9	t55	7
Jackson, Mark, *Den.*	738	38	19.4	53	1
Fryar, Irving, *N.E.*	737	43	17.1	t69	6
Winslow, Kellen, *S.D.*	728	64	11.4	t28	5
Watson, Steve, *Den.*	699	45	15.5	46	3
Brooks, James, *Cin.*	686	54	12.7	54	4
Collins, Tony, *N.E.*	684	77	8.9	49	5
Langhorne, Reggie, *Clev.*	678	39	17.4	66	1
Shuler, Mickey, *Jets*	675	69	9.8	t36	4
Marshall, Henry, *K.C.*	652	46	14.2	31	1
Hester, Jessie, *Raiders*	632	23	27.5	t81	6
Lipps, Louis, *Pitt.*	590	38	15.5	48	3
Slaughter, Webster, *Clev.*	577	40	14.4	t47	4
Holman, Rodney, *Cin.*	570	40	14.3	t34	2
Fontenot, Herman, *Clev.*	559	47	11.9	t72	1
Franklin, Byron, *Buff.*	547	33	16.6	49	2

t = Touchdown

AFC RUSHERS

	Att	Yards	Ave	Long	TD
Warner, Curt, *Sea.*	319	1481	4.6	t60	13
Brooks, James, *Cin.*	205	1087	5.3	t56	5
Jackson, Earnest, *Pitt.*	216	910	4.2	31	5
Abercrombie, Walter, *Pitt.*	214	877	4.1	t38	6
McNeil, Freeman, *Jets*	214	856	4.0	40	5
Hampton, Lorenzo, *Mia.*	186	830	4.5	t54	9
Winder, Sammy, *Den.*	240	789	3.3	31	9
Allen, Marcus, *Raiders*	208	759	3.6	t28	5
Mack, Kevin, *Clev.*	174	665	3.8	20	10
Rozier, Mike, *Hou.*	199	662	3.3	t19	4
Riddick, Robb, *Buff.*	150	632	4.2	t41	4
McMillan, Randy, *Ind.*	189	609	3.2	28	3
Hector, Johnny, *Jets*	164	605	3.7	41	8
Williams, John L., *Sea.*	129	538	4.2	36	0
McCallum, Napoleon, *Raiders*	142	536	3.8	18	1
Dickey, Curtis, *Clev.*	135	523	3.9	47	6
Kinnebrew, Larry, *Cin.*	131	519	4.0	39	8
Pruitt, Mike, *K.C.*	139	448	3.2	16	2
Anderson, Gary, *S.D.*	127	442	3.5	17	1
James, Craig, *N.E.*	154	427	2.8	16	4
Collins, Tony, *N.E.*	156	412	2.6	17	3
Wilson, Stanley, *Cin.*	68	379	5.6	t58	8
Bell, Greg, *Buff.*	90	377	4.2	42	4
Adams, Curtis, *S.D.*	118	366	3.1	22	4
Willhite, Gerald, *Den.*	85	365	4.3	42	5
Bentley, Albert, *Ind.*	73	351	4.8	t70	3
Spencer, Tim, *S.D.*	99	350	3.5	23	6
Davenport, Ron, *Mia.*	75	314	4.2	35	0
Green, Boyce, *K.C.*	90	314	3.5	27	3
Heard, Herman, *K.C.*	71	295	4.2	40	2
Byner, Earnest, *Clev.*	94	277	2.9	37	2
Elway, John, *Den.*	52	257	4.9	24	1
Moriarty, Larry, *Hou.-K.C.*	90	252	2.8	11	1
Hawkins, Frank, *Raiders*	58	245	4.2	15	0
Smith, Jeff, *K.C.*	54	238	4.4	t32	3
Gill, Owen, *Ind.*	53	228	4.3	18	1
Johnson, Bill, *Cin.*	39	226	5.8	34	0
Pinkett, Allen, *Hou.*	77	225	2.9	14	2
James, Lionel, *S.D.*	51	224	4.4	24	0
Wallace, Ray, *Hou.*	52	218	4.2	19	3
Wonsley, George, *Ind.*	60	214	3.6	46	1
Nathan, Tony, *Mia.*	27	203	7.5	20	0
Kelly, Jim, *Buff.*	41	199	4.9	20	0
McGee, Buford, *S.D.*	63	187	3.0	20	7
Harmon, Ronnie, *Buff.*	54	172	3.2	38	0
Tatupu, Mosi, *N.E.*	71	172	2.4	13	1
Eason, Tony, *N.E.*	35	170	4.9	26	0
Erenberg, Rich, *Pitt.*	42	170	4.0	17	1
Bennett, Woody, *Mia.*	36	162	4.5	16	0
Moon, Warren, *Hou.*	42	157	3.7	19	2
Byrum, Carl, *Buff.*	38	156	4.1	18	0
Morris, Randall, *Sea.*	19	149	7.8	t49	1
Givins, Ernest, *Hou.*	9	148	16.4	t43	1

t = Touchdown

AFC SCORING – Kickers

	XP	XPA	FG	FGA	PTS
Franklin, Tony, *N.E.*	44	45	32	41	140
Johnson, Norm, *Sea.*	42	42	22	35	108
Karlis, Rich, *Den.*	44	45	20	28	104
Breech, Jim, *Cin.*	50	51	17	32	101
Lowery, Nick, *K.C.*	43	43	19	26	100
Bahr, Chris, *Raiders*	36	36	21	28	99
Anderson, Gary, *Pitt.*	32	32	21	32	95
Reveiz, Fuad, *Mia.*	52	55	14	22	94
Zendejas, Tony, *Hou.*	28	29	22	27	94
Leahy, Pat, *Jets*	44	44	16	19	92
Bahr, Matt, *Clev.*	30	30	20	26	90
Benirschke, Rolf, *S.D.*	39	41	16	25	87
Norwood, Scott, *Buff.*	32	34	17	27	83
Biasucci, Dean, *Ind.*	26	27	13	25	65
Moseley, Mark, *Wash.-Clev.*	25	28	12	19	61

Above: Tim McGee.
Left: Sammy Winder led the AFC in touchdowns.

AFC SCORING – Touchdowns

	TD	TDR	TDP	TDM	PTS
Winder, Sammy, *Den.*	14	9	5	0	84
Warner, Curt, *Sea.*	13	13	0	0	78
Hampton, Lorenzo, *Mia.*	12	9	3	0	72
Walker, Wesley, *Jets*	12	0	12	0	72
Duper, Mark, *Mia.*	11	0	11	0	66
Paige, Stephone, *K.C.*	11	0	11	0	66
Clayton, Mark, *Mia.*	10	0	10	0	60
Collinsworth, Cris, *Cin.*	10	0	10	0	60
Mack, Kevin, *Clev.*	10	10	0	0	60
Morgan, Stanley, *N.E.*	10	0	10	0	60
Anderson, Gary, *S.D.*	9	1	8	0	54
Brooks, James, *Cin.*	9	5	4	0	54
Kinnebrew, Larry, *Cin.*	9	8	1	0	54
Largent, Steve, *Sea.*	9	0	9	0	54
Willhite, Gerald, *Den.*	9	5	3	1	54

AFC KICKOFF RETURNERS

	No	Yards	Ave	Long	TD
Sanchez, Lupe, *Pitt.*	25	591	23.6	64	0
McGee, Tim, *Cin.*	43	1007	23.4	94	0
Humphery, Bobby, *Jets*	28	655	23.4	t96	1
Bell, Ken, *Den.*	23	531	23.1	42	0
Lang, Gene, *Den.*	21	480	22.9	42	0
Edmonds, Bobby Joe, *Sea.*	34	764	22.5	46	0
Starring, Stephen, *N.E.*	36	802	22.3	52	0
Ellis, Craig, *Mia.*	25	541	21.6	41	0
Bentley, Albert, *Ind.*	32	687	21.5	37	0
Adams, Stefon, *Raiders*	27	573	21.2	51	0
McNeil, Gerald, *Clev.*	47	997	21.2	t100	1
Morris, Randall, *Sea.*	23	465	20.2	38	0
Anderson, Gary, *S.D.*	24	482	20.1	35	0
Drewrey, Willie, *Hou.*	25	500	20.0	32	0
Pinkett, Allen, *Hou.*	26	519	20.0	48	0
Smith, Jeff, *K.C.*	29	557	19.2	29	0
Martin, Robbie, *Ind.*	21	385	18.3	27	0
Walker, Fulton, *Raiders*	23	368	16.0	27	0

t = Touchdown
Leader based on average return, minimum 20 returns

AFC PUNTERS

	No	Yards	Long	Ave	Total Punts	TB	Blk	Opp Ret	Ret Yds	In 20	Net Ave
Stark, Rohn, *Ind.*	76	3432	63	45.2	76	5	0	48	502	22	37.2
Roby, Reggie, *Mia.*	56	2476	73	44.2	56	9	0	23	200	13	37.4
Camarillo, Rich, *N.E.*	89	3746	64	42.1	92	7	3	60	565	16	33.1
Mojsiejenko, Ralf, *S.D.*	72	3026	62	42.0	74	11	2	42	368	15	32.9
Gossett, Jeff, *Clev.*	83	3423	61	41.2	83	10	0	44	268	21	35.6
Johnson, Lee, *Hou.*	88	3623	66	41.2	88	9	0	40	303	26	35.7
Colbert, Lewis, *K.C.*	99	4033	56	40.7	99	6	0	52	572	23	33.7
Kidd, John, *Buff.*	75	3031	57	40.4	75	9	0	32	260	14	34.5
Guy, Ray, *Raiders*	90	3620	64	40.2	90	11	0	42	357	20	33.8
Newsome, Harry, *Pitt.*	86	3447	64	40.1	89	11	3	34	364	18	32.2
Jennings, Dave, *Jets*	85	3353	55	39.4	85	6	0	36	165	27	36.1
Gamache, Vince, *Sea.*	79	3048	55	38.6	79	7	0	38	298	10	33.0
Hayes, Jeff, *Cin.*	56	1965	52	35.1	58	3	2	19	182	11	29.7

Leader based on gross average, minimum 40 punts

AFC SACKERS

	No
Jones, Sean, *Raiders*	15.5
Smith, Bruce, *Buff.*	15.0
Williams, Lee, *S.D.*	15.0
Jones, Rulon, *Den.*	13.5
O'Neal, Leslie, *S.D.*	12.5
Green, Jacob, *Sea.*	12.0
Willis, Keith, *Pitt.*	12.0
Pickel, Bill, *Raiders*	11.5
Townsend, Greg, *Raiders*	11.5
Smith, Billy Ray, *S.D.*	11.0
Veris, Garin, *N.E.*	11.0
Still, Art, *K.C.*	10.5
Mecklenburg, Karl, *Den.*	9.5
Tippett, Andre, *N.E.*	9.5
Hairston, Carl, *Clev.*	9.0
King, Emanuel, *Cin.*	9.0
Blackmon, Don, *N.E.*	7.5
Long, Howie, *Raiders*	7.5
Camp, Reggie, *Clev.*	7.0
Maas, Bill, *K.C.*	7.0
Williams, Brent, *N.E.*	7.0
Browner, Ross, *Cin.*	6.5
Clancy, Sam, *Clev.*	6.5
Edwards, Eddie, *Cin.*	6.5
Gary, Keith, *Pitt.*	6.5
Hardison, Dee, *S.D.*	6.5
McNanie, Sean, *Buff.*	6.5
Merriweather, Mike, *Pitt.*	6.0
Puzzuoli, Dave, *Clev.*	6.0
Toran, Stacey, *Raiders*	6.0
Young, Fredd, *Sea.*	6.0
Fletcher, Simon, *Den.*	5.5
Koch, Pete, *K.C.*	5.5
Wilson, Earl, *S.D.*	5.5
Benson, Thomas, *S.D.*	5.0
Bickett, Duane, *Ind.*	5.0
Brown, Mark, *Mia.*	5.0
Childress, Ray, *Hou.*	5.0
Cofield, Tim, *K.C.*	5.0
Gaines, Greg, *Sea.*	5.0
Hand, Jon, *Ind.*	5.0
Martin, Rod, *Raiders*	5.0
Nash, Joe, *Sea.*	5.0
Nelson, Edmund, *Pitt.*	5.0
Banks, Chip, *Clev.*	4.5
Cooper, Louis, *K.C.*	4.5
Hinkle, Bryan, *Pitt.*	4.5
Williams, Reggie, *Cin.*	4.5
Betters, Doug, *Mia.*	4.0
Bryant, Jeff, *Sea.*	4.0

AFC PUNT RETURNERS

	No	FC	Yards	Ave	Long	TD
Edmonds, Bobby Joe, *Sea.*	34	14	419	12.3	t75	1
Willhite, Gerald, *Den.*	42	8	468	11.1	t70	1
Pitts, Ron, *Buff.*	18	11	194	10.8	t49	1
Fryar, Irving, *N.E.*	35	10	366	10.5	t59	1
Anderson, Gary, *S.D.*	25	10	227	9.1	30	0
Walker, Fulton, *Raiders*	49	15	440	9.0	t70	1
Woods, Rick, *Pitt.*	33	12	294	8.9	41	0
McNeil, Gerald, *Clev.*	40	10	348	8.7	t84	1
Smith, Jeff, *K.C.*	29	11	245	8.4	48	0
Sohn, Kurt, *Jets*	35	8	289	8.3	27	0
Brooks, Bill, *Ind.*	18	7	141	7.8	18	0
Drewrey, Willie, *Hou.*	34	13	262	7.7	25	0
Martin, Robbie, *Ind.*	17	5	109	6.4	25	0
Ellis, Craig, *Mia.*	24	1	149	6.2	17	0

t = Touchdown
Leader based on average return, minimum 15 returns

Left: Bobby Joe Edmonds led the NFL on punt return average.

Below: Deron Cherry led the AFC in pass interceptions.

AFC INTERCEPTORS

	No	Yards	Ave	Long	TD
Cherry, Deron, *K.C.*	9	150	16.7	49	0
Lippett, Ronnie, *N.E.*	8	76	9.5	43	0
McElroy, Vann, *Raiders*	7	105	15.0	28	0
Breeden, Louis, *Cin.*	7	72	10.3	t36	1
Harden, Mike, *Den.*	6	179	29.8	52	2
Holmes, Jerry, *Jets*	6	29	4.8	28	0
Burruss, Lloyd, *K.C.*	5	193	38.6	t72	3
Brown, Dave, *Sea.*	5	58	11.6	24	1
Byrd, Gill, *S.D.*	5	45	9.0	18	0
Lyles, Lester, *Jets*	5	36	7.2	22	0
Lynn, Johnny, *Jets*	5	36	7.2	26	0
Dixon, Hanford, *Clev.*	5	35	7.0	19	0
Dale, Jeffery, *S.D.*	4	153	38.3	50	0
Ross, Kevin, *K.C.*	4	66	16.5	35	0
Robinson, Jerry, *Raiders*	4	42	10.5	t32	1
Coleman, Leonard, *Ind.*	4	36	9.0	31	0
Justin, Kerry, *Sea.*	4	29	7.3	18	0
Romes, Charles, *Buff.*	4	23	5.8	23	0
Fulcher, David, *Cin.*	4	20	5.0	15	0
Lewis, Albert, *K.C.*	4	18	4.5	13	0
Seale, Sam, *Raiders*	4	2	0.5	2	0
Sanchez, Lupe, *Pitt.*	3	71	23.7	t67	1
Hill, Greg, *K.C.*	3	64	21.3	t26	1
Wright, Louis, *Den.*	3	56	18.7	56	0
Williams, Eric, *Pitt.*	3	44	14.7	25	0
Robinson, Eugene, *Sea.*	3	39	13.0	25	0
Moyer, Paul, *Sea.*	3	38	12.7	20	0
Wright, Felix, *Clev.*	3	33	11.0	33	0

t = Touchdown

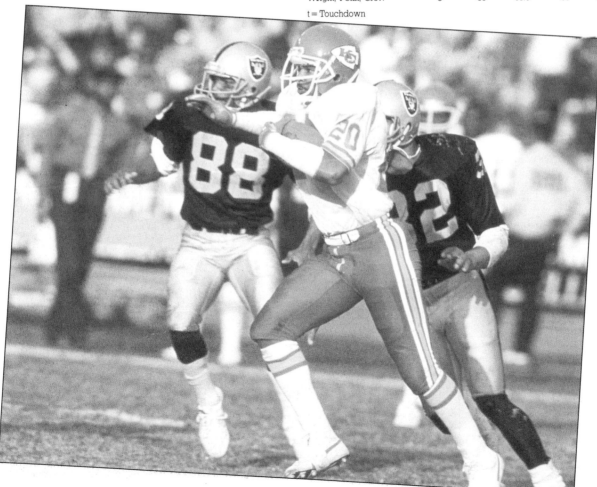

BUFFALO BILLS

Address One Bills Drive, Orchard Park, New York 14127.
Stadium Rich Stadium, Orchard Park.
  Capacity 80,290 *Playing Surface* AstroTurf.
Team Colours Royal Blue, Scarlet Red, and White.
Head Coach Marv Levy – second year.
Championships Division 1980; AFL 1964,'65.
History AFL 1960-69, AFC 1970-

Offense

Even by their own estimate, the Bills are two or three years away from making a serious challenge for a title, but there can be no mistaking the new-found purpose of a club which, for too long, has been out of the reckoning. Last year, with just a little more tenacity in the closing stages of their games – in six of their losses they led inside the final quarter – they could have bettered par. New quarterback Jim Kelly, then, was not an instant winner, but he brought stature and promise to an offense which had faltered for several seasons. Kelly was the Bills' second pick in the first round of the 1983 collegiate draft, but he had opted for the USFL, where he was the premier quarterback. Last year, his first season with the Bills, he established club records for pass completions (285) and completion percentage (59.4). One unexpected feature of the Bills' passing game was the emergence of tight end Pete Metzelaars, who caught 49 passes after catching only 39 in his previous four years as a pro. The play of second-year wide receiver Andre Reed was more predictable. Reed, who became the Bills' primary threat at wide receiver, confirmed the quality of his rookie year and appears set to play a significant role for the foreseeable future. The veteran Jerry Butler should be back after recovering from his leg fracture, but he may not displace Chris Burkett, who averaged a breathtaking 22.9 yards on 34 receptions. If there appear to be few problems at wide receiver, the position at running back is less clear. With the senior player, Greg Bell, out of the lineup for much of the season with a nagging groin injury, Robb Riddick stepped in to have the best of his four years as a pro (he has missed another two because of injury), leading the club in rushing and ranking second-equal with 49 pass receptions. Even so, he would not be regarded as a top-class halfback. A fully-fit Bell would regain his seniority but he is rumoured to be unsettled, and last year's premier draft selection, Ronnie Harmon, does not appear to be ready to move up to start. Draftees Jamie Mueller and Kerry Porter will bid for roster spots. The starting position at fullback is open to competition, with last year's fifth-round pick, Carl Byrum, appearing to have the best credentials. Happily, the offensive line is beginning to look solid. Center Kent Hull, guards Jim Ritcher and Will Wolford, and right tackle Joe Devlin started in all sixteen games and should continue. Ken Jones, who missed four games through injury, makes up the quintet, with Tim Vogler, Mark Traynowicz and Justin Cross in reserve.

Defense

'We are in desperate need of speed, especially at outside linebacker,' admitted head coach Marv Levy. And true to his word, he selected the Penn State star, Shane Conlan, with the Bills' first option in the draft. Conlan is an impact player who responds to the big occasion and should be an instant starter, at the expense of either Darryl Talley or Lucius Sanford. Eugene Marve, who led the club in tackles for the third time in the last five years, will remain at right inside linebacker, partnered by former USFL star Ray Bentley. Conlan's arrival will be of enormous help to defensive end Bruce Smith, who led the club with 15.0 quarterback sacks and is the one genuine super player in the entire defense. Not very long ago, nose tackle Fred Smerlas was in that class, but he is beginning to slow. Nonetheless, he remains a valuable starter with the reliable Sean McNanie now established at defensive left end. There could be some shuffling in the defensive secondary following the unexpected trade of former starting free safety Steve Freeman to the Vikings. Dwight Drane will probably move up to start at safety in partnership with Martin Bayless. Charles Romes has been the starter at right cornerback since 1978 and would be expected to continue, despite suggestions that he has lost a step or two of speed. On the other corner, former first-round pick Derrick Burroughs has edged ahead of Rodney Bellinger. However, they will face competition from both Nate Odomes and Roland Mitchell, two second-round draftees who are outstanding athletes with exceptional speed.

Special Teams

Last year, placekicker Scott Norwood was perfect inside the 40-yard range but kicked only three of thirteen field goal attempts from further out. However, both Norwood and punter John Kidd, the latter whose form was a minor disappointment after his 1985 showing, will be retained. Defensive back Ron Pitts was the one bright spot, return-

1987 SCHEDULE OF GAMES		
September		
13 NEW YORK JETS		1:00
20 HOUSTON		1:00
27 at Dallas		12:00
October		
4 INDIANAPOLIS		1:00
11 at New England		1:00
18 NEW YORK GIANTS		4:00
25 at Miami		1:00
November		
1 WASHINGTON		1:00
8 DENVER		1:00
15 at Cleveland		1:00
22 at New York Jets		1:00
29 MIAMI		1:00
December		
6 at Los Angeles Raiders		1:00
13 at Indianapolis		1:00
20 NEW ENGLAND		1:00
27 at Philadelphia		1:00

ing eighteen punts at an average of 10.8 yards, but no one was able to break free from the coverage returning kickoffs. Draftee Odomes has the speed to return both kickoffs and punts.

1987 DRAFT

Round	Name	Pos.	Ht.	Wt.	College
1.	Conlan, Shane	LB	6-2	227	Penn State
2.	Odomes, Nate	CB	5-9	185	Wisconsin
2.	Mitchell, Roland	CB	5-11	180	Texas Tech
3.	Brandon, David	LB	6-3	218	Memphis State
3.	Mueller, Jamie	RB	6-1	223	Benedictine College
4.	Seals, Leon	DE	6-4	250	Jackson State
7.	Porter, Kerry	RB	6-1	203	Washington State
8.	Mesner, Bruce	DE	6-5	279	Maryland
9.	McKeller, Keith	TE	6-4	243	Jacksonville State
11.	Ballard, Howard	T	6-6	285	Alabama A&M
12.	McGrail, Joe	DT	6-3	269	Delaware

VETERAN ROSTER

No.	Name	Pos.	Ht.	Wt.	NFL Year	College
43	Bayless, Martin	S	6-2	195	4	Bowling Green
28	Bell, Greg	RB	5-10	210	4	Notre Dame
36	Bellinger, Rodney	CB	5-8	189	4	Miami
50	Bentley, Ray	LB	6-2	250	2	Central Michigan
81	Brookins, Mitchell	WR	5-11	196	3	Illinois
	Broughton, Walter	WR	5-10	180	2	Jacksonville State
85	Burkett, Chris	WR	6-4	198	3	Jackson State
29	Burroughs, Derrick	CB	6-1	180	3	Memphis State
61	Burton, Leonard	C	6-3	265	2	South Carolina
80	Butler, Jerry	WR	6-0	178	8	Clemson
35	Byrum, Carl	RB	6-0	232	2	Miss. Valley State
	Caron, Roger	G-T	6-5	275	4	Harvard
69	Christy, Greg	G	6-4	285	2	Pittsburgh
41	Clark, Steve	S	6-3	186	1	Liberty
63	Cross, Justin	T	6-6	265	6	Western State, Colo.
70	Devlin, Joe	T	6-5	280	11	Iowa
45	Drane, Dwight	S	6-1	200	2	Oklahoma
53	Furjanic, Tony	LB	6-1	228	2	Notre Dame
99	Garner, Hal	LB	6-4	225	3	Utah State
8	Gelbaugh, Stan	QB	6-3	207	2	Maryland
75	Hamby, Mike	DE	6-4	270	2	Utah State
33	Harmon, Ronnie	RB	5-11	192	2	Iowa
55	Haslett, Jim	LB	6-3	236	8	Indiana, Pa.
71	Hellestrae, Dale	T	6-5	275	3	Southern Methodist
67	Hull, Kent	C	6-4	262	2	Mississippi State
48	Johnson, Lawrence	CB	5-11	202	7	Wisconsin
72	Jones, Ken	T	6-5	285	12	Arkansas State
12	Kelly, Jim	QB	6-3	215	2	Miami
38	Kelso, Mark	S	5-11	177	2	William & Mary
84	Kern, Don	TE	6-4	235	3	Arizona State
4	Kidd, John	P	6-3	208	4	Northwestern
49	King, Bruce	RB	6-1	219	3	Purdue
54	Marve, Eugene	LB	6-2	240	6	Saginaw Valley State
13	McClure, Brian	QB	6-6	222	1	Bowling Green
95	McNanie, Sean	DE	6-5	270	4	San Diego State
60	Melka, Jim	LB	6-1	228	1	Wisconsin
88	Metzelaars, Pete	TE	6-7	243	6	Wabash
11	Norwood, Scott	K	6-0	207	3	James Madison
64	Pike, Mark	LB	6-4	257	1	Georgia Tech
27	Pitts, Ron	S	5-10	175	2	UCLA
68	Ploeger, Kurt	DE	6-5	260	2	Gustavus Adolphus
79	Prater, Dean	DE	6-4	256	6	Oklahoma State
83	Reed, Andre	WR	6-0	186	3	Kutztown State, Pa.
14	Reich, Frank	QB	6-3	208	3	Maryland
82	Richardson, Eric	WR	6-1	185	3	San Jose State
40	Riddick, Robb	RB	6-0	195	5	Millersville State, Pa.
51	Ritcher, Jim	G	6-3	265	8	North Carolina State
87	Rolle, Butch	TE	6-3	242	2	Michigan State
26	Romes, Charles	CB	6-1	190	11	North Carolina Central
57	Sanford, Lucius	LB	6-2	220	10	Georgia Tech
52	Seawright, James	LB	6-2	219	1	South Carolina
76	Smerlas, Fred	NT	6-3	270	9	Boston College
78	Smith, Bruce	DE	6-4	280	3	Virginia Tech
74	Smith, Don	NT	6-5	262	9	Miami
56	Talley, Darryl	LB	6-4	227	5	West Virginia
89	Tasker, Steve	WR-KR	5-9	185	3	Northwestern
86	Teal, Jimmy	WR	5-10	170	3	Texas A&M
62	Traynowicz, Mark	G	6-5	275	3	Nebraska
65	Vogler, Tim	G	6-3	285	9	Ohio State
34	Wilkins, Gary	RB-TE	6-1	235	2	Georgia Tech
	Williams, Bob	TE	6-3	238	1	Penn State
23	Williams, Kevin	DB	5-9	170	3	Iowa State
94	Witt, Billy	DE	6-5	265	1	North Alabama
73	Wolford, Will	G	6-5	276	2	Vanderbilt

Bruce Smith is living up to all his promise.

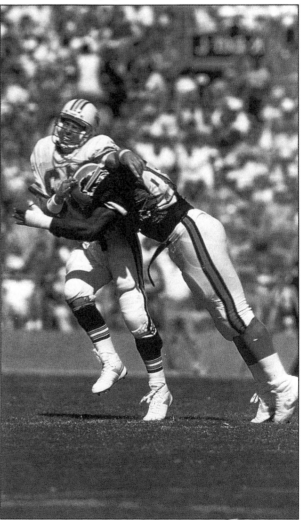

INDIANAPOLIS COLTS

Address P.O. Box 24100 Indianapolis, Indiana 46224-0100.
Stadium Hoosier Dome, Indianapolis.
Capacity 60,127 *Playing Surface* AstroTurf.
Team Colours Royal Blue, White, and Silver.
Head Coach Ron Meyer – second year.
Championships Division 1970, '75, '76, '77; Conference 1970;
NFL 1958, '59, '68; Super Bowl 1970.
History NFL 1953-69, AFC 1970-
(Until 1984, they were known as the Baltimore Colts. A
team of the same name played in the AAFC, from 1947
to 1949, and in the NFL in 1950, at the end of which they
went out of business.)

Offense

In early December 1986, new head coach Ron Meyer (he
was the head coach of the Patriots for 34 games spanning
the years 1982-84) arrived to take over a listless group that
stood at 0-13. He gambled that quarterback Gary Hogeboom's shoulder had mended and re-installed him as the
starter ahead of the rookie, Jack Trudeau. The transformation was astounding, as the Colts beat Atlanta and Buffalo,
before travelling to Los Angeles, where they overwhelmed the mighty Raiders with a 24-point second-half
scoring burst. Over the three-game spell, Hogeboom
completed 62 per cent of his passes for a rating of 85.6. It's
the kind of performance which could quickly bring the
club back into contention. Trudeau will serve as a good
backup after the experiences of a rookie campaign in
which he attempted 417 passes – the third-most by any
rookie in league history. For the first time in many years,
the Colts enter a season armed with the certainty of having
a passing offense. Veteran wide receiver Matt Bouza is
coming off by far his best year as a pro (he led the
club with 71 receptions) and Bill Brooks was a rookie
sensation, catching 65 passes for 1,131 yards and eight
touchdowns. In the search for a third player of class, the
Colts dealt a second-round draft option to Washington in
exchange for 1986 draftee Walter Murray. Under Meyer's
new system, tight ends Pat Beach and Mark Boyer may be
given the opportunity to catch more passes. The rushing
offense could have its difficulties, following the loss of the
senior player, Randy McMillan, who suffered a broken leg
in an offseason car accident and will be out for the entire
season. Albert Bentley appears to have the edge over
George Wonsley to start at halfback, and Owen Gill could
fill in as a blocking fullback. Certainly, they'll be helped by
the most talented offensive line in recent Colts history. Pro
Bowler Chris Hinton will return to left guard, teaming up
with Pro Bowl center Ray Donaldson and right guard Ron
Solt, who is a former first-round pick. Kevin Call started at
right tackle all last year. One of Chris Gambol and Randy
Dixon, two highly-regarded draftees, could step in at left
tackle.

Defense

The Colts are hoping that draftee Cornelius Bennett will
do for them what Lawrence Taylor did for the Giants.
Indeed, Bennett has been described as a faster variety of
the great Taylor. His acquisition means that the Colts could
field four first-round picks at linebacker. This, however,
would need Barry Krauss to make a full recovery from a
knee injury which has required extensive surgery. The
probable starting quartet would have Bennett and Duane
Bickett on the outsides, with leading tackler Cliff Odom
joined by Johnie Cooks, who is felt able to make the
transition to inside linebacker. Alternatively, the Colts
may use Bennett as a dual-purpose defender, swapping
between inside linebacker and defensive end. This would
enable Cooks to remain on the outside, where he has
looked most comfortable. Bennett could be a terror in his
own right and must take some of the load off Bickett, who is
without doubt the Colts' best defensive player. Again,
Bennett's pass rushing could help the development of the
1986 first-round pick, defensive end Jon Hand, who came
on well after a slow start. Defensive left end Donnell
Thompson and nose tackle Scott Kellar complete the front
three. The secondary is looking more solid after the
acquisition of Dwight Hicks, Dexter Clinkscale and Kirk
Springs. But the real boost came from former first-round
pick Leonard Coleman, who has begun to look the part at
left cornerback. Right cornerback Eugene Daniel led the
team with fifteen passes defensed and is something of a
ball-hawker, having picked off seventeen passes in the
last three seasons. It was his touchdown, on a return of a
blocked punt, which lifted the Colts to their first win of the
1986 season. Nesby Glasgow led the defensive secondary
in tackles for the seventh consecutive year and forms a
secure partnership with Hicks in the safety positions.

Special Teams

Rohn Stark went to his second successive Pro Bowl after
topping the league with a 45.2-yard gross average, and he
remains as the NFL all-time career leader in this category.

1987 SCHEDULE OF GAMES		
September		
13	CINCINNATI	12:00
20	MIAMI	12:00
27	at St Louis	12:00
October		
4	at Buffalo	1:00
11	NEW YORK JETS	12:00
18	at Pittsburgh	1:00
25	NEW ENGLAND	1:00
November		
1	at New York Jets	1:00
8	SAN DIEGO	1:00
15	at Miami	1:00
22	at New England	1:00
29	HOUSTON	1:00
December		
6	at Cleveland	1:00
13	BUFFALO	1:00
20	at San Diego	1:00
27	TAMPA BAY	1:00

Surprisingly, Dean Biasucci beat out Raul Allegre for the job of placekicker and though his statistics were not impressive, closer analysis reveals that, of his twelve field goal failures, six were from 50 or more yards out. Newcomer Kirk Springs, who in 1983 led the AFC in punt returns and came fifth in kickoff returns, could add glitter to the special teams.

1987 DRAFT

Round	Name	Pos.	Ht.	Wt.	College
1.	Bennett, Cornelius	LB	6-2	230	Alabama
3.	Gambol, Chris	T	6-6	282	Iowa
4.	Dixon, Randy	T	6-3	293	Pittsburgh
5.	Banks, Roy	WR	5-9	190	Eastern Illinois
6.	Robinson, Freddie	S	6-0	182	Alabama
7.	Bellini, Mark	WR	5-11	180	Brigham Young
8.	Miller, Chuckie	CB	5-8	178	UCLA
9.	Ontko, Bob	LB	6-4	230	Penn State
10.	Goode, Chris	CB	6-0	186	Alabama
11.	Reynosa, Jim	DE	6-3	255	Arizona State
12.	Adams, David	RB	5-6	167	Arizona

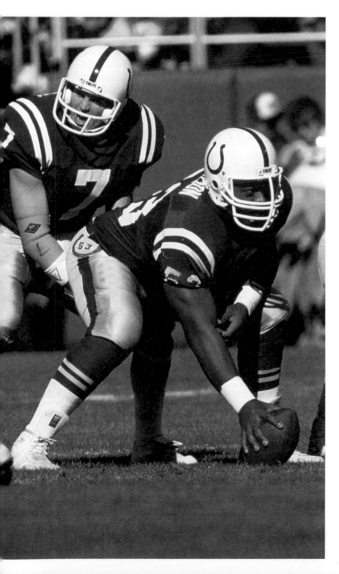

VETERAN ROSTER

No.	Name	Pos.	Ht.	Wt.	NFL Year	College
57	Ahrens, Dave	LB	6-3	245	7	Wisconsin
62	Anderson, Pete	C	6-4	270	1	Georgia
79	Armstrong, Harvey	NT	6-3	261	5	Southern Methodist
72	Baldischwiler, Karl	T	6-5	276	9	Oklahoma
40	Ballage, Pat	S	6-1	200	1	Notre Dame
81	Beach, Pat	TE	6-4	244	5	Washington State
20	Bentley, Albert	RB	5-11	210	3	Miami
4	Biasucci, Dean	K	6-0	198	3	Western Carolina
50	Bickett, Duane	LB	6-5	241	3	Southern California
85	Bouza, Matt	WR	6-3	208	6	California
84	Boyer, Mark	TE	6-4	239	3	Southern California
80	Brooks, Bill	WR	5-11	190	2	Boston University
74	Brotzki, Bob	T	6-5	269	2	Syracuse
68	Broughton, Willie	DE	6-5	277	3	Miami
71	Call, Kevin	T	6-7	293	4	Colorado State
47	Clinkscale, Dextor	S	5-11	195	7	South Carolina State
31	Coleman, Leonard	S	6-2	197	3	Vanderbilt
98	Cooks, Johnie	LB	6-4	251	6	Mississippi State
38	Daniel, Eugene	CB	6-0	178	4	Louisiana State
23	Daniel, Kenny	CB	5-10	180	3	San Jose State
53	Donaldson, Ray	C	6-4	282	8	Georgia
44	Gill, Owen	RB	6-1	230	3	Iowa
25	Glasgow, Nesby	S	5-10	186	9	Washington
90	Haines, John	DL	6-7	266	3	Texas
78	Hand, Jon	DE	6-6	280	2	Alabama
87	Harbour, James	WR	6-1	192	2	Mississippi
29	Hicks, Dwight	S	6-1	192	9	Michigan
75	Hinton, Chris	T	6-4	288	5	Northwestern
7	Hogeboom, Gary	QB	6-4	207	8	Central Michigan
21	Holt, John	CB	5-11	180	7	West Texas State
56	Hunley, Lamonte	LB	6-2	241	3	Arizona
94	Kellar, Scott	NT	6-3	278	2	Northern Illinois
5	Kiel, Blair	QB	6-0	200	3	Notre Dame
55	Krauss, Barry	LB	6-3	239	9	Alabama
92	Leiding, Jeff	LB	6-3	232	2	Texas
59	Lowry, Orlando	LB	6-4	237	3	Ohio State
88	Martin, Robbie	WR-PR	5-8	187	7	Cal Poly-SLO
32	McMillan, Randy	RB	6-0	216	7	Pittsburgh
86	Murray, Walter	WR	6-4	200	2	Hawaii
93	Odom, Cliff	LB	6-2	241	7	Texas-Arlington
35	Randle, Tate	S	6-0	204	6	Texas Tech
58	Redd, Glen	LB	6-1	232	6	Brigham Young
	Reilly, Dameon	WR	5-11	179	1	Rhode Island
83	Sherwin, Tim	TE	6-6	246	7	Boston College
45	Sims, Tommy	S	6-0	190	1	Tennessee
66	Solt, Ron	G	6-3	279	4	Maryland
	Springs, Kirk	S-KR	6-0	197	7	Miami, Ohio
3	Stark, Rohn	P	6-3	202	6	Florida State
99	Thompson, Donnell	DE	6-5	272	7	North Carolina
10	Trudeau, Jack	QB	6-3	211	2	Illinois
64	Utt, Ben	G	6-5	281	6	Georgia Tech
60	Walker, Gary	C	6-3	263	1	Boston University
34	Wonsley, George	RB	6-0	220	4	Mississippi State

Gary Hogeboom could spark a Colts renaissance.

MIAMI DOLPHINS

Address 4770 Biscayne Boulevard, Suite 1440, Miami, Florida 33137.

Stadium Robbie Stadium, Miami.
Capacity 75,500 *Playing Surface* Grass.

Team Colours Aqua, Coral, and White.

Head Coach Don Shula – eighteenth year.

Championships Division 1971, '72, '73, '74, '79, '81, '83, '84, '85; Conference 1971, '72, '73, '82, '84; Super Bowl 1972, '73.

History AFL 1966-69, AFC 1970-

Offense

'We've got a lot of work to do in many areas,' reflected Miami head coach Don Shula. Perhaps it was the memory of seeing his team slither to 2-5 after seven weeks, his worst start as a head coach, which lingered in Shula's mind. The plain fact is that the Dolphins have been leading a charmed existence for some years, one way or another disguising their defensive weaknesses. But it is equally true that to do it required coaching skills and organisation of a high order. Also, they have one of the best offenses in football. Quarterback Dan Marino has scaled such heights that yet another catalogue of amazing achievements went largely unnoticed. He established NFL single-season records for passing attempts (623) and completions (378), the latter record which he already held, logged the second-best mark for touchdown passes (44) and the third-best total for passing yardage (4,746). The 'Mark Brothers', wide receivers Clayton and Duper, are classed amongst the best pairings in the league, and the veteran Nat Moore continues as an outstanding third receiver. Running backs Lorenzo Hampton and Tony Nathan chipped in with 61 and 48 pass receptions respectively. It was, then, unexpected when the Dolphins selected Scott Schwedes in the second round of the draft. The rushing game was much less effective, ranking 25th in the NFL. And though the club can be pleased with the steady emergence of former first-round draftee Hampton, who was the leading rusher and scored all nine of the Dolphins' rushing touchdowns, the lack of a big-play threat simmering on the back burner is a weakness. Hampton and Woody Bennett form the senior pairing, backed up by Nathan and Ron Davenport. Despite losing players to early-season injuries, the offensive line gave up only 17 quarterback sacks, the lowest total in the entire NFL. Dwight Stephenson is the league's best center and he has at his left hand a Pro Bowler in guard Roy Foster. Ronnie Lee has an edge over Larry Lee at right guard. Jeff Dellenbach took his chance to start at left tackle when Jon Giesler went down with injury and could retain his seniority. Former Green Bay player Greg Koch was an insurance acquisition when the Dolphins were hit with injuries in training camp, and it was a pleasant surprise that he came through to start in every game. Bruce Hardy, who is coming off the most productive campaign by a tight end in Miami history, plays a vital role in the whole package, backed up by the reliable Dan Johnson.

Defense

Defensively, the Dolphins ended the season tied for 26th place in the league, and you can't go much lower than that. The problems cannot be solved at a stroke but there are several grounds for optimism. Firstly, linebacker Hugh Green may return after the injury which kept him out for all but the first ten quarters of the season. In that brief period, he logged four quarterback sacks. Green could form a dominating partnership with last year's rookie revelation, inside linebacker John Offerdahl, who capped an outstanding season by starting in the Pro Bowl. Second-round draftee linebacker Rick Graf, who, in college, was nicknamed 'Thunder' for the sound of his tackles, could have an immediate impact and will challenge Bob Brudzinski to start outside Larry Kolic. The same is true of first-round draftee John Bosa, who specialises against the run and, at the very least, will compete for playing time with the current starting linemen, T.J. Turner, Bob Baumhower and George Little. The defensive secondary struggled last year with almost the entire personnel suffering significant injuries. Strong safety Glenn Blackwood remains as the 'brains' of the outfit, whilst Bud Brown is a big hitter. William Judson has made the right cornerback position his own but, sadly, left cornerback Don McNeal was again hit by injuries, as was his replacement, Paul Lankford.

Special Teams

Placekicker Fuad Reveiz is coming off a marginal year, when he never seemed to establish the kind of mechanical consistency and timing needed for success in this pressure position. Similarly, punter Reggie Roby, who is not far behind Rohn Stark of Indianapolis in leg strength, was occasionally insecure, mishandling a few snaps. Draftee Schwedes may play a part in the kick return department, where only punt returner James Pruitt, who scored on a 71-yard return, rang any alarm bells.

1987 SCHEDULE OF GAMES		
September		
13 at New England	1:00	
20 at Indianapolis	12:00	
27 NEW YORK GIANTS	1:00	
October		
4 at Seattle	1:00	
11 KANSAS CITY	1:00	
18 at New York Jets	1:00	
25 BUFFALO	1:00	
November		
1 PITTSBURGH	1:00	
8 at Cincinnati	4:00	
15 INDIANAPOLIS	1:00	
22 at Dallas	7:00	
29 at Buffalo	1:00	
December		
7 NEW YORK JETS (Mon.)	9:00	
13 at Philadelphia	1:00	
20 WASHINGTON	8:00	
28 NEW ENGLAND (Mon.)	9:00	

1987 DRAFT

Round	Name	Pos.	Ht.	Wt.	College
1.	Bosa, John	DE	6-4	258	Boston College
2.	Graf, Rick	LB	6-5	232	Wisconsin
2.	Schwedes, Scott	WR	5-11	170	Syracuse
4.	Stradford, Troy	RB-WR	5-8	185	Boston College
5.	Conlin, Chris	T	6-3	290	Penn State
6.	Sellers, Lance	LB	6-2	228	Boise State
7.	Brown, Tom	RB	6-1	225	Pittsburgh
8.	Williams, Joel	TE	6-4	234	Notre Dame
8.	Dennis, Mark	T	6-6	282	Illinois
9.	Pidgeon, Tim	LB	5-11	238	Syracuse
10.	Taylor, Bobby	CB	5-9	175	Wisconsin
11.	Mann, Terence	DT	6-3	268	Southern Methodist
12.	Karsatos, Jim	QB	6-3	238	Ohio State

VETERAN ROSTER

No.	Name	Pos.	Ht.	Wt.	NFL Year	College
73	Baumhower, Bob	NT	6-5	265	10	Alabama
34	Bennett, Woody	RB	6-2	225	9	Miami
75	Betters, Doug	DE	6-7	265	10	Nevada-Reno
47	Blackwood, Glenn	S	6-0	190	9	Texas
43	Brown, Bud	S	6-0	194	4	Southern Mississippi
32	Brown, Donald	CB	5-11	189	2	Maryland
51	Brown, Mark	LB	6-2	230	5	Purdue
59	Brudzinski, Bob	LB	6-4	223	11	Ohio State
71	Charles, Mike	NT	6-4	287	5	Syracuse
	Clark, Steve	G	6-4	260	5	Utah
83	Clayton, Mark	WR	5-9	175	5	Louisville
30	Davenport, Ron	RB	6-2	230	3	Louisville
65	Dellenbach, Jeff	T	6-6	280	3	Wisconsin
85	Duper, Mark	WR	5-9	187	6	N.W. State, Louisiana
61	Foster, Roy	G	6-4	275	6	Southern California
53	Frye, David	LB	6-2	227	5	Purdue
79	Giesler, Jon	T	6-5	265	9	Michigan
74	Green, Cleveland	T	6-3	262	9	Southern
55	Green, Hugh	LB	6-2	225	7	Pittsburgh
27	Hampton, Lorenzo	RB	6-0	212	3	Florida
84	Hardy, Bruce	TE	6-5	232	10	Arizona State
90	Hendel, Andy	LB	6-1	230	2	North Carolina State
11	Jensen, Jim	WR	6-4	215	7	Boston University
87	Johnson, Dan	TE	6-3	240	5	Iowa State
49	Judson, William	CB	6-2	190	6	South Carolina State
64	Katolin, Mike	C	6-3	270	1	San Jose State
68	Koch, Greg	T	6-4	276	11	Arkansas
94	Kolic, Larry	LB	6-1	242	2	Ohio State
40	Kozlowski, Mike	S	6-1	198	8	Colorado
44	Lankford, Paul	CB	6-2	184	6	Penn State
66	Lee, Larry	G-C	6-2	263	7	UCLA
72	Lee, Ronnie	G	6-4	265	9	Baylor
99	Little, George	DE	6-4	278	3	Iowa
13	Marino, Dan	QB	6-4	214	5	Pittsburgh
28	McNeal, Don	CB	5-11	192	7	Alabama
89	Moore, Nat	WR	5-9	188	14	Florida
22	Nathan, Tony	RB	6-0	206	9	Alabama
56	Offerdahl, John	LB	6-2	232	2	Western Michigan
82	Pruitt, James	WR-PR	6-2	199	2	Cal State-Fullerton
7	Reveiz, Fuad	K	5-11	222	3	Tennessee
4	Roby, Reggie	P	6-2	243	5	Iowa
26	Rose, Donovan	S	6-1	190	3	Hampton Institute
80	Rose, Joe	TE	6-3	230	7	California
52	Sendlein, Robin	LB	6-3	225	7	Texas
50	Shipp, Jackie	LB	6-2	236	4	Oklahoma
25	Smith, Mike	CB	6-0	171	3	Texas-El Paso
70	Sochia, Brian	NT	6-3	274	5	N.W. Oklahoma State
57	Stephenson, Dwight	C	6-2	255	8	Alabama
10	Strock, Don	QB	6-5	225	14	Virginia Tech
24	Thompson, Reyna	CB	5-11	194	2	Baylor
76	Toth, Tom	T	6-5	275	2	Western Michigan
95	Turner, T.J.	DE	6-4	265	2	Houston

Linebacker John Offerdahl gives 'heart' to the Miami defense.

NEW ENGLAND PATRIOTS

Address Sullivan Stadium, Route 1, Foxboro, Mass. 02035.
Stadium Sullivan Stadium, Foxboro.
   Capacity 61,000 *Playing Surface* Super Turf.
Team Colours Red, White, and Blue.
Head Coach Raymond Berry – fourth year.
Championships Division 1978, '86; Conference 1985.
History AFL 1960-69, AFC 1970-
   (Until 1971, they were known as the Boston Patriots.)

Offense

It was in character when the 1986 Patriots clinched the AFC Eastern division title with a late drive in the final game of the season. But there was a key ingredient missing from the team which went to Super Bowl XX, and that was the great left guard, John Hannah. Everyone knew that his retirement would be felt but no one realised just how much. From having a sound rushing game, the Patriots slumped to dead last in the league, averaging a depressing 2.9 yards per carry. As a remedial step, they dealt with Tampa Bay for Sean Farrell, a former first-round pick who has been on the verge of Pro Bowl selection for most of his career. Farrell will probably step in at left guard alongside left tackle Brian Holloway, while Trevor Matich, who has played at guard, may now be ready to take over from Pete Brock at center. Darryl Haley will probably retain his spot at right tackle, with Paul Fairchild, Ron Wooten and first-round draftee Bruce Armstrong competing for the right guard position. Setting aside a poor 1986 performance, in which the malaise was evenly spread between Craig James, Tony Collins and Mosi Tatupu, the Patriots are as solid as any NFL club at running back. Both James and Collins have had 1,000-yards-rushing seasons, and Tatupu has all the power needed for those short-yardage downs. Tony Eason will retain his status as the senior quarterback, despite the impressive claims of the respected veteran, Steve Grogan. However, Grogan gives the Patriots one of the best reserves in pro football and he will continue in his vital role of calling the plays from the sideline. Without ever attracting the kind of attention heaped on Dan Marino, Ken O'Brien, Dan Fouts and the like, Eason has become one of the NFL's finest quarterbacks. And he could not wish for a better set of receivers. Collins made an invaluable contribution with a personal career-best 77 catches. Of all the major active wide receivers in the league, Stanley Morgan is the only one with a career average per reception of 20 or more yards. In terms of receptions and yardage, he is coming off the finest season of his glittering ten-year career. His starting partner, Irving Fryar, has yet to live up to his collegiate reputation, but there's no doubting his status as a starter and he shows every sign of coming to his best. Tight end Lin Dawson's knee injury kept him out all year but rookie Greg Baty took his chance well, with 37 pass receptions, and he may hang onto the starting job.

Defense

On defense the Patriots were adequate without ever dominating, ranking 16th in the league. Injuries were a major factor, with former first-round pick defensive end Ken Sims playing in only a handful of games, and line-backers Andre Tippett, Lawrence McGrew and Steve Nelson all missing playing time. Sims' injury obliged the Patriots to make changes to the defensive line, but here there were encouraging signs for the future. Toby Williams did well in attempting the conversion to nose tackle, and rookie defensive end Brent Williams made an excellent contribution with seven quarterback sacks. Firing off from the right defensive end position, Garin Veris led the club with 11 sacks. Veris really has developed into an all-star performer and must soon be attracting votes to the Pro Bowl. At linebacker, Andre Tippett came through what was, for him, a steady season. But he is still regarded as the AFC's best in the outside position. Tippett and right outside linebacker Don Blackmon combined for 17 sacks. In the absence of Nelson, Johnny Rembert came in at the left inside position and led all the linebackers with 98 tackles. The four starters in the secondary are first class. Left cornerback Ronnie Lippett led the team with eight pass interceptions while safeties Fred Marion and Roland James were the only Patriots players to log more than one hundred tackles (they had 122 and 112 respectively). Right cornerback Ray Clayborn had only three pass interceptions, but that's a measure of the respect in which he is held by opposing quarterbacks, who simply choose not to challenge him. The secondary, then, would have to rank amongst the NFL's best but, beyond the starters, they're a little thin on talent.

Special Teams

It was a year for placekicker Tony Franklin to remember, as he set personal best marks for field goals (32), points (140) and celebrated his first selection to the Pro Bowl. Punter Rich Camarillo continues to boom the ball into the

1987 SCHEDULE OF GAMES		
September		
13 MIAMI		1:00
21 at New York Jets (Mon.)		9:00
27 at Washington		1:00
October		
4 CLEVELAND		1:00
11 BUFFALO		1:00
18 at Houston		12:00
25 at Indianapolis		1:00
November		
1 LOS ANGELES RAIDERS		1:00
8 at New York Giants		8:00
15 DALLAS		1:00
22 INDIANAPOLIS		1:00
29 PHILADELPHIA		1:00
December		
6 at Denver		2:00
13 NEW YORK JETS		1:00
20 at Buffalo		1:00
28 at Miami (Mon.)		9:00

distance. Fryar underlined his value by averaging 10.5 yards over 35 punt returns, while Stephen Starring did well enough to retain his job as the senior kickoff returner.

1987 DRAFT

Round	Name	Pos.	Ht.	Wt.	College
1.	Armstrong, Bruce	T-G	6-3	264	Louisville
3.	Perryman, Bob	RB	6-1	225	Michigan
4.	Gannon, Rich	QB-RB	6-2	200	Delaware
4.	Beasley, Derrick	S	6-1	205	Winston-Salem State
4.	Jordan, Tim	LB	6-2	219	Wisconsin
5.	Villa, Danny	T	6-4	295	Arizona State
5.	Gibson, Tom	DE	6-7	250	Northern Arizona
6.	Taylor, Gene	WR	6-1	183	Fresno State
11.	Reveiz, Carlos	K	5-8	188	Tennessee
12.	Davis, Elgin	RB	5-10	195	Central Florida

VETERAN ROSTER

No.	Name	Pos.	Ht.	Wt.	NFL Year	College
62	Bain, Bill	T	6-4	260	13	Southern California
48	Baty, Greg	TE	6-5	241	2	Stanford
94	Black, Mel	LB	6-2	228	2	Eastern Illinois
55	Blackmon, Don	LB	6-3	235	7	Tulsa
28	Bowman, Jim	S	6-2	210	3	Central Michigan
58	Brock, Pete	C	6-5	275	12	Colorado
3	Camarillo, Rich	P	5-11	185	7	Washington
26	Clayborn, Raymond	CB	6-0	186	11	Texas
33	Collins, Tony	RB	5-11	212	7	East Carolina
87	Dawson, Lin	TE	6-3	240	6	North Carolina State
59	Doig, Steve	LB	6-2	240	5	New Hampshire
21	Dupard, Reggie	RB	5-11	205	2	Southern Methodist
11	Eason, Tony	QB	6-4	212	5	Illinois
66	Fairchild, Paul	G	6-4	270	4	Kansas
	Farrell, Sean	G	6-3	260	6	Penn State
1	Franklin, Tony	K	5-8	182	9	Texas A&M
80	Fryar, Irving	WR	6-0	200	4	Nebraska
43	Gibson, Ernest	CB	5-10	185	4	Furman
14	Grogan, Steve	QB	6-4	210	13	Kansas State
68	Haley, Darryl	T-G	6-4	265	5	Utah
27	Hawthorne, Greg	TE	6-2	235	9	Baylor
97	Hodge, Milford	DE	6-3	278	2	Washington State
76	Holloway, Brian	T	6-7	288	7	Stanford
51	Ingram, Brian	LB	6-4	235	5	Tennessee
32	James, Craig	RB	6-0	215	4	Southern Methodist
38	James, Roland	S	6-2	191	8	Tennessee
83	Jones, Cedric	WR	6-1	184	6	Duke
42	Lippett, Ronnie	CB	5-11	180	5	Miami
31	Marion, Fred	S	6-2	191	6	Miami
64	Matich, Trevor	G-C	6-4	270	3	Brigham Young
50	McGrew, Lawrence	LB	6-5	233	7	Southern California
23	McSwain, Rod	CB	6-1	198	4	Clemson
67	Moore, Steve	G-T	6-4	285	5	Tennessee State
86	Morgan, Stanley	WR	5-11	181	11	Tennessee
75	Morriss, Guy	C-G	6-4	275	15	Texas Christian
57	Nelson, Steve	LB	6-2	230	14	North Dakota State
70	Plunkett, Art	T	6-7	260	6	Nevada-Las Vegas
22	Profit, Eugene	DB	5-10	165	2	Yale
12	Ramsey, Tom	QB	6-1	189	3	UCLA
52	Rembert, Johnny	LB	6-3	234	5	Clemson
95	Reynolds, Ed	LB	6-5	242	5	Virginia
65	Ruth, Mike	NT	6-1	266	2	Boston College
77	Sims, Ken	DE	6-5	271	6	Texas
81	Starring, Stephen	WR-KR	5-10	172	5	McNeese State
30	Tatupu, Mosi	RB	6-0	227	10	Southern California
56	Tippett, Andre	LB	6-3	241	6	Iowa
60	Veris, Garin	DE	6-4	255	3	Stanford
24	Weathers, Robert	RB	6-2	222	6	Arizona State
53	Weishuhn, Clayton	LB	6-1	218	4	Angelo State
96	Williams, Brent	DE	6-3	278	2	Toledo
82	Williams, Derwin	WR	6-1	185	3	New Mexico
54	Williams, Ed	LB	6-4	244	4	Texas
90	Williams, Toby	DE	6-4	270	5	Nebraska
61	Wooten, Ron	G	6-4	273	6	North Carolina

Andre Tippett is still the AFC's premier outside linebacker.

NEW YORK JETS

Address 598 Madison Avenue, New York, N.Y. 10022.
Stadium Giants Stadium, East Rutherford, N.J. 07073.
　　Capacity 76,891 *Playing Surface* AstroTurf.
Team Colours Kelly Green and White.
Head Coach Joe Walton – fifth year.
Championships AFL 1968; Super Bowl 1968.
History AFL 1960-69, AFC 1970-
　　(Until 1963, they were known as the New York Titans.)

Offense

After standing at 10-1 after eleven weeks which had included a barnstorming nine consecutive victories, the Jets didn't win another regular season game and almost missed the playoffs. The major reason for their collapse was a sequence of terrible injuries, and the story will continue into the 1987 season as several players seek to come back after major reconstructive surgery. When healthy, the offensive line is super, featuring its natural leader, former Pro Bowler Joe Fields, at center. Last year's preseason shuffling left Jim Sweeney at left tackle, Reggie McElroy at right tackle and Ted Banker at left guard. However, all four players had injury problems, the most serious being those of McElroy and Sweeney, who may not be ready for the start of the season. Dan Alexander managed to stay clear of knocks and had a fine year at right guard. The backups include Guy Bingham, a solid guard who doubles as a center, and last year's first-round pick, Mike Haight. At quarterback, the Jets can call on two first-class operators, Ken O'Brien and Pat Ryan. O'Brien is the more polished and he can be quite devastating, as he showed last season when, week after week, he roasted the opposition with his big-play style. After the tenth game, his passer rating stood at a heady 111. However, he went into a slump which would see him replaced by Ryan in the playoffs. O'Brien is the favourite to start but he'll have to regain his spurs in training camp. The reward will be the opportunity of passing to an outstanding set of receivers, with Wesley Walker and Al Toon split wide and Mickey Shuler at tight end. Both Walker and Toon caught their passes for over 1,000 yards and, between them, accounted for twenty touchdowns. Shuler finally earned the recognition he has deserved for some time, namely, that of being selected to the Pro Bowl. The Jets' rushing game is as good as any in the league with the proviso that Freeman McNeil remains healthy. Good as McNeil is, Johnny Hector showed that he could be a genuine starter when given the chance, and they are now joined by the powerful Roger Vick, who came in the first round of the draft.

Defense

It was on defense that the injuries had their most telling effect, as the heart was ripped out of the unit. The injuries to both All-Pro nose tackle Joe Klecko and Pro Bowl inside linebacker Lance Mehl are such that they may not return. Starting defensive end Marty Lyons has had surgery on both shoulders and another All-Pro, defensive end Mark Gastineau, was slowed all season with a series of problems. Head coach Joe Walton is keeping a brave face and he is helped by his realism, to quote, 'You have to play the cards you are dealt'. The chances are that both Gastineau and Lyons will be back to full health and, together with nose tackle Tom Baldwin and defensive end Barry Bennett, they form a group out of which a good three-man defensive line could emerge. At left outside linebacker, Bob Crable had his first injury-free campaign and was almost back to his best form. Rusty Guilbeau has made the right outside linebacker spot his own. Inside linebacker Kyle Clifton took over as the defensive signal-caller and led the club in tackles for the second straight year, while Kevin McArthur was a pleasant surprise. They are reinforced by draftees Alex Gordon and Onzy Elam, who join Troy Benson and Matt Monger in reserve. The secondary had a difficult time against the pass – they ranked dead last in the league – but it is far from a shambles and could turn around very quickly. Jerry Holmes returned from a stay in the USFL and led the team in interceptions from the left cornerback position. Holmes helped to weld together three young players, cornerback Russell Carter and safeties Lester Lyles and Harry Hamilton, all of whom retain the confidence of head coach Walton.

Special Teams

Placekicker Pat Leahy, an old pro who is dedicated to his craft, had an excellent year and should continue in the same vein. Dave Jennings came back from foot surgery, and although his gross average was an unspectacular 39.4 yards, he led the AFC with 27 punts inside the 20-yard line. Both Bobby Humphery and JoJo Townsell can return the kickoffs all the way for touchdowns – last season they scored touchdowns on returns of 96 and 93 yards respectively. Kurt Sohn is a sure-handed punt returner but he may have to step aside more often for Townsell in the coming season.

1987 SCHEDULE OF GAMES	September	
	13 at Buffalo	1:00
	21 NEW ENGLAND (Mon.)	9:00
	27 at Pittsburgh	4:00
	October	
	4 DALLAS	4:00
	11 at Indianapolis	12:00
	18 MIAMI	1:00
	25 at Washington	1:00
	November	
	1 INDIANAPOLIS	1:00
	9 SEATTLE (Mon.)	9:00
	15 at Kansas City	12:00
	22 BUFFALO	1:00
	29 CINCINNATI	1:00
	December	
	7 at Miami (Mon.)	9:00
	13 at New England	1:00
	20 PHILADELPHIA	1:00
	27 at New York Giants	1:00

1987 DRAFT

Round	Name	Pos.	Ht.	Wt.	College
1.	Vick, Roger	RB	6-2	220	Texas A&M
2.	Gordon, Alex	LB	6-4	238	Cincinnati
3.	Elam, Onzy	LB	6-2	214	Tennessee State
5.	Jackson, Kirby	CB	5-11	180	Mississippi State
6.	Martin, Tracy	WR	6-2	200	North Dakota
7.	Nichols, Gerald	NT	6-2	265	Florida State
8.	Hunter, Eddie	RB	5-10	191	Virginia Tech
8.	Rice, Mike	P-WR	5-11	190	Montana
9.	McLean, Ron	DE	6-3	260	Cal State-Fullerton
10.	Lewis, Sid	DB	5-11	180	Penn State
11.	Timmer, Kirk	LB	6-3	232	Montana State
12.	Ransdell, Bill	QB	6-2	215	Kentucky

VETERAN ROSTER

No.	Name	Pos.	Ht.	Wt.	NFL Year	College
60	Alexander, Dan	G	6-4	268	11	Louisiana State
43	Amoia, Vince	RB	5-11	220	1	Arizona State
95	Baldwin, Tom	NT	6-4	270	4	Tulsa
63	Banker, Ted	G-T-C	6-2	265	4	Southeast Missouri
31	Barber, Marion	RB	6-3	228	6	Minnesota
78	Bennett, Barry	DE	6-4	260	10	Concordia, Minn.
54	Benson, Troy	LB	6-2	235	2	Pittsburgh
64	Bingham, Guy	C-G	6-3	260	8	Montana
	Brophy, Jay	LB	6-3	233	3	Miami
22	Bruckner, Nick	RB	5-11	185	4	Syracuse
27	Carter, Russell	CB-S	6-2	195	4	Southern Methodist
	Clark, Randy	C	6-4	270	8	Northern Illinois
59	Clifton, Kyle	LB	6-4	230	4	Texas Christian
50	Crable, Bob	LB	6-3	230	6	Notre Dame
52	Crawford, Tim	LB	6-4	230	1	Texas Tech
30	Faaola, Nuu	RB	5-11	215	2	Hawaii
65	Fields, Joe	C	6-2	253	13	Widener
98	Foster, Jerome	DE	6-3	235	4	Ohio State
99	Gastineau, Mark	DE	6-5	270	9	East Central Oklahoma
35	Glenn, Kerry	CB	5-9	175	2	Minnesota
81	Griggs, Billy	TE	6-3	230	3	Virginia
94	Guilbeau, Rusty	LB	6-4	235	6	McNeese State
79	Haight, Mike	G-T	6-4	270	2	Iowa
39	Hamilton, Harry	S	6-0	195	4	Penn State
	Hamm, Bob	DE	6-4	257	4	Nevada-Reno
84	Harper, Michael	WR	5-10	180	2	Southern California
34	Hector, Johnny	RB	5-11	200	5	Texas A&M
47	Holmes, Jerry	CB	6-2	175	6	West Virginia
28	Howard, Carl	CB-S	6-2	190	4	Rutgers
48	Humphery, Bobby	CB-KR	5-10	180	4	New Mexico State
55	Jackson, Charles	LB	6-2	224	10	Washington
13	Jennings, Dave	P	6-4	200	14	St Lawrence
80	Jones, Johnny 'Lam'	WR	6-11	180	6	Texas
71	King, Gordon	T-G	6-6	270	9	Stanford
73	Klecko, Joe	NT	6-3	263	11	Temple
89	Klever, Rocky	TE	6-3	228	5	Montana
5	Leahy, Pat	K	6-0	200	14	St Louis University
26	Lyles, Lester	S-LB	6-3	218	3	Virginia
29	Lynn, Johnny	CB-S	6-0	198	8	UCLA
93	Lyons, Marty	DE-NT	6-5	269	9	Alabama
57	McArthur, Kevin	LB	6-2	230	2	Lamar
68	McElroy, Reggie	T	6-6	270	5	West Texas State
24	McNeil, Freeman	RB	5-11	214	7	UCLA
56	Mehl, Lance	LB	6-3	233	8	Penn State
36	Miano, Rich	S	6-0	200	3	Hawaii
58	Monger, Matt	LB	6-1	238	3	Oklahoma State
74	Moore, Derland	NT	6-4	273	15	Oklahoma
7	O'Brien, Ken	QB	6-4	208	5	Cal-Davis
49	Paige, Tony	RB	5-10	225	4	Virginia Tech
10	Ryan, Pat	QB	6-3	210	10	Tennessee
82	Shuler, Mickey	TE	6-3	231	10	Penn State
87	Sohn, Kurt	WR-KR	5-11	180	6	Fordham
53	Sweeney, Jim	T-G	6-4	260	4	Pittsburgh
88	Toon, Al	WR	6-4	205	3	Wisconsin
83	Townsell, JoJo	WR	5-9	180	3	UCLA
70	Waldemore, Stan	G-C-T	6-4	269	8	Nebraska
85	Walker, Wesley	WR	6-0	182	11	California

Freeman McNeil needs to stay free of injuries.

CINCINNATI BENGALS

Address 200 Riverfront Stadium, Cincinnati, Ohio 45202.
Stadium Riverfront Stadium, Cincinnati.
  Capacity 59,754 *Playing Surface* AstroTurf.
Team Colours Black, Orange, and White.
Head Coach Sam Wyche – fourth year.
Championships Division 1970, '73, '81; Conference 1981.
History AFL 1968-69, AFC 1970-

Offense

There can now be little argument that head coach Sam Wyche has assembled the best offense in pro football. Furthermore, unlike the Dolphins, who could also make a claim to the top spot, the Bengals are balanced – they ranked second in the league in rushing and third in passing. It all begins with a monster offensive line, featuring Pro Bowlers in left tackle Anthony Munoz and right guard Max Montoya. Center Dave Rimington is a former first-round pick, while another first-rounder, Brian Blados, has to settle for reserve status. Last season, Blados lost his starting spot at left guard to Bruce Kozerski and, again, Blados lost out to second-year player Joe Walter in the competition to replace the departed Mike Wilson at right tackle. The line is very sound and yet there still remains room for improvement. Last year, starting quarterback Boomer Esiason added steel resolve to the list of his outstanding talents as a pure passer. He was a little inconsistent and, briefly, was benched. But, typically, on that occasion, against Houston on Week Ten with the Bengals trailing 26-0, he came back on to throw three touchdown passes, albeit in a losing cause. His wide receivers, Cris Collinsworth and Eddie Brown, are highly dangerous. Collinsworth caught his passes for over 1,000 yards for the fourth time in his career, while Brown gave almost a repeat of his rookie season, catching 58 passes for 964 yards and four touchdowns. The backups, Tim McGee and Steve Kreider, are as good as most reserves around the league. Tight end Rodney Holman was another who showed that his form of the previous year was genuine, as he caught 40 passes for 570 yards. In reserve, the Bengals have the fast-improving Eric Kattus. San Diego must regret the trade which sent running back James Brooks to the Bengals in 1984. Brooks put on a superb show, rushing for 1,087 yards and catching 54 passes for 686 yards to establish himself as one of the league's finest dual-purpose backs. Stanley Wilson emerged as a runner of frightening potential, averaging 5.6 yards over 68 carries and scoring eight rushing touchdowns. The blockbusting Larry Kinnebrew matched that total while averaging 4.0 yards on 131 carries, and there's yet more talent in the form of Bill Johnson, who was a 1,000-yard rusher in the USFL before joining Cincinnati in 1985.

Defense

Defensively, the Bengals were poor and this was acknowledged by their use of the top four picks in the draft to look for help. The existing defensive line is solid enough but, although nose tackle Tim Krumrie is becoming respected around the conference, defensive ends Ross Browner and Eddie Edwards are beginning to slow. Of the reserves, Jim Skow is considered to be ahead of Mike Hammerstein but both men may have to step aside for Jason Buck, who, as the top interior lineman in collegiate football last season, won the Outland Trophy. Again, draftee Skip McClendon, a rangy player who has played outside linebacker, may find a role as a specialist pass rusher. The Bengals are not noted for their intensity at linebacker and it may be that last year's first-round draftee, Joe Kelly, is not the answer to their problems on the inside. On the other hand, he took time to warm up after missing training camp. Left outside linebacker Emanuel King led the club with nine sacks and the ageless Reggie Williams logged 4.5 from the right outside position. Carl Zander, who was a second-round pick in 1985, has settled in at left inside linebacker. The defensive secondary could be set for a big improvement with the maturing of last year's rookie finds, strong safety David Fulcher and right cornerback Lewis Billups, both of whom started immediately. Fulcher is a crunching tackler and, despite being considered suspect against the pass, he grabbed four interceptions to rank second in the club. Veteran left cornerback Louis Breeden led the team with seven interceptions, matching his previous best which came in the 1980 campaign. During Billups' four-week absence through injury, the Bengals lost twice, underlining their lack of depth. But this may have been rectified by the drafting of Eric Thomas and Leonard Bell, who will provide quality depth and may even challenge the incumbent at free safety, Robert Jackson.

Special Teams

Punter Jeff Hayes was released in the offseason after seeing two of his efforts blocked and averaging a poor 35.1 yards. Draftee Greg Horne has a great chance to take his

1987 SCHEDULE OF GAMES	September	
	13 at Indianapolis	12:00
	20 SAN FRANCISCO	1:00
	27 at Los Angeles Rams	1:00
	October	
	4 SAN DIEGO	1:00
	11 at Seattle	1:00
	18 CLEVELAND	1:00
	25 at Pittsburgh	1:00
	November	
	1 HOUSTON	1:00
	8 MIAMI	4:00
	15 at Atlanta	4:00
	22 PITTSBURGH	1:00
	29 at New York Jets	1:00
	December	
	6 KANSAS CITY	1:00
	13 at Cleveland	1:00
	20 NEW ORLEANS	1:00
	27 at Houston	12:00

place. Placekicker Jim Breech, too, was disappointing, though he did kick two 51-yard field goals. The one success was Tim McGee, who averaged 23.4 yards over 43 kickoff returns and may apply his outstanding speed more often as a punt returner, paired with Ray Horton.

1987 DRAFT

Round	Name	Pos.	Ht.	Wt.	College
1.	Buck, Jason	DE	6-5	260	Brigham Young
2.	Thomas, Eric	CB	5-10	179	Tulane
3.	Bell, Leonard	S	5-10	200	Indiana
3.	McClendon, Skip	DE	6-4	258	Arizona State
4.	Riggs, Jim	TE	6-5	245	Clemson
5.	Logan, Mark	RB	5-10	206	Kentucky
5.	Horne, Greg	P	5-11	185	Arkansas
6.	Gordon, Sonny	S	5-11	192	Ohio State
7.	Thatcher, Chris	G	6-4	275	Lafayette
8.	Wilcots, Solomon	CB	5-10	182	Colorado
9.	Raddatz, Craig	LB	6-3	235	Wisconsin
10.	McCluskey, David	RB	6-0	220	Georgia
11.	Warne, Jim	T	6-6	300	Arizona State
12.	Holifield, John	RB	6-0	193	West Virginia

VETERAN ROSTER

No.	Name	Pos.	Ht.	Wt.	NFL Year	College
53	Barker, Leo	LB	6-2	227	4	New Mexico State
24	Billups, Lewis	CB	5-11	190	2	North Alabama
74	Blados, Brian	G	6-5	295	4	North Carolina
55	Brady, Ed	LB	6-2	235	4	Illinois
3	Breech, Jim	K	5-6	161	9	California
34	Breeden, Louis	CB	5-11	185	10	North Carolina Central
21	Brooks, James	RB	5-10	182	7	Auburn
81	Brown, Eddie	WR	6-0	185	3	Miami
79	Browner, Ross	DE	6-3	265	10	Notre Dame
27	Bussey, Barney	S	6-0	195	2	South Carolina State
80	Collinsworth, Cris	WR	6-5	192	7	Florida
93	DeAyala, Kiki	LB	6-1	225	2	Texas
67	Douglas, David	T	6-4	280	2	Tennessee
73	Edwards, Eddie	DE	6-5	256	11	Miami
7	Esiason, Boomer	QB	6-4	220	4	Maryland
33	Fulcher, David	S	6-3	228	2	Arizona State
11	Gaynor, Doug	QB	6-2	205	2	Long Beach State
71	Hammerstein, Mike	DE	6-4	270	2	Michigan
95	Herrmann, James	DE	6-6	266	1	Brigham Young
43	Hillary, Ira	WR	5-11	190	1	South Carolina
82	Holman, Rodney	TE	6-3	238	6	Tulane
20	Horton, Ray	CB	5-11	190	5	Washington
37	Jackson, Robert	S	5-10	186	6	Central Michigan
36	Jennings, Stanford	RB	6-1	205	4	Furman
30	Johnson, Bill	RB	6-2	230	3	Arkansas State
84	Kattus, Eric	TE	6-5	235	2	Michigan
58	Kelly, Joe	LB	6-2	227	2	Washington
90	King, Emanuel	LB	6-4	251	3	Alabama
28	Kinnebrew, Larry	RB	6-1	258	5	Tennessee State
64	Kozerski, Bruce	C	6-4	275	4	Holy Cross
86	Kreider, Steve	WR	6-4	192	9	Lehigh
69	Krumrie, Tim	NT	6-2	262	5	Wisconsin
88	Martin, Mike	WR	5-10	186	5	Illinois
85	McGee, Tim	WR	5-10	175	2	Tennessee
65	Montoya, Max	G	6-5	275	9	UCLA
78	Munoz, Anthony	T	6-6	278	8	Southern California
75	Reimers, Bruce	T	6-7	280	4	Iowa State
50	Rimington, Dave	C	6-3	288	5	Nebraska
96	Shaw, Jeff	NT	6-1	280	1	Salem College
56	Simpkins, Ron	LB	6-1	235	7	Michigan
70	Skow, Jim	DE	6-3	250	2	Nebraska
63	Walter, Joe	T	6-6	290	3	Texas Tech
51	White, Leon	LB	6-2	236	2	Brigham Young
57	Williams, Reggie	LB	6-0	228	12	Dartmouth
32	Wilson, Stanley	RB	6-1	210	4	Oklahoma
91	Zander, Carl	LB	6-2	235	3	Tennessee

Cris Collinsworth is coming off his fourth 1,000-yards-receiving season.

CLEVELAND BROWNS

Address Tower B, Cleveland Stadium, Cleveland, Ohio 44114.
Stadium Cleveland Stadium, Cleveland.
Capacity 80,098 *Playing Surface* Grass.
Team Colours Seal Brown, Orange, and White.
Head Coach Marty Schottenheimer – fourth year.
Championships Division 1971, '80, '85, '86; AAFC 1946, '47, '48, '49; NFL 1950, '54, '55, '64.
History AAFC 1946-49, NFL 1950-69, AFC 1970-

Offense

Many pro football experts remain unconvinced by the Browns, citing the fact that only rarely did they dominate their opponents. But the record shows that, after losing narrowly to Miami the previous year, they then came within 37 seconds of reaching the Super Bowl. Another opinion of the Browns is that they're a young team, which is well coached and is on schedule for winning a league championship in the next two or three years. Second-year quarterback Bernie Kosar improved dramatically after a hesitant first term. He was the NFL's seventh-best rated passer, threw for the fourth-highest yardage and had the lowest interception percentage, en route to confirming the judgement of the club which paid a high price to Buffalo to select him in the 1985 supplemental draft. Furthermore, he displayed that extra key quality, leadership. His willingness to go for the killer passes brought the best out of a collection of receivers who aren't exactly household names. Wide receiver Brian Brennan had his best year as a pro, leading the club with 55 receptions, the versatile Herman Fontenot came second with 47, rookie Webster Slaughter had a fine debut, catching 40 passes, and Reginald Langhorne started in fifteen games, confounding those who felt that his only chance of making the roster would be as a special-teamer. Tight end Ozzie Newsome was slowed by early-season shoulder and ankle injuries but, by his very presence on the field, served as a threat. It augurs well for 1987. The starting offensive line is a collection of players who have come through despite, in many cases, having slipped into the NFL long after the cameras had stopped clicking and the pressmen had returned to their favourite watering holes. Paul Farren was a 12th-round pick, and Larry Williams spent all of 1985 on injured reserve after being picked in the 10th round. Right guard Dan Fike was a 10th-round pick of the Jets and subsequently was released, while right tackle Cody Risien was a seventh-round draftee. By comparison, center Mike Baab was a 'big shot', being selected in the fifth round. Rickey Bolden, who started in the first five games before breaking his arm, will return at left tackle, meaning that Farren will probably revert to left guard, displacing Williams who will join second-round draftee Gregg Rakoczy in reserve. The rushing game suffered through injury – Earnest Byner and Kevin Mack played as a pairing in only eight quarters – and it is hardly surprising that the Browns slipped to 22nd place in the NFL. But both men, who are former 1,000-yard rushers, are fully fit to resume as starters, backed up by Fontenot, Curtis Dickey and draftee Tim Manoa.

Defense

The Browns shuffle their defensive linemen according to circumstances. Carl Hairston and Reggie Camp are the defensive ends in the starting three-man line, with Pro Bowler Bob Golic at nose tackle. When they switch to a four-man front, Sam Clancy takes an inside position with Dave Puzzuoli coming on as a defensive end. It's a system which gives everyone a shot at sacking the quarterback and, excluding Golic from the group, they led the club in the order listed. The linebacking unit will be without Pro Bowler Chip Banks, who has been traded. For his spot at left outside linebacker, the Browns drafted Mike Junkin, who is said to be a one-man wrecking crew. He joins a group of highly-respected veterans, including outside linebacker Clay Matthews, who played for much of the season with a torn groin muscle but still came close to Pro Bowl selection. The inside positions are held down by two intimidating tacklers, Eddie Johnson and former Eagles player Anthony Griggs, with the highly-impressive Mike Johnson as the senior reserve. Strong safety Ray Ellis was an excellent signing after having been released by Philadelphia. He replaced the injured Al Gross and started fifteen games. At free safety, Chris Rockins is a gifted athlete with the speed to play at cornerback and all the toughness of a prize fighter. As a pair, cornerbacks Frank Minnifield and Hanford Dixon are widely regarded as the best in the business when it comes to man-on-man coverage.

Special Teams

With the status of Matt Bahr uncertain (he needed surgery after injuring his knee when making a tackle on Week Twelve of the season), and Mark Moseley having been

1987 SCHEDULE OF GAMES		
September		
13 at New Orleans		12:00
20 PITTSBURGH		1:00
28 DENVER (Mon.)		9:00
October		
4 at New England		1:00
11 HOUSTON		1:00
18 at Cincinnati		1:00
26 LOS ANGELES RAMS (Mon.)		9:00
November		
1 at San Diego		1:00
8 ATLANTA		1:00
15 BUFFALO		1:00
22 at Houston		12:00
29 at San Francisco		5:00
December		
6 INDIANAPOLIS		1:00
13 CINCINNATI		1:00
20 at Los Angeles Raiders		1:00
26 at Pittsburgh (Sat.)		12:30

released, draftee Jeff Jaeger would appear to have an outstanding opportunity of winning the job of placekicker. Jeff Gossett is secure and so is his record of never having had a punt blocked. There's excitement in the air whenever Gerald 'Ice Cube' McNeil embarks on a kick return. A spectacular runner, he returned a punt 84 yards for a touchdown and scored on a 100-yard kickoff return.

1987 DRAFT

Round	Name	Pos.	Ht.	Wt.	College
1.	Junkin, Mike	LB	6-3	235	Duke
2.	Rakoczy, Gregg	C	6-5	280	Miami
3.	Manoa, Tim	RB	6-0	227	Penn State
3.	Jaeger, Jeff	K	5-11	193	Washington
6.	Braggs, Stephen	S	5-9	173	Texas
8.	Bullitt, Steve	LB	6-2	227	Texas A&M
10.	Winters, Frank	C	6-2	270	Western Illinois
11.	Brewton, Larry	DB	5-9	185	Temple

VETERAN ROSTER

No.	Name	Pos.	Ht.	Wt.	NFL Year	College
66	Andrews, Tom	G	6-4	267	3	Louisville
61	Baab, Mike	C	6-4	270	6	Texas
9	Bahr, Matt	K	5-10	175	9	Penn State
99	Baldwin, Keith	DE	6-4	270	5	Texas A&M
77	Bolden, Rickey	T	6-6	280	4	Southern Methodist
93	Bolzan, Scott	T	6-3	270	1	Northern Illinois
54	Bowser, Charles	LB	6-3	235	5	Duke
86	Brennan, Brian	WR	5-9	178	4	Boston College
44	Byner, Earnest	RB	5-10	215	4	East Carolina
96	Camp, Reggie	DE	6-4	280	5	California
91	Clancy, Sam	DE	6-7	260	4	Pittsburgh
18	Danielson, Gary	QB	6-2	196	10	Purdue
38	Davis, Johnny	RB	6-1	235	10	Alabama
33	Dickey, Curtis	RB	6-1	220	8	Texas A&M
29	Dixon, Hanford	CB	5-11	186	7	Southern Mississippi
24	Ellis, Ray	S	6-1	196	7	Ohio State
39	Everett, Major	RB	5-10	218	5	Mississippi College
74	Farren, Paul	T	6-5	280	5	Boston University
69	Fike, Dan	G	6-7	280	3	Florida
28	Fontenot, Herman	RB-KR	6-0	206	3	Louisiana State
79	Golic, Bob	NT	6-2	270	8	Notre Dame
7	Gossett, Jeff	P	6-2	200	6	Eastern Illinois
80	Greer, Terry	WR	6-2	197	2	Alabama State
53	Griggs, Anthony	LB	6-3	230	6	Ohio State
27	Gross, Al	S	6-3	195	5	Arizona
78	Hairston, Carl	DE	6-4	260	12	Maryland Eastern Shore
23	Harper, Mark	CB	5-9	174	2	Alcorn State
48	Hoggard, D.D.	CB	6-0	188	2	North Carolina State
81	Holt, Harry	TE	6-4	240	5	Arizona
51	Johnson, Eddie	LB	6-1	225	7	Louisville
59	Johnson, Mike	LB	6-1	228	2	Virginia Tech
19	Kosar, Bernie	QB	6-5	210	3	Miami
88	Langhorne, Reginald	WR	0-2	195	3	Elizabeth City State
02	Lilja, George	G	6-4	270	6	Michigan
34	Mack, Kevin	RB	6-0	212	3	Clemson
90	Malone, Ralph	DE	6-5	225	2	Georgia Tech
57	Matthews, Clay	LB	6-2	235	10	Southern California
89	McNeil, Gerald	WR-PR	5-7	140	2	Baylor
71	Meyer, Jim	T	6-5	295	1	Illinois State
52	Miller, Nick	LB	6-2	238	1	Arkansas
31	Minnifield, Frank	CB	5-9	180	4	Louisville
82	Newsome, Ozzie	TE	6-2	232	10	Alabama
58	Nicolas, Scott	LB	6-3	226	6	Miami
12	Norseth, Mike	QB	6-2	200	1	Kansas
10	Pagel, Mike	QB	6-2	200	6	Arizona State
72	Puzzuoli, Dave	NT	6-3	260	5	Pittsburgh
63	Risien, Cody	T	6-7	280	8	Texas A&M
37	Rockins, Chris	S	6-0	195	4	Oklahoma State
40	Simmons, King	S	6-2	200	1	Texas Tech
84	Slaughter, Webster	WR	6-0	170	2	San Diego State
87	Tucker, Travis	TE	6-3	240	3	South Connecticut State
50	Van Pelt, Brad	LB	6-5	235	15	Michigan State
85	Weathers, Clarence	WR	5-9	170	5	Delaware State
55	Weathers, Curtis	LB	6-5	230	8	Mississippi
95	White, James	DE	6-3	245	1	Louisiana State
70	Williams, Larry	G	6-5	290	2	Notre Dame
22	Wright, Felix	CB-S	6-2	190	3	Drake

Former Pro Bowler Ozzie Newsome will be hoping to bounce back after the least-productive of his nine seasons in the NFL.

HOUSTON OILERS

AFC CENTRAL DIVISION

Address Box 1516, Houston, Texas 77001.
Stadium Astrodome, Houston.
   Capacity 50,496 *Playing Surface* AstroTurf.
Team Colours Columbia Blue, Scarlet, and White.
Head Coach Jerry Glanville – third year.
Championships AFL 1960,'61.
History AFL 1960-69, AFC 1970-

Offense

If good drafting makes good football teams, the Oilers must surely be ready to break the shackles which have held them in check for the past six years. Considering their 4-3 record over the final seven weeks of last season, they may already be on the march. It was after nine weeks that Oilers quarterback Warren Moon talked head coach Jerry Glanville into opening up the offense, and the show took to the road. Moon went on to pass for a season total of 3,489 yards, breaking his own Oilers record. Wide receivers Drew Hill and the super rookie, Ernest Givins, each caught passes for over 1,000 yards on the season, a feat previously achieved by only eighteen pairs on the same team in league history. Tight end Jamie Williams, who started in all sixteen games for the third year in a row, had a quiet year but the club is well pleased with his progress. The passing attack was further strengthened in the draft, when the imposing Haywood Jeffires was selected with the second of the Oilers' two first-round options. It meant that they could afford to trade Tim Smith, who had slipped into obscurity, after three really fine seasons over which he caught 198 passes for 2,977 yards. Last year, the rushing game was a disappointment, but all that could change with the return of left guard Mike Munchak, a Pro Bowler who started 53 times in that position before going out with injury on Week Six. A fully-fit Munchak joining center Jim Romano, tackles Bruce Matthews and Dean Steinkuhler and the former Rams All-Pro, right guard Kent Hill, would form a potentially awesome offensive line. Also, draftee Alonzo Highsmith could play a major role in sparking an Oilers return to competitiveness. Highsmith, who came with the Oilers' premier option, was another inspired selection. He didn't rack up big numbers at the University of Miami, simply because the rushing game was not their style. However, he certainly can motor in the right circumstances and, perhaps more importantly, he is an outstanding blocker. In addition to giving Moon a little more time on passing plays, he could be the man to spring the senior running back, Mike Rozier, into the open spaces.

Defense

Satisfied that the offense had been catered for, Glanville began the search for linebackers and came up with five from the draft. Defense against the run was the weakness in 1986, despite the sterling efforts of inside linebackers Robert Abraham and John Grimsley, the latter who displaced Avon Riley after six games. Starting outside linebackers Robert Lyles and Johnny Meads did not pose a serious threat as pass rushers (they registered 3.0 and 3.5 sacks respectively) and they will be under pressure from second-round draftee Walter Johnson, who played defensive end in college where he earned a reputation as a ferocious blitzer. The three-man defensive line, on which defensive end Ray Childress was outstanding for the second straight year, could use a little assistance from someone with a wild streak. Taking every defensive lineman into account, the group logged only sixteen sacks, and of those Childress had five. In mitigation for the starting trio of Childress, nose tackle Doug Smith and defensive right end Richard Byrd, each was in only his second year in what was the NFL's youngest three-man front. The defensive secondary suffered only the injury to free safety Bo Eason, who went out on Week Nine. His replacement, Jeff Donaldson, started for the remainder of the season, alongside strong safety Keith Bostic. On the corners, Steve Brown and Patrick Allen are unchallenged, and while that observation might suggest security and quality, it also reminds us that former first-round pick Richard Johnson has yet to play up to his potential. The secondary is young and is hardly the most feared in the NFL. However, they played their part in a defense which earned a few interesting statistics which the Oilers' 1987 opponents might do well to remember. Specifically, they gave up the fewest first downs on passing in the NFL, opposing quarterbacks completed just 46.5 per cent of their passes which, again, was a league-best figure, and only four quarterbacks managed to complete more than 50 per cent of their passes.

Special Teams

The Oilers have a splendid kicking game. Second-year punter Lee Johnson had a gross average of 41.2 yards while planting 26 of his efforts inside the opposing 20-yard line. Tony Zendejas failed on only five of 27 field goal

1987 SCHEDULE OF GAMES		
September		
13 LOS ANGELES RAMS		12:00
20 at Buffalo		1:00
27 LOS ANGELES RAIDERS		12:00
October		
4 at Denver		2:00
11 at Cleveland		1:00
18 NEW ENGLAND		12:00
25 ATLANTA		12:00
November		
1 at Cincinnati		1:00
8 at San Francisco		1:00
15 at Pittsburgh		1:00
22 CLEVELAND		12:00
29 at Indianapolis		1:00
December		
6 SAN DIEGO		12:00
13 at New Orleans		12:00
20 PITTSBURGH		12:00
27 CINCINNATI		12:00

attempts, underlining his value to the club. Reserve wide receiver Willie Drewrey manfully shouldered the burden of punt returns and shared the kickoff returns with Allen Pinkett, but with only modest success.

Ernest Givins became only the ninth rookie in league history to catch passes for over 1,000 yards.

1987 DRAFT

Round	Name	Pos.	Ht.	Wt.	College
1.	Highsmith, Alonzo	RB	6-1	235	Miami
1.	Jeffires, Haywood	WR	6-2	198	North Carolina State
2.	Johnson, Walter	LB	5-11	235	Louisiana Tech
3.	Carlson, Cody	QB	6-3	200	Baylor
4.	Dusbabek, Mark	LB	6-3	235	Minnesota
5.	Tillman, Spencer	RB	5-10	204	Oklahoma
6.	Smith, Al	LB	6-0	230	Utah State
6.	Caston, Toby	LB	6-0	235	Louisiana State
7.	Banks, Robert	LB-DE	6-4	247	Notre Dame
8.	James, Michel	WR	5-11	188	Washington State
9.	Neighbors, Wes	C	6-0	260	Alabama
10.	Duncan, Curtis	WR	5-10	183	Northwestern
11.	Davis, John	G-C	6-4	304	Georgia Tech
12.	Valentine, Ira	RB	6-0	207	Texas A&M

VETERAN ROSTER

No.	Name	Pos.	Ht.	Wt.	NFL Year	College
56	Abraham, Robert	LB	6-1	230	6	North Carolina State
86	Akiu, Mike	WR	5-9	182	3	Hawaii
29	Allen, Patrick	CB	5-10	179	4	Utah State
75	Baker, Jesse	DE	6-5	271	9	Jacksonville State
36	Banks, Chuck	RB	6-2	225	2	West Virginia Tech
25	Bostic, Keith	S	6-1	223	5	Michigan
92	Briehl, Tom	LB	6-3	247	2	Stanford
24	Brown, Steve	CB	5-11	187	5	Oregon
94	Bush, Frank	LB	6-1	218	3	North Carolina State
71	Byrd, Richard	DE	6-3	264	3	Southern Mississippi
79	Childress, Ray	DE	6-6	276	3	Texas A&M
50	Dodge, Kirk	LB	6-1	231	3	Nevada-Las Vegas
31	Donaldson, Jeff	S	6-0	194	4	Colorado
88	Dressel, Chris	TE	6-4	239	5	Stanford
82	Drewrey, Willie	WR-KR	5-7	164	3	West Virginia
31	Eason, Bo	S	6-2	200	4	Cal-Davis
32	Edwards, Stan	RB	6-0	210	5	Michigan
51	Fairs, Eric	LB	6-3	235	2	Memphis State
95	Fuller, William	DE	6-3	255	2	North Carolina
81	Givins, Ernest	WR	5-9	175	2	Louisville
68	Golic, Mike	NT	6-5	272	2	Notre Dame
59	Grimsley, John	LB	6-2	236	4	Kentucky
85	Hill, Drew	WR	5-9	168	8	Georgia Tech
72	Hill, Kent	G	6-5	260	9	Georgia Tech
22	Johnson, Kenny	S	5-11	172	7	Mississippi State
11	Johnson, Lee	P	6-1	199	3	Brigham Young
23	Johnson, Richard	CB	6-1	190	3	Wisconsin
58	Kelley, Mike	C-G	6-5	266	2	Notre Dame
37	Kush, Rod	S	6-1	195	7	Nebraska-Omaha
10	Luck, Oliver	QB	6-2	196	6	West Virginia
28	Lyday, Allen	S	5-10	197	4	Nebraska
93	Lyles, Robert	LB	6-1	225	4	Texas Christian
98	Madsen, Lynn	DE	6-4	260	2	Washington
78	Maggs, Don	T-G	6-5	279	4	Tulane
74	Matthews, Bruce	T	6-4	283	5	Southern California
26	McMillian, Audrey	CB	6-0	190	3	Houston
91	Meads, Johnny	LB	6-2	235	4	Nicholls State
1	Moon, Warren	QB	6-3	210	4	Washington
76	Moran, Eric	T-G	6-5	294	4	Washington
67	Morgan, Karl	NT	6-1	255	4	UCLA
63	Munchak, Mike	G	6-3	286	6	Penn State
39	Oliver, Hubert	RB	5-10	230	5	Arizona
89	Parks, Jeff	TE	6-3	240	2	Auburn
52	Pennison, Jay	C	6-1	265	2	Nicholls State
20	Pinkett, Allen	RB	5-9	185	2	Notre Dame
53	Riley, Avon	LB	6-3	240	7	UCLA
55	Romano, Jim	C	6-3	255	6	Penn State
33	Rozier, Mike	RB	5-10	211	3	Nebraska
99	Smith, Doug	NT	6-4	287	3	Auburn
70	Steinkuhler, Dean	T-G	6-3	275	4	Nebraska
35	Wallace, Ray	RB	6-0	221	2	Purdue
69	Williams, Doug	T-G	6-5	285	2	Texas A&M
87	Williams, Jamie	TE	6-4	245	5	Nebraska
12	Witkowski, John	QB	6-1	205	3	Columbia
40	Woolfolk, Butch	RB	6-1	215	6	Michigan
7	Zendejas, Tony	K	5-8	165	3	Nevada-Reno

DENVER BRONCOS

Address 5700 Logan Street, Denver, Colorado 80216.
Stadium Denver Mile High Stadium.
    Capacity 75,100 *Playing Surface* Grass (Prescription
    Athletic Turf).
Team Colours Orange, Royal Blue, and White.
Head Coach Dan Reeves – seventh year.
Championships Division 1977, '78, '84, '86; Conference 1977
    '86.
History AFL 1960-69, AFC 1970-

Offense

It's difficult to establish a form-line on a club which won its first six games before going 5-5 the rest of the way. Again, in the playoffs, when it mattered against both New England and Cleveland, they could chew up the yards. But against the Giants in Super Bowl XXI, they couldn't make that one vital yard in three attempts when success would have given them a 17-7 lead. Towards the end of last season, increasingly, the offense became a one-man show. That man was quarterback John Elway, who took it upon himself to get the job done. His passing still is erratic, but he became the leader which the club wanted when they traded with the Colts in 1983. His has become the responsibility of nursing the best out of a unit which, in what seems a Denver tradition, has no genuine stars amongst its strike players. But they're all steady and reliable, none more so than running backs Sammy Winder and Gerald Willhite. They are expected to continue as the starters, ahead of Ken Bell and Gene Lang respectively. Of Steve Sewell, it's not clear which direction his career will take. He has the perfect size and speed for the modern prototype running back, but his talents make him equally valuable as a receiver, possibly even split wide. In that area, the receivers, rookie sixth-round pick Mark Jackson proved to be a super acquisition as he led the club with 738 yards at a big-time average of 19.4 per catch but, still, is regarded as a backup to Vance Johnson. Steve Watson is coming off a sub-par year and it could be that he adopts a reserve role, allowing Jackson to step into his spot, wide to the right. The arrival of first-round draftee Ricky Nattiel puts further pressure on Watson. Another 1986 sixth-round pick, Orson Mobley, came on well, even evoking comparison with the former Broncos favourite, Riley Odoms. All it needed was for one commentator to suggest it and, before long, it was common 'knowledge'. If the Broncos are perhaps deficient in any one area, it is in reserve strength for the offensive line, which really felt the loss of starting right guard Paul Howard during the later stages of the playoffs. Howard will try to return, joining center Billy Bryan, right tackle Ken Lanier, left guard Keith Bishop and, probably, last year's fourth-round draftee, Jim Juriga, who had apparently beaten out Dave Studdard for the starting left tackle spot before being injured during the preseason. As a group they are one of the lightest in the NFL but they are well respected. Last

year, Bishop became the first Denver offensive lineman selected to the Pro Bowl.

Defense

Denver's style on defense is to hustle, harry and chase, never allowing its opponent to settle into its game-plan. Up front, the charge is led by the one-two combination of defensive end Rulon Jones, a player of great force and vision, together with Karl Mecklenburg, who is nominally an inside linebacker but reverts to pass rusher when the occasion demands. They led the club with 13.5 and 9.5 sacks respectively. The supporting cast on the line includes starting nose tackle Greg Kragen and starting defensive end Andre Townsend. Backup defensive end Simon Fletcher may be used more often as the starting left outside linebacker, in place of Jim Ryan, the latter who is projected to shift to the right side, occupying the space vacated by the venerated Tom Jackson who has retired. The other starter is fourth-year player Ricky Hunley, a collision merchant who led the club with 164 tackles starting at right inside linebacker. Hunley could show significant improvement as he learns the subtle art of reading the game. Again, this area, linebacking, was helped by the drafting of Michael Brooks and Marc Munford. It's tempting to say that the defensive secondary is almost too well stocked with talent. Former Pro Bowl cornerback Mark Haynes can't break into the starting lineup, which has Mike Harden and Louis Wright on the corners. Harden, who led the club with six interceptions, is unchallenged, but there's just a possibility that Wright is beginning to slow. At free safety, Steve Foley has the edge over another splendid reserve, Tony Lilly, while Pro Bowl starter Dennis Smith keeps out yet another potential starter, Randy Robbins, at strong safety.

Special Teams

It would be wrong for the memory of two misses in the

1987 SCHEDULE OF GAMES	September	
	13 SEATTLE	2:00
	20 vs. Green Bay at Milwaukee	12:00
	28 at Cleveland (Mon.)	9:00
	October	
	4 HOUSTON	2:00
	12 LOS ANGELES RAIDERS	
	(Mon.)	7:00
	18 at Kansas City	3:00
	25 at Minnesota	12:00
	November	
	1 DETROIT	2:00
	8 at Buffalo	1:00
	16 CHICAGO (Mon.)	7:00
	22 at Los Angeles Raiders	1:00
	29 at San Diego	1:00
	December	
	6 NEW ENGLAND	2:00
	13 at Seattle	5:00
	19 KANSAS CITY (Sat.)	2:00
	27 SAN DIEGO	2:00

Super Bowl to cloud what was, for placekicker Rich Karlis, a solid performance in the regular season. Mike Horan found his timing as the season wore on and is one of the better punters. Gerald Willhite has developed into a punt returner of consistently high quality – averaging 10.7 yards on 78 returns over the last three seasons – whilst the partnership of running backs Lang and Bell takes good care of the kickoff returns.

1987 DRAFT

Round	Name	Pos.	Ht.	Wt.	College
1.	Nattiel, Ricky	WR	5-9	180	Florida
3.	Brooks, Michael	LB	6-0	235	Louisiana State
4.	Munford, Marc	LB	6-1	230	Nebraska
6.	Marshall, Warren	RB	6-0	215	James Madison
7.	Strozier, Wilbur	TE-G	6-4	264	Georgia
8.	Morgan, Dan	G	6-6	280	Penn State
9.	Plummer, Bruce	CB	6-0	190	Mississippi State
10.	Wilkinson, Rafe	LB	6-2	235	Richmond
11.	Roberts, Steve	DE	6-4	239	Washington
11.	Neal, Tommy	RB	5-9	206	Maryland
12.	Braxton, Tyrone	CB	5-10	173	North Dakota State

VETERAN ROSTER

No.	Name	Pos.	Ht.	Wt.	NFL Year	College
35	Bell, Ken	RB	5-10	190	2	Boston College
54	Bishop, Keith	G	6-3	265	7	Baylor
64	Bryan, Billy	C	6-2	255	10	Duke
72	Cameron, Dallas	LB	6-2	242	1	Miami
69	Colorito, Tony	NT	6-5	260	2	Southern California
59	Comeaux, Darren	LB	6-1	227	6	Arizona State
63	Cooper, Mark	G	6-5	267	5	Miami
55	Dennison, Rick	LB	6-3	220	6	Colorado State
32	Dudek, Joe	RB	6-0	181	1	Plymouth State
7	Elway, John	QB	6-3	210	5	Stanford
73	Fletcher, Simon	DE	6-5	240	3	Houston
43	Foley, Steve	S	6-3	190	11	Tulane
62	Freeman, Mike	G	6-3	256	3	Arizona
90	Gilbert, Freddie	DE	6-4	275	2	Georgia
85	Hackett, Joey	TE	6-5	267	2	Elon College
31	Harden, Mike	CB	6-1	192	8	Michigan
36	Haynes, Mark	CB	5-11	195	8	Colorado
2	Horan, Mike	P	5-11	190	4	Long Beach State
60	Howard, Paul	G	6-3	260	14	Brigham Young
98	Hunley, Ricky	LB	6-2	238	4	Arizona
80	Jackson, Mark	WR	5-9	174	2	Purdue
82	Johnson, Vance	WR	5-11	174	3	Arizona
75	Jones, Rulon	DE	6-6	260	8	Utah State
66	Juriga, Jim	T	6-6	269	1	Illinois
3	Karlis, Rich	K	6-0	180	6	Cincinnati
88	Kay, Clarence	TE	6-2	237	4	Georgia
97	Klostermann, Bruce	LB	6-4	225	1	South Dakota State
71	Kragen, Greg	NT	6-3	245	3	Utah State
8	Kubiak, Gary	QB	6-0	192	5	Texas A&M
33	Lang, Gene	RB	5-10	196	4	Louisiana State
76	Lanier, Ken	T	6-3	269	7	Florida State
22	Lilly, Tony	S	6-0	199	4	Florida
77	Mecklenburg, Karl	DE-LB	6-3	230	5	Minnesota
87	Micho, Bobby	TE	6-3	240	3	Texas
89	Mobley, Orson	TE	6-5	256	2	Salem College
74	Remsberg, Dan	T	6-6	275	2	Abilene Christian
48	Robbins, Randy	S	6-2	189	4	Arizona
83	Rolle, Gary	WR	5-11	174	1	Florida
50	Ryan, Jim	LB	6-1	218	9	William & Mary
84	Sampson, Clint	WR	5-11	183	5	San Diego State
30	Sewell, Steve	RB	6-3	210	3	Oklahoma
71	Short, Stan	G-T	6-4	269	1	Penn State
49	Smith, Dennis	S	6-3	200	7	Southern California
70	Studdard, Dave	T	6-4	260	9	Texas
61	Townsend, Andre	DE-NT	6-3	265	4	Mississippi
81	Watson, Steve	WR	6-4	195	9	Temple
47	Willhite, Gerald	RB	5-10	200	6	San Jose State
45	Wilson, Steve	CB	5-10	195	9	Howard
23	Winder, Sammy	RB	5-11	203	6	Southern Mississippi
52	Woodard, Ken	LB	6-1	218	6	Tuskegee Institute
99	Woodard, Raymond	DE	6-6	290	1	Texas
20	Wright, Louis	CB	6-3	200	13	San Jose State

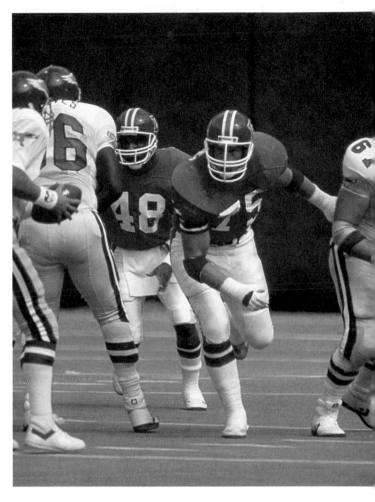

Randy Robbins (# 48) will challenge for greater playing time.

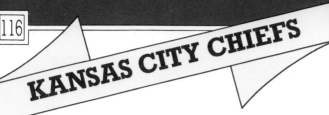

KANSAS CITY CHIEFS

AFC WESTERN DIVISION

Address One Arrowhead Drive, Kansas City, Missouri 64129.

Stadium Arrowhead Stadium, Kansas City.
Capacity 78,067 *Playing Surface* AstroTurf-8.

Team Colours Red, Gold, and White.

Head Coach Frank Gansz – first year.

Championships Division 1971; AFL 1962, '66, '69;
Super Bowl 1969.

History AFL 1960-69, AFC 1970-
(Until 1963, they were known as the Dallas Texans.)

Offense

The Chiefs were not the best-fancied team to reach the playoffs but they did, thanks mostly to tenacity and an outstanding special-teams effort. The signs are that they may find their way into the playoffs a little more easily this year. The major reason would have to be their offensive line, which has the potential to become the AFC's best in double-quick time. Right guard Mark Adickes and left tackle Irv Eatman arrived from the USFL and performed at top level. Center Rick Donnalley, formerly of Washington, became the third new starter. Dave Lutz improved dramatically and Brad Budde had another strong year. In reserve, they have the immensely-powerful Brian Jozwiak, who was their 1986 first-round pick, and former first-rounder John Alt. If this line can give reasonable pass protection, as it should, the Chiefs' aerial attack could be as good as any in the conference. Henry Marshall and Stephone Paige ended the season as the senior pairing, but Carlos Carson is a genuine starter in his own right and Emile Harry hovers as a fine deep threat. Tight end Walt Arnold is the steady sort and may be pressured by Jonathan Hayes. Looking at the quarterback position, it will be interesting to see if Todd Blackledge, who was preferred by departed head coach John Mackovic to the more-experienced Bill Kenney, occupies the same favouritism with new head coach Frank Gansz. Last year there was little to choose between them, but it would appear that the veteran experience of Kenney would be of greater value in what will be a new-style offense. The change in emphasis will come about because, almost certainly, the Chiefs have found themselves a running back from the draft. Ever since the days of the late Joe Delaney, the club has stumbled around vainly in the search for a first-class running back. Astonishingly, since that time, 1982, the Chiefs' top rushing performance has been Herman Heard's 684 yards in 1984. Heard is still on the roster, along with veterans Boyce Green, Mike Pruitt, Larry Moriarty and Jeff Smith, but they may all soon find themselves watching from the sideline as first-round draftee Paul Palmer rips off his yards. Palmer, who is a halfback, could be a franchise player, but the possibilities for second-rounder Christian Okoye are mind-boggling. The word is that the Nigerian-born Okoye, a big, raw, rangy, fire engine of a running back, gave only a taste of

what he could do at tiny Azusa Pacific, where, in that modest company, he was 'Superman'.

Defense

The Chiefs' weakest area of defense, linebacking, was improved considerably by the arrival of last year's second-round pick, Dino Hackett, and they may have found a good backup in draftee Todd Howard. Otherwise, the existing group of Hackett, Louis Cooper, Tim Cofield, Scott Radecic and Gary Spani can maintain par. To the front and behind the linebackers, there is sheer excellence. The return of defensive end Mike Bell, to join defensive end Art Still and nose tackle Bill Maas, could give the Chiefs as good a three-man defensive line as there exists. Pete Koch would come in when the Chiefs use a four-man line. The secondary is nothing less than excellent. Safeties Deron Cherry and Lloyd Burruss are Pro Bowlers, and Albert Lewis was unlucky not to travel with them. Third-year cornerback Kevin Ross did not look out of place. Backups Sherman Cocroft, J.C. Pearson and Mark Robinson have been given few opportunities.

Special Teams

The special teams are indeed special, not only in the formal sense of punting, kicking, returning punts and kickoffs, but also in stopping the other team, forcing errors and turning them into scores. The squads have been honed and primed to kill by the same Frank Gansz, who was a favourite of the players and now has overall charge of the team. All told, the special team blocked 11 kicks (seven punts, three field goal attempts and a one-point conversion attempt) and twice actually tackled the punter in possession. Six of the turnovers which they forced resulted directly in touchdowns. They maintained the momentum when the offense, as mostly was the case, was unable to make any headway, and they ended the regular season in fine style, scoring all three touchdowns in the win over Pittsburgh which took the club into the playoffs.

1987 SCHEDULE OF GAMES		
September		
13 SAN DIEGO		12:00
20 at Seattle		1:00
27 MINNESOTA		12:00
October		
4 at Los Angeles Raiders		1:00
11 at Miami		1:00
18 DENVER		3:00
25 at San Diego		1:00
November		
1 at Chicago		12:00
8 PITTSBURGH		12:00
15 NEW YORK JETS		12:00
22 GREEN BAY		12:00
26 at Detroit (Thanksgiving)		12:30
December		
6 at Cincinnati		1:00
13 LOS ANGELES RAIDERS		3:00
19 at Denver (Sat.)		2:00
27 SEATTLE		12:00

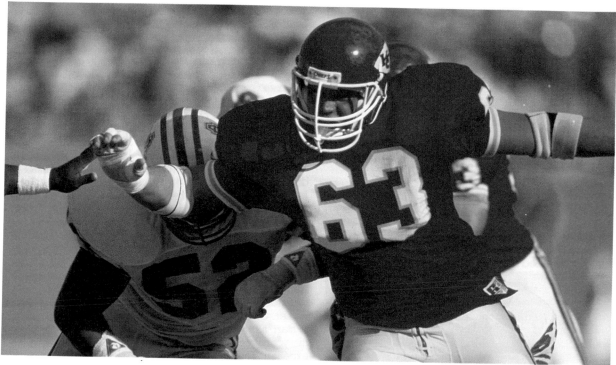

Nose tackle Bill Maas was the AFC starter in the 1987 Pro Bowl.

In the more formal roles, placekicker Nick Lowery had an off year by his standards, but Lewis Colbert did well enough in his rookie year, landing 23 punts inside the opposing 20-yard line. Jeff Smith was more effective returning punts than kickoffs, the latter role in which Boyce Green scored on a 97-yard return and may have earned himself a permanent job.

1987 DRAFT

Round	Name	Pos.	Ht.	Wt.	College
1.	Palmer, Paul	RB	5-9	190	Temple
2.	Okoye, Christian	RB	6-2	250	Azusa Pacific
3.	Howard, Todd	LB	6-2	235	Texas A&M
5.	Taylor, Kitrick	WR	5-11	178	Washington State
7.	Hudson, Doug	QB	6-3	205	Nicholls State
8.	Clemons, Michael	RB	5-5	160	William & Mary
9.	Watts, Randy	DE	6-6	275	Catawba
10.	Evans, James	RB	5-10	202	Southern University
11.	Richardson, Craig	WR	5-11	192	Eastern Washington
12.	Holmes, Bruce	LB	6-2	222	Minnesota

VETERAN ROSTER

No.	Name	Pos.	Ht.	Wt.	NFL Year	College
61	Adickes, Mark	T	6-4	274	2	Baylor
76	Alt, John	T	6-7	282	4	Iowa
87	Arnold, Walt	TE	6-3	224	8	New Mexico
77	Baldinger, Rich	G-T	6-4	285	5	Wake Forest
58	Baugh, Tom	C	6-3	274	2	Southern Illinois
99	Bell, Mike	DE	6-4	259	7	Colorado State
81	Bergmann, Paul	TE	6-2	235	1	UCLA
14	Blackledge, Todd	QB	6-3	223	5	Penn State
66	Budde, Brad	G	6-4	271	8	Southern California
34	Burruss, Lloyd	S	6-0	209	7	Maryland
88	Carson, Carlos	WR	5-11	184	8	Louisiana State
20	Cherry, Deron	S	5-11	196	7	Rutgers
22	Cocroft, Sherman	S	6-1	195	4	San Jose State
84	Coffman, Paul	TE	6-3	225	10	Kansas State
54	Cofield, Tim	LB	6-2	245	2	Elizabeth City State
5	Colbert, Lewis	P	5-11	180	2	Auburn
55	Cooper, Louis	LB	6-2	235	3	Western Carolina
51	Donnalley, Rick	C	6-2	270	6	North Carolina
75	Eatman, Irv	T	6-7	293	2	UCLA
48	Garron, Andre	RB	5-11	193	1	New Hampshire
40	Green, Boyce	RB	5-11	215	5	Carson-Newman
98	Griffin, Leonard	DE	6-4	252	2	Grambling State
56	Hackett, Dino	LB	6-3	225	2	Appalachian State
82	Hancock, Anthony	WR-KR	6-0	204	6	Tennessee
86	Harry, Emile	WR	5-11	175	2	Stanford
85	Hayes, Jonathan	TE	6-5	236	3	Iowa
44	Heard, Herman	RB	5-10	190	4	Southern Colorado
23	Hill, Greg	CB	6-1	199	5	Oklahoma State
93	Holle, Eric	DE-NT	6-5	265	4	Texas
73	Jozwiak, Brian	T-G	6-5	308	2	West Virginia
9	Kenney, Bill	QB	6-4	211	9	Northern Colorado
74	Koch, Pete	DE	6-6	275	4	Maryland
70	Lathrop, Kit	DE	6-5	261	4	Arizona State
29	Lewis, Albert	CB	6-2	192	5	Grambling State
8	Lowery, Nick	K	6-4	189	8	Dartmouth
72	Lutz, David	T	6-5	287	5	Georgia Tech
63	Maas, Bill	NT	6-5	268	4	Pittsburgh
89	Marshall, Henry	WR	6-2	216	12	Missouri
94	McAlister, Ken	LB	6-5	220	5	San Francisco
32	Moriarty, Larry	RB	6-1	237	5	Notre Dame
83	Paige, Stephone	WR	6-2	183	5	Fresno State
96	Pearson, Aaron	LB	6-0	236	5	Mississippi State
24	Pearson, J.C.	CB	5-11	183	2	Washington
43	Pruitt, Mike	RB	6-0	235	12	Purdue
97	Radecic, Scott	LB	6-3	242	4	Penn State
30	Robinson, Mark	S	5-11	206	4	Penn State
31	Ross, Kevin	CB	5-9	182	4	Temple
10	Seurer, Frank	QB	6-1	195	2	Kansas
42	Smith, Jeff	RB-KR	5-9	201	3	Nebraska
59	Spani, Gary	LB	6-2	229	10	Kansas State
67	Still, Art	DE	6-7	255	10	Kentucky

SEATTLE SEAHAWKS

Address 11220 N.E. 53rd Street, Kirkland, Washington 98033.

Stadium Kingdome, Seattle.

Capacity 64,984 *Playing Surface* AstroTurf.

Team Colours Blue, Green, and Silver.

Head Coach Chuck Knox – fifth year.

Championships None.

History NFC 1976, AFC 1977-

Offense

Over the final few weeks of the 1986 regular season, Seattle was the hottest team around and, one day, they might be asking the trivia question, 'Name the club which didn't reach the playoffs despite beating both the eventual Super Bowl participants'. One reason for the Seahawks' return to prominence was the play of the offensive line, which underwent reconstruction and featured four new starters. Ron Mattes and Mike Wilson (ex-Bengals) took over in the tackle positions and Bryan Millard moved in at right guard. Will Grant became the fourth new starter when he took over from Kani Kauahi for the final six games. Kauahi had started in three games after the regular starter, Blair Bush, had been injured on Week Seven. Bush is expected to regain his seniority and Edwin Bailey will continue at left guard. Hovering in the offensive backfield, Curt Warner and his rookie teammate, John L. Williams, were primed to take advantage of the authority established by the offensive line. Warner responded with a repeat performance of his remarkable rookie year, well and truly dismissing any last doubts about his recovery from knee surgery early in the 1984 season. As expected, Williams' blocking was superb and, in his own right, he turned out to be a real handful for the opposition, rushing for 538 yards at an average of 4.2 and catching 33 passes. Randall Morris is available for spot duty. Dave Krieg had his problems and, for a time in midseason, so did the Seahawks. While Krieg was out of favour – he was benched in favour of Gale Gilbert – the Seahawks lost four straight games. But when he returned, they looked like world-beaters. It's a measure of his quality that Krieg moved up to third place in the all-time passer ratings. However, the Seahawks felt it prudent to pick up the former Rams and 49ers quarterback, Jeff Kemp, who would ensure continuity should Krieg be injured. Conceivably, he might even start ahead of Krieg. There are no problems at wide receiver, where the great veteran, Steve Largent, continues his assault on the league all-time receiving records. One more season should be enough to take him past Charlie Joiner's new marks. The club still regards Daryl Turner as the other starting wide receiver, despite the fact that Byron Franklin caught almost twice as many passes. Ray Butler, too, matched Turner pass-for-pass and yard-for-yard, but Turner has a nose for the end zone (he has scored 30 touchdowns on 87 receptions over the last three years). On the down side, starting tight end

Mike Tice and his backup, Gordon Hudson, would grade out at no better than average.

Defense

Over the final five weeks of last season, the Seahawks allowed an average of only 13.8 points per game. With a repeat of that form they would stroll into the playoffs. At last, defensive end Jacob Green earned a Pro Bowl selection after years of knocking on the door. He was at his predatory best, registering 12 sacks, including a club-record four against the Giants. The other starting defensive end, Jeff Bryant, and his backup, Randy Edwards, each had four sacks. Reggie Kinlaw won his battle with former Pro Bowler Joe Nash to start at nose tackle but was injured on Week Fourteen against his old club, the Raiders. Recognising the importance of linebacking, the Seahawks used their first two options to draft reinforcements. Tony Woods, who has been compared with other former University of Pittsburgh stars, Rickey Jackson (New Orleans) and Hugh Green (Miami), may sharpen his teeth as a specialist pass rusher. The existing starters on the left side are Fredd Young, a three-time Pro Bowler whose tackles are guaranteed to loosen your fillings, and outside him, Bruce Scholtz, who had three sacks, two interceptions and forced a team-high four fumbles. Greg Gaines had five sacks starting on the right outside while Keith Butler concentrated on the run, logging 96 tackles to rank third on the team. The Seahawks welcome back the NFL's best strong safety, Kenny Easley, from injury, to rejoin his free safety partner, Eugene Robinson. Dave Brown and Terry Taylor take care of the corners, and there is exceptionally good reserve strength in backups Kerry Justin and Patrick Hunter.

Special Teams

In Bobby Joe Edmonds, the Seahawks have found the latest dual-purpose phenomenon to hit the AFC.

1987 SCHEDULE OF GAMES		
September		
13 at Denver		2:00
20 KANSAS CITY		1:00
27 at San Diego		1:00
October		
4 MIAMI		1:00
11 CINCINNATI		1:00
18 at Detroit		1:00
25 at Los Angeles Raiders		1:00
November		
1 MINNESOTA		1:00
9 at New York Jets (Mon.)		9:00
15 GREEN BAY		1:00
22 SAN DIEGO		1:00
30 LOS ANGELES RAIDERS (Mon.)		6:00
December		
6 at Pittsburgh		1:00
13 DENVER		5:00
20 at Chicago		12:00
27 at Kansas City		12:00

Edmonds, a rookie fifth-round pick, led the NFL in punt returns and finished sixth in the AFC returning kickoffs. Placekicker Norm Johnson was tremendous over long range – he had the four longest field goals in the AFC (a 54-yarder and three 53-yarders). By contrast, punter Vince Gamache was a couple of yards below par on his gross punting average and faces a struggle in training camp to retain his job.

Fredd Young demonstrates how to feel a collar.

1987 DRAFT

Round	Name	Pos.	Ht.	Wt.	College
1.	Woods, Tony	LB	6-2	248	Pittsburgh
2.	Wyman, Dave	LB	6-2	230	Stanford
4.	Moore, Mark	S	5-11	195	Oklahoma State
5.	Agee, Tommie	RB	5-11	210	Auburn
5.	Rodriguez, Ruben	P	6-2	222	Arizona
7.	Barbay, Roland	DT	6-3	265	Louisiana State
7.	Tennell, Derek	TE	6-4	233	UCLA
8.	Garza, Sammy	QB	6-1	185	Texas-El Paso
9.	Johnson, M.L.	LB	6-2	228	Hawaii
10.	Clark, Louis	TE-WR	6-1	210	Mississippi State
11.	Oliver, Darryl	RB	5-11	190	Miami
12.	Dove, Wes	DE	6-6	265	Syracuse
12.	Burse, Tony	RB	5-11	215	Middle Tennessee State

VETERAN ROSTER

No.	Name	Pos.	Ht.	Wt.	NFL Year	College
47	Anderson, Eddie	S	6-1	199	2	Fort Valley State
65	Bailey, Edwin	G	6-4	276	7	South Carolina State
76	Borchardt, Jon	G	6-5	272	9	Montana State
22	Brown, Dave	CB	6-1	197	13	Michigan
77	Bryant, Jeff	DE	6-5	272	6	Clemson
59	Bush, Blair	C	6-3	272	10	Washington
53	Butler, Keith	LB	6-4	239	10	Memphis State
83	Butler, Ray	WR	6-3	206	8	Southern California
87	Davis, Tony	TE	6-5	239	1	Missouri
45	Easley, Ken	S	6-3	206	7	UCLA
30	Edmonds, Bobby Joe	RB-KR	5-11	186	2	Arkansas
68	Edwards, Randy	DE	6-4	267	4	Alabama
66	Eisenhooth, Stan	C	6-5	278	1	Towson State
64	Essink, Ron	T	6-6	302	7	Grand Valley State
88	Franklin, Byron	WR	6-1	183	6	Auburn
56	Gaines, Greg	LB	6-3	222	6	Tennessee
2	Gamache, Vince	P	5-11	176	2	Cal State-Fullerton
7	Gilbert, Gale	QB	6-3	206	3	California
52	Grant, Will	C	6-3	268	10	Kentucky
69	Graves, Rory	T	6-6	290	1	Ohio State
79	Green, Jacob	DE	6-3	252	8	Texas A&M
84	Greene, Danny	WR	5-11	190	2	Washington
85	Hudson, Gordon	TE	6-4	241	2	Brigham Young
23	Hunter, Patrick	CB	5-11	185	2	Nevada-Reno
27	Johnson, Greggory	S	6-1	195	5	Oklahoma State
9	Johnson, Norm	K	6-2	198	6	UCLA
26	Justin, Kerry	C	5-11	175	7	Oregon State
54	Kaiser, John	LB	6-3	233	4	Arizona
62	Kauahi, Kani	C	6-2	261	6	Hawaii
	Kemp, Jeff	QB	6-0	201	7	Dartmouth
63	Kinlaw, Reggie	NT	6-2	249	8	Oklahoma
17	Krieg, Dave	QB	6-1	196	8	Milton, Wis.
37	Lane, Eric	RB	6-0	201	7	Brigham Young
80	Largent, Steve	WR	5-11	191	12	Tulsa
70	Mattes, Ron	T	6-6	306	2	Virginia
51	Merriman, Sam	LB	6-3	232	5	Idaho
71	Millard, Bryan	G	6-5	284	4	Texas
61	Mitz, Alonzo	DE	6-3	275	2	Florida
43	Morris, Randall	RB	6-0	200	4	Tennessee
21	Moyer, Paul	S	6-1	203	4	Arizona State
72	Nash, Joe	NT	6-2	257	6	Boston College
73	Powell, Alvin	G	6-5	296	2	Winston-Salem State
41	Robinson, Eugene	S	6-0	186	3	Colgate
8	Salisbury, Sean	QB	6-5	215	2	Southern California
58	Scholtz, Bruce	LB	6-6	244	6	Texas
74	Singer, Curt	T	6-5	279	2	Tennessee
82	Skansi, Paul	WR	5-11	183	5	Washington
20	Taylor, Terry	CB	5-10	191	4	Southern Illinois
86	Tice, Mike	TE	6-7	247	7	Maryland
81	Turner, Daryl	WR	6-3	194	4	Michigan State
89	Walker, Byron	WR	6-4	188	6	Citadel
28	Warner, Curt	RB	5-11	204	4	Penn State
32	Williams, John L.	RB	5-11	226	2	Florida
75	Wilson, Mike	T	6-5	280	10	Georgia
50	Young, Fredd	LB	6-1	233	4	New Mexico State

CHAPTER SEVEN

NATIONAL FOOTBALL CONFERENCE

TEAM RANKINGS

Art Monk.

	OFFENSE						DEFENSE					
	Total Yds.	Rushing	Passing	Points For	%Intercepted	%Sacked	Total Yds.	Rushing	Passing	Points Against	%Interceptions	%Sacks
Atlanta	7	2	11	9	6	13	6	8	6	6	4 =	13
Chicago	5	1	8	5	14	3	1	2	2	1	2	1
Dallas	4	8	4	6	9	10	7	11	3	11	11	2
Detroit	11	11	7	10	7	7	11	13	4	10	6	7
Green Bay	8	14	5	12	11	5	9	10	5	13	8	12
L.A. Rams	10	3	14	7	4 =	6	4	5	7	4	3	11
Minnesota	2	12	2	1	1	8	8	6	8	5	4 =	10
New Orleans	9	5	10	8	13	4	10	4	13	7	7	9
N.Y. Giants	6	4	6	3	10	9	2	1	11	2	10	4
Philadelphia	12	6	12	11	2	14	12	9	9	9	9	5
St Louis	13	10	9	14	4 =	11	3	12	1	12	14	6
San Francisco	1	7	1	2	3	1	5	3	10	3	1	8
Tampa Bay	14	9	13	13	12	12	14	14	14	14	13	14
Washington	3	13	3	4	8	2	13	7	12	8	12	3

NFC PASSERS

	Att	Comp	% Comp	Yards	Ave Gain	TD	% TD	Long	Int	% Int	Rating Points
Kramer, Tommy, *Minn.*	372	208	55.9	3000	8.06	24	6.5	t76	10	2.7	92.6
Montana, Joe, *S.F.*	307	191	62.2	2236	7.28	8	2.6	48	9	2.9	80.7
Hipple, Eric, *Det.*	305	192	63.0	1919	6.29	9	3.0	46	11	3.6	75.6
Simms, Phil, *Giants*	468	259	55.3	3487	7.45	21	4.5	49	22	4.7	74.6
Lomax, Neil, *St L.*	421	240	57.0	2583	6.14	13	3.1	t48	12	2.9	73.6
Schroeder, Jay, *Wash.*	541	276	51.0	4109	7.60	22	4.1	t71	22	4.1	72.9
Archer, David, *Atl.*	294	150	51.0	2007	6.83	10	3.4	65	9	3.1	71.6
Jaworski, Ron, *Phil.*	245	128	52.2	1405	5.73	8	3.3	56	6	2.4	70.2
Pelluer, Steve, *Dall.*	378	215	56.9	2727	7.21	8	2.1	t84	17	4.5	67.9
Wright, Randy, *G.B.*	492	263	53.5	3247	6.60	17	3.5	62	23	4.7	66.2
Wilson, Dave, *N.O.*	342	189	55.3	2353	6.88	10	2.9	t63	17	5.0	65.8
Young, Steve, *T.B.*	363	195	53.7	2282	6.29	8	2.2	46	13	3.6	65.5
Non-qualifiers											
White, Danny, *Dall.*	153	95	62.1	1157	7.56	12	7.8	63	5	3.3	97.9
Kemp, Jeff, *S.F.*	200	119	59.5	1554	7.77	11	5.5	t66	8	4.0	85.7
Wilson, Wade, *Minn.*	143	80	55.9	1165	8.15	7	4.9	39	5	3.5	84.4
Cunningham, Randall, *Phil.*	209	111	53.1	1391	6.66	8	3.8	t75	7	3.3	72.9
Schonert, Turk, *Atl.*	154	95	61.7	1032	6.70	4	2.6	41	8	5.2	68.4
Everett, Jim, *Rams*	147	73	49.7	1018	6.93	8	5.4	t60	8	5.4	67.8
Ferguson, Joe, *Det.*	155	73	47.1	941	6.07	7	4.5	73	7	4.5	62.9
McMahon, Jim, *Chi.*	150	77	51.3	995	6.63	5	3.3	t58	8	5.3	61.4
Dils, Steve, *Rams*	129	59	45.7	693	5.37	4	3.1	t65	4	3.1	60.0
Bartkowski, Steve, *Rams*	126	61	48.4	654	5.19	2	1.6	42	3	2.4	59.4
Tomczak, Mike, *Chi.*	151	74	49.0	1105	7.32	2	1.3	85	10	6.6	50.2
DeBerg, Steve, *T.B.*	96	50	52.1	610	6.35	5	5.2	45	12	12.5	49.7

t = Touchdown
Leader based on rating points, minimum 224 attempts

NFC RECEIVERS – Most Receptions

	No	Yards	Ave	Long	TD
Rice, Jerry, *S.F.*	86	1570	18.3	t66	15
Craig, Roger, *S.F.*	81	624	7.7	48	0
Smith, J.T., *St L.*	80	1014	12.7	45	6
Walker, Herschel, *Dall.*	76	837	11.0	t84	2
Clark, Gary, *Wash.*	74	1265	17.1	55	7
Monk, Art, *Wash.*	73	1068	14.6	69	4
Bavaro, Mark, *Giants*	66	1001	15.2	41	4
Lofton, James, *G.B.*	64	840	13.1	36	4
Brown, Charlie, *Atl.*	63	918	14.6	42	4
Clark, Dwight, *S.F.*	61	794	13.0	t45	2
Quick, Mike, *Phil.*	60	939	15.7	t75	9
Jordan, Steve, *Minn.*	58	859	14.8	t68	6
Ferrell, Earl, *St L.*	56	434	7.8	t30	3
Jones, James, *Det.*	54	334	6.2	21	1
Chadwick, Jeff, *Det.*	53	995	18.8	73	5
Nelson, Darrin, *Minn.*	53	593	11.2	34	3
Hill, Tony, *Dall.*	49	770	15.7	63	3
Epps, Phillip, *G.B.*	49	612	12.5	t53	4
Jones, Mike, *N.O.*	48	625	13.0	45	3
Newsome, Tim, *Dall.*	48	421	8.8	30	3
Magee, Calvin, *T.B.*	45	564	12.5	45	5
Bland, Carl, *Det.*	44	511	11.6	34	2
Bryant, Kelvin, *Wash.*	43	449	10.4	40	3
Wilder, James, *T.B.*	43	326	7.6	25	1
Gault, Willie, *Chi.*	42	818	19.5	t53	5
Carter, Gerald, *T.B.*	42	640	15.2	46	2
Dixon, Floyd, *Atl.*	42	617	14.7	65	2
Green, Roy, *St L.*	42	517	12.3	t48	6
Sherrard, Mike, *Dall.*	41	744	18.1	t68	5
Francis, Russ, *S.F.*	41	505	12.3	52	1
Tautalatasi, Junior, *Phil.*	41	325	7.9	56	2
Mitchell, Stump, *St L.*	41	276	6.7	24	0
Spagnola, John, *Phil.*	39	397	10.2	38	1
Carter, Anthony, *Minn.*	38	686	18.1	t60	7
Martin, Eric, *N.O.*	37	675	18.2	84	5

t = Touchdown

NFC RECEIVERS – Most Yards

	Yards	No	Ave	Long	TD
Rice, Jerry, *S.F.*	1570	86	18.3	t66	15
Clark, Gary, *Wash.*	1265	74	17.1	55	7
Monk, Art, *Wash.*	1068	73	14.6	69	4
Smith, J.T., *St L.*	1014	80	12.7	45	6
Bavaro, Mark, *Giants*	1001	66	15.2	41	4
Chadwick, Jeff, *Det.*	995	53	18.8	73	5
Quick, Mike, *Phil.*	939	60	15.7	t75	9
Brown, Charlie, *Atl.*	918	63	14.6	42	4
Jordan, Steve, *Minn.*	859	58	14.8	t68	6
Lofton, James, *G.B.*	.840	64	13.1	36	4
Walker, Herschel, *Dall.*	837	76	11.0	t84	2
Gault, Willie, *Chi.*	818	42	19.5	t53	5
Clark, Dwight, *S.F.*	794	61	13.0	t45	2
Hill, Tony, *Dall.*	770	49	15.7	63	3
Sherrard, Mike, *Dall.*	744	41	18.1	t68	5
Stanley, Walter, *G.B.*	723	35	20.7	62	2
Didier, Clint, *Wash.*	691	34	20.3	t71	4
Carter, Anthony, *Minn.*	686	38	18.1	t60	7
Martin, Eric, *N.O.*	675	37	18.2	84	5
Carter, Gerald, *T.B.*	640	42	15.2	46	2
Jones, Mike, *N.O.*	625	48	13.0	45	3
Craig, Roger, *S.F.*	624	81	7.7	48	0
Dixon, Floyd, *Atl.*	617	42	14.7	65	2
Epps, Philip, *G.B.*	612	49	12.5	t53	4
Lewis, Leo, *Minn.*	600	32	18.8	t76	2
Nelson, Darrin, *Minn.*	593	53	11.2	34	3
Jones, Hassan, *Minn.*	570	28	20.4	t55	4
Magee, Calvin, *T.B.*	564	45	12.5	45	5
Johnson, Bobby, *Giants*	534	31	17.2	t44	5
Green, Roy, *St L.*	517	42	12.3	t48	6
Bland, Carl, *Det.*	511	44	11.6	34	2
Jackson, Kenny, *Phil.*	506	30	16.9	49	6
Francis, Russ, *S.F.*	505	41	12.3	52	1
Robinson, Stacy, *Giants*	494	29	17.0	49	2
Bryant, Kelvin, *Wash.*	449	43	10.4	40	3

t = Touchdown

NFC RUSHERS

	Att	Yards	Ave	Long	TD		Att	Yards	Ave	Long	TD
Dickerson, Eric, *Rams*	404	1821	4.5	t42	11	Austin, Cliff, *Atl.*	62	280	4.5	22	1
Morris, Joe, *Giants*	341	1516	4.4	54	14	Haddix, Michael, *Phil.*	79	276	3.5	18	0
Mayes, Rueben, *N.O.*	286	1353	4.7	50	8	Suhey, Matt, *Chi.*	84	270	3.2	17	2
Payton, Walter, *Chi.*	321	1333	4.2	41	8	Carthon, Maurice, *Giants*	72	260	3.6	12	0
Riggs, Gerald, *Atl.*	343	1327	3.9	31	9	Bryant, Kelvin, *Wash.*	69	258	3.7	t22	4
Rogers, George, *Wash.*	303	1203	4.0	42	18	Pelluer, Steve, *Dall.*	41	255	6.2	21	1
Jones, James, *Det.*	252	903	3.6	39	8	Brown, Ted, *Minn.*	63	251	4.0	60	4
Craig, Roger, *S.F.*	204	830	4.1	25	7	Anderson, Ottis, *St L.-Giants*	75	237	3.2	16	3
Mitchell, Stump, *St L.*	174	800	4.6	44	5	Sanders, Thomas, *Chi.*	27	224	8.3	t75	5
Nelson, Darrin, *Minn.*	191	793	4.2	42	4	Thomas, Calvin, *Chi.*	56	224	4.0	23	0
Dorsett, Tony, *Dall.*	184	748	4.1	33	5	Rice, Allen, *Minn.*	73	220	3.0	19	2
Walker, Herschel, *Dall.*	151	737	4.9	t84	12	Stamps, Sylvester, *Atl.*	30	220	7.3	48	0
Wilder, James, *T.B.*	190	704	3.7	t45	2	Andrews, William, *Atl.*	52	214	4.1	13	1
James, Garry, *Det.*	159	688	4.3	t60	3	Jordan, Buford, *N.O.*	68	207	3.0	10	1
Cribbs, Joe, *S.F.*	152	590	3.9	19	5	Griffin, Keith, *Wash.*	62	197	3.2	12	0
Byars, Keith, *Phil.*	177	577	3.3	32	1	Rouson, Lee, *Giants*	54	179	3.3	t21	2
Ferrell, Earl, *St L.*	124	548	4.4	25	0	Tautalatasi, Junior, *Phil.*	51	163	3.2	50	0
Cunningham, Randall, *Phil.*	66	540	8.2	20	5	McMahon, Jim, *Chi.*	22	152	6.9	23	1
Davis, Kenneth, *G.B.*	114	519	4.6	50	0	Lomax, Neil, *St L.*	35	148	4.2	18	1
Redden, Barry, *Rams*	110	467	4.2	t41	4	Anderson, Neal, *Chi.*	35	146	4.2	23	0
Hilliard, Dalton, *N.O.*	121	425	3.5	36	5	Rathman, Tom, *S.F.*	33	138	4.2	t29	1
Young, Steve, *T.B.*	74	425	5.7	31	5	Tyler, Wendell, *S.F.*	31	127	4.1	14	0
Anderson, Alfred, *Minn.*	83	347	4.2	29	2	White, Charles, *Rams*	22	126	5.7	19	0
Ellis, Gerry, *G.B.*	84	345	4.1	24	2	Tomczak, Mike, *Chi.*	23	117	5.1	16	3
Wonsley, Nathan, *T.B.*	73	339	4.6	t59	3	Howard, Bobby, *T.B.*	30	110	3.7	16	1
Carruth, Paul, *G.B.*	81	308	3.8	42	2	Newsome, Tim, *Dall.*	34	110	3.2	13	2
Archer, David, *Atl.*	52	298	5.7	22	0	Gentry, Dennis, *Chi.*	11	103	9.4	29	1
Ellerson, Gary, *G.B.*	90	287	3.2	18	3	Crawford, Charles, *Phil.*	28	88	3.1	15	1
Springs, Ron, *T.B.*	74	285	3.9	40	0	Gault, Willie, *Chi.*	8	79	9.9	33	0
Toney, Anthony, *Phil.*	69	285	4.1	43	1	t = Touchdown					

NFC SCORING – Kickers

	XP	XPA	FG	FGA	PTS
Butler, Kevin, *Chi.*	36	37	28	41	120
Wersching, Ray, *S.F.*	41	42	25	35	116
Nelson, Chuck, *Minn.*	44	47	22	28	110
Andersen, Morten, *N.O.*	30	30	26	30	108
Allegre, Raul, *Giants*	33	33	24	32	105
Septien, Rafael, *Dall.*	43	43	15	21	88
McFadden, Paul, *Phil.*	26	27	20	31	86
Lansford, Mike, *Rams*	34	35	17	24	85
Murray, Ed, *Det.*	31	32	18	25	85
Del Greco, Al, *G.B.*	29	29	17	27	80
Igwebuike, Donald, *T.B.*	26	27	17	24	77
Luckhurst, Mick, *Atl.*	21	21	14	24	63
Zendejas, Max, *Wash.*	23	28	9	14	50
Lee, John, *St L.*	14	17	8	13	38
Haji-Sheikh, Ali, *Atl.*	7	8	9	12	34
Schubert, Eric, *St L.*	9	9	3	11	18
Cooper, Joe, *Giants*	4	4	2	4	10
Cox, Steve, *Wash.*	0	0	3	5	9
Thomas, Bob, *Giants*	4	4	0	1	4
Atkinson, Jess, *Wash.*	3	3	0	0	3
Donnelly, Rick, *Atl.*	1	1	0	0	1

NFC SCORING – Touchdowns

	TD	TDR	TDP	TDM	PTS
Rogers, George, *Wash.*	18	18	0	0	108
Rice, Jerry, *S.F.*	16	1	15	0	96
Morris, Joe, *Giants*	15	14	1	0	90
Walker, Herschel, *Dall.*	14	12	2	0	84
Dickerson, Eric, *Rams*	11	11	0	0	66
Payton, Walter, *Chi.*	11	8	3	0	66
Jones, James, *Det.*	9	8	1	0	54
Quick, Mike, *Phil.*	9	0	9	0	54
Riggs, Gerald, *Atl.*	9	9	0	0	54
Mayes, Rueben, *N.O.*	8	8	0	0	48
Bryant, Kelvin, *Wash.*	7	4	3	0	42
Carter, Anthony, *Minn.*	7	0	7	0	42
Clark, Gary, *Wash.*	7	0	7	0	42
Craig, Roger, *S.F.*	7	7	0	0	42
Nelson, Darrin, *Minn.*	7	4	3	0	42

NFC KICKOFF RETURNERS

	No	Yards	Ave	Long	TD
Gentry, Dennis, *Chi.*	20	576	28.8	t91	1
Gray, Mel, *N.O.*	31	866	27.9	t101	1
Sikahema, Vai, *St L.*	37	847	22.9	44	0
Bess, Rufus, *Minn.*	31	705	22.7	43	0
Brown, Ron, *Rams*	36	794	22.1	55	0
Stamps, Sylvester, *Atl.*	24	514	21.4	35	0
Hunter, Herman, *Det.*	49	1007	20.6	54	0
Jenkins, Ken, *Wash.*	27	554	20.5	37	0
Stanley, Walter, *G.B.*	28	559	20.0	55	0
Elder, Donnie, *Pitt.-Det.*	22	435	19.8	36	0
McConkey, Phil, *Giants*	24	471	19.6	27	0
Lavette, Robert, *Dall.*	36	699	19.4	37	0
Freeman, Phil, *T.B.*	31	582	18.8	33	0
Crawford, Charles, *Phil.*	27	497	18.4	36	0
Sanders, Thomas, *Chi.*	22	399	18.1	44	0

t = Touchdown
Leader based on average return, minimum 20 returns

Left: George Rogers led the NFL with 18 touchdowns.

Right: Eric Dickerson was 305 yards ahead of his nearest challenger.

NFC PUNTERS

	No	Yards	Long	Ave	Total Punts	TB	Blk	Opp Ret	Ret Yds	In 20	Net Ave
Landeta, Sean, *Giants*	79	3539	61	44.8	79	11	0	41	386	24	37.1
Donnelly, Rick, *Atl.*	78	3421	71	43.9	79	9	1	47	477	19	35.0
Cox, Steve, *Wash.*	75	3271	58	43.6	75	16	0	36	220	21	36.4
Hansen, Brian, *N.O.*	81	3456	66	42.7	82	11	1	37	234	17	36.6
Teltschik, John, *Phil.*	108	4493	62	41.6	109	10	1	62	631	20	33.6
Runager, Max, *S.F.*	83	3450	62	41.6	85	8	2	49	373	23	34.3
Coleman, Greg, *Minn.*	67	2774	69	41.4	67	4	0	39	353	15	34.9
Buford, Maury, *Chi.*	69	2850	59	41.3	70	8	1	23	110	20	36.9
Saxon, Mike, *Dall.*	86	3498	58	40.7	87	10	1	41	301	28	34.4
Garcia, Frank, *T.B.*	77	3089	60	40.1	77	8	0	38	410	19	32.7
Bracken, Don, *G.B.*	55	2203	63	40.1	57	5	2	33	235	6	32.8
Black, Mike, *Det.*	46	1819	57	39.5	47	5	1	21	250	11	31.3
Hatcher, Dale, *Rams*	97	3740	57	38.6	98	5	1	47	416	26	32.9
Cater, Greg, *St L.*	61	2271	52	37.2	62	4	1	24	130	16	33.2

Leader based on gross average, minimum 40 punts

NFC PUNT RETURNERS

	No	FC	Yards	Ave	Long	TD
Sikahema, Vai, *St L.*	43	16	522	12.1	t71	2
Garrity, Gregg, *Phil.*	17	7	187	11.0	t76	1
Griffin, Don, *S.F.*	38	18	377	9.9	t76	1
Mandley, Pete, *Det.*	43	9	420	9.8	t81	1
Jenkins, Ken, *Wash.*	28	11	270	9.6	39	0
Stanley, Walter, *G.B.*	33	7	316	9.6	t83	1
Martin, Eric, *N.O.*	24	9	227	9.5	39	0
Cooper, Evan, *Phil.*	16	7	139	8.7	58	0
Barnes, Lew, *Chi.*	57	9	482	8.5	35	0
Sutton, Mickey, *Rams*	28	5	234	8.4	32	0
McConkey, Phil, *Giants*	32	12	253	7.9	22	0
Bess, Rufus, *Minn.*	23	10	162	7.0	15	0
Banks, Gordon, *Dall.*	27	14	160	5.9	20	0
Dixon, Floyd, *Atl.*	26	3	151	5.8	16	0
Lavette, Robert, *Dall.*	18	3	92	5.1	28	0

t = Touchdown

Leader based on average return, minimum 15 returns

Right: Ronnie Lott led the NFL with ten pass interceptions.

Below: Vai Sikahema was the only man in the NFL to score two touchdowns on punt returns.

NFC INTERCEPTORS

	No	Yards	Ave	Long	TD
Lott, Ronnie, *S.F.*	10	134	13.4	t57	1
Waymer, Dave, *N.O.*	9	48	5.3	17	0
Lee, Mark, *G.B.*	9	33	3.7	11	0
Gray, Jerry, *Rams*	8	101	12.6	28	0
Holt, Issiac, *Minn.*	8	54	6.8	27	0
Richardson, Mike, *Chi.*	7	69	9.9	32	0
Irvin, LeRoy, *Rams*	6	150	25.0	t50	1
Duerson, Dave, *Chi.*	6	139	23.2	38	0
Downs, Michael, *Dall.*	6	54	9.0	31	0
Waters, Andre, *Phil.*	6	39	6.5	21	0
McKyer, Tim, *S.F.*	6	33	5.5	t21	1
Young, Roynell, *Phil.*	6	9	1.5	9	0
Cromwell, Nolan, *Rams*	5	101	20.2	t80	1
Clark, Bret, *Atl.*	5	94	18.8	34	0
Marshall, Wilber, *Chi.*	5	68	13.6	t58	1
Fellows, Ron, *Dall.*	5	46	9.2	t34	1
Mitchell, Devon, *Det.*	5	41	8.2	17	0
Green, Darrell, *Wash.*	5	9	1.8	7	0
Browner, Joey, *Minn.*	4	62	15.5	t39	1
Galloway, Duane, *Det.*	4	58	14.5	36	0
Fahnhorst, Jim, *S.F.*	4	52	13.0	46	0
Kinard, Terry, *Giants*	4	52	13.0	25	0
Fuller, Jeff, *S.F.*	4	44	11.0	26	0
Mack, Cedric, *St L.*	4	42	10.5	24	0
Poe, Johnnie, *N.O.*	4	42	10.5	30	0
Case, Scott, *Atl.*	4	41	10.3	41	0
Williams, Perry, *Giants*	4	31	7.8	15	0
Cade, Mossy, *G.B.*	4	26	6.5	18	0
McNorton, Bruce, *Det.*	4	10	2.5	10	0
Holmoe, Tom, *S.F.*	3	149	49.7	t78	2
Harris, John, *Minn.*	3	69	23.0	28	0
Jordan, Curtis, *Wash.*	3	46	15.3	20	0
Walls, Everson, *Dall.*	3	46	15.3	24	0
Newsome, Vince, *Rams*	3	45	15.0	34	0
Fencik, Gary, *Chi.*	3	37	12.3	24	0
Wattelet, Frank, *N.O.*	3	34	11.3	22	0
Hill, Kenny, *Giants*	3	25	8.3	23	0
Cooper, Evan, *Phil.*	3	20	6.7	20	0
McKeever, Vito, *T.B.*	3	12	4.0	10	0
Lee, Carl, *Minn.*	3	10	3.3	10	0
Johnson, Alonzo, *Phil.*	3	6	2.0	9	0
Williamson, Carlton, *S.F.*	3	3	1.0	2	0
Griffin, Don, *S.F.*	3	0	0.0	0	0
Jackson, Vestee, *Chi.*	3	0	0.0	0	0
Nixon, Tory, *S.F.*	2	106	53.0	t88	1

t = Touchdown

NFC SACKERS

	No		No
Taylor, Lawrence, *Giants*	20.5	Bryan, Rick, *Atl.*	7.0
Manley, Dexter, *Wash.*	18.5	Duerson, Dave, *Chi.*	7.0
White, Reggie, *Phil.*	18.0	Greene, Kevin, *Rams*	7.0
Jeffcoat, Jim, *Dall.*	14.0	Nunn, Freddie Joe, *St L.*	7.0
Haley, Charles, *S.F.*	12.0	Banks, Carl, *Giants*	6.5
Marshall, Leonard, *Giants*	12.0	Gay, William, *Det.*	6.5
Dent, Richard, *Chi.*	11.5	Reed, Doug, *Rams*	6.5
Stover, Jeff, *S.F.*	11.0	White, Randy, *Dall.*	6.5
Baker, Al, *St L.*	10.5	Butz, Dave, *Wash.*	6.0
Millard, Keith, *Minn.*	10.5	Clark, Bruce, *N.O.*	6.0
Hampton, Dan, *Chi.*	10.0	Cobb, Garry, *Phil.*	6.0
Mann, Charles, *Wash.*	10.0	Gann, Mike, *Atl.*	5.5
Ferguson, Keith, *Det.*	9.5	Jones, Ed, *Dall.*	5.5
Brown, Greg, *Phil.*	9.0	Marshall, Wilber, *Chi.*	5.5
Geathers, James, *N.O.*	9.0	Pitts, Mike, *Atl.*	5.5
Jackson, Rickey, *N.O.*	9.0	Roberts, Larry, *S.F.*	5.5
Martin, Doug, *Minn.*	9.0	Wilcher, Mike, *Rams*	5.5
Board, Dwaine, *S.F.*	8.0	Dutton, John, *Dall.*	5.0
Clarke, Ken, *Phil.*	8.0	Lockhart, Eugene, *Dall.*	5.0
Harris, Timothy, *G.B.*	8.0	Miller, Shawn, *Rams*	5.0
Jeter, Gary, *Rams*	8.0	Newton, Tim, *Minn.*	5.0
McMichael, Steve, *Chi.*	8.0	Perry, William, *Chi.*	5.0
Wilson, Otis, *Chi.*	8.0	Galloway, David, *St L.*	4.5
Cofer, Mike, *Det.*	7.5	Hamilton, Steve, *Wash.*	4.5
Warren, Frank, *N.O.*	7.5	Smerek, Don, *Dall.*	4.5

DALLAS COWBOYS

Address One Cowboy Parkway, Irving, Texas 75063.
Stadium Texas Stadium, Irving.
  Capacity 63,749 *Playing Surface* Texas Turf.
Team Colours Royal Blue, Metallic Silver Blue, and White.
Head Coach Tom Landry – twenty-eighth year.
Championships Division 1970,'71,'73,'76,'77,'78,'79,'81,'85;
  Conference 1970,'71,'75,'77,'78; Super Bowl 1971,'77.
History NFL 1960-69, NFC 1970-

Offense

The Dallas Cowboys are coming off their first net losing season since 1964, and that could spell trouble for everybody, since they'll be looking to bounce back immediately. On the offensive line, Tom Rafferty is unchallenged at center but, in the words of head coach Tom Landry, 'Everything else is up for grabs'. Those who may have an edge include guards Crawford Ker and Glen Titensor, while the obvious candidates for the tackle spots would be Mark Tuinei and Phil Pozderac. There's good news about former starting guard Kurt Petersen, who missed all of last year but has recovered from his knee injury. Former first-round pick Howard Richards has been a disappointment but he, too, has had injuries. The Cowboys haven't given up on 'The Kitchen', Nate Newton, a 317-pound guard, though it is hoped that he will trim down a little. And they selected an even bigger guard, Jeff Zimmerman, with their third option in the draft. There's so much talent at running back that the only problem will be in using it to its best effect. Tony Dorsett will start at halfback with Herschel Walker nominally at fullback, but no one believes that Walker's role will be that of a conventional fullback. It means that the Cowboys will threaten a big gain on every down, whether rushing or by passing. The reserve pairing will be Darryl Clack at halfback and Timmy Newsome at fullback with two good players, Robert Lavette and Todd Fowler, giving further depth. The success of the passing game depends on the return of quarterback Danny White, for whom the system is tailor-made. However, it would appear that his wrist injury was more complicated than a standard fracture, and it is said that he may have to change his style of delivery. If White is not fully fit, the Cowboys do have a worry, for he is some way ahead of Steve Pelluer. Nonetheless, Pelluer gained valuable experience as the starter in nine of the last ten games of last year. His great advantages are quickness and pure speed, the latter which enables him to out-run many defenders. The wide receivers suffered from an inconsistent service in 1987, but the probable starting pair of Tony Hill and Mike Sherrard compares with the best. Hill is a classy veteran while Sherrard has breathtaking speed and good hands. Mike Renfro, who was not a serious factor last year after injuring his shoulder in the American Bowl, is an excellent third wide receiver. Productivity at tight end has slipped a little, and the return of Doug Cosbie to his Pro Bowl form would be welcome.

Defense

After going through a period of uncertainty, the Cowboys are ready to reassert their traditional authority on the defensive line. Defensive tackle Randy White is coming off a sub-par year, but, subsequently, it has been revealed that he was carrying injuries to both his shoulder and hamstring. Defensive end Jim Jeffcoat, too, had ankle problems but still managed to log a club-leading 14 sacks. John Dutton was supposed to be past it – 'Too old,' said the experts – but he responded by having his best season for years. Ed 'Too Tall' Jones has, however, slowed, and seems sure to step aside for the exciting Kevin Brooks at defensive left end. First-round draftee Danny Noonan will probably be used in relief of Dutton, while there's extra backup help from Don Smerek and last year's third-rounder, Mark Walen. It's more difficult to be optimistic about the Cowboys at linebacker, where they are no better than ordinary in an era of pro football when line-backing is assuming extra importance. Jeff Rohrer held off the challenge from Jesse Penn and started in company with the aggressive Eugene Lockhart and the reliable Mike Hegman. They are well supported by steady players in Penn, Steve DeOssie and Garth Jax, but the unit as a whole could use an impact player. Cornerbacks Everson Walls and Ron Fellows complement each other really well. Walls, who is the only player to have led the NFL in interceptions three times, has just been signed to a new long-term contract. Free safety Michael Downs has emerged as the inspirational leader of the secondary and, last year, topped the club list with six interceptions. Strong safety Bill Bates is a crunching tackler. The pool is enriched by the arrival of second-round draftee Ron Francis.

Special Teams

Placekicker Rafael Septien has been released for reasons not connected with football, thus giving 11th-round draftee

1987 SCHEDULE OF GAMES	September	
	13 at St Louis	12:00
	20 at New York Giants	4:00
	27 BUFFALO	12:00
	October	
	4 at New York Jets	4:00
	11 PHILADELPHIA	12:00
	19 WASHINGTON (Mon.)	8:00
	25 at Philadelphia	1:00
	November	
	2 NEW YORK GIANTS (Mon.)	8:00
	8 at Detroit	1:00
	15 at New England	1:00
	22 MIAMI	7:00
	26 MINNESOTA (Thanksgiving)	3:00
	December	
	6 ATLANTA	12:00
	13 at Washington	1:00
	21 at Los Angeles Rams (Mon.)	6:00
	27 ST LOUIS	12:00

Jeff Ward a golden opportunity. Mike Saxon is an adequate punter with quarterback White as a fine backup. Returning kickoffs was not a Dallas strength last year, and the sparkle they need in the punt return department could come from draftee Kelvin Martin.

1987 DRAFT

Round	Name	Pos.	Ht.	Wt.	College
1.	Noonan, Danny	DT	6-3	281	Nebraska
2.	Francis, Ron	CB	5-9	200	Baylor
3.	Zimmerman, Jeff	G	6-3	325	Florida
4.	Martin, Kelvin	WR-KR	5-9	160	Boston College
5.	Gay, Everett	WR	6-2	206	Texas
6.	Onosai, Joe	G-C	6-2	265	Hawaii
7.	Sweeney, Kevin	QB	5-11	190	Fresno State
8.	Gogan, Kevin	T	6-7	300	Washington
9.	Blount, Alvin	RB	5-9	198	Maryland
10.	Jones, Dale	LB	6-1	229	Tennessee
11.	Ward, Jeff	K	5-9	172	Texas
12.	Armstrong, Scott	LB	6-1	228	Florida

VETERAN ROSTER

No.	Name	Pos.	Ht.	Wt.	NFL Year	College
36	Albritton, Vince	S	6-2	210	4	Washington
62	Baldinger, Brian	G	6-4	261	5	Duke
87	Banks, Gordon	WR	5-10	173	5	Stanford
40	Bates, Bill	S	6-1	204	5	Tennessee
99	Brooks, Kevin	DL	6-6	273	3	Michigan
85	Chandler, Thornton	TE	6-5	245	2	Alabama
42	Clack, Darryl	RB	5-10	218	2	Arizona State
10	Collier, Reggie	QB	6-3	207	2	So. Mississippi
84	Cosbie, Doug	TE	6-6	238	9	Santa Clara
55	DeOssie, Steve	LB	6-2	245	4	Boston College
33	Dorsett, Tony	RB	5-11	189	11	Pittsburgh
26	Downs, Michael	S	6-3	204	7	Rice
78	Dutton, John	DT	6-7	261	14	Nebraska
27	Fellows, Ron	CB	6-0	173	7	Missouri
46	Fowler, Todd	FB	6-3	221	3	Stephen F. Austin
28	Granger, Norm	RB	5-10	225	2	Iowa
58	Hegman, Mike	LB	6-1	227	12	Tennessee State
45	Hendrix, Manny	DB	5-10	178	2	Utah
80	Hill, Tony	WR	6-2	205	11	Stanford
23	Holloway, Johnny	CB	5-11	182	2	Kansas
53	Jax, Garth	LB	6-2	225	2	Florida State
77	Jeffcoat, Jim	DE	6-5	260	5	Arizona State
72	Jones, Ed	DE	6-9	273	13	Tennessee State
68	Ker, Crawford	G	6-3	285	3	Florida
29	Lavette, Robert	RB	5-11	190	3	Georgia Tech
56	Lockhart, Eugene	LB	6-2	235	4	Houston
14	McDonald, Paul	QB	6-2	185	8	Southern California
30	Newsome, Timmy	RB	6-1	237	8	Winston-Salem State
61	Newton, Nate	G	6-3	317	2	Florida A&M
16	Pelluer, Steve	QB	6-4	208	4	Washington
59	Penn, Jesse	LB	6-3	218	3	Virginia Tech
65	Petersen, Kurt	G	6-4	272	7	Missouri
81	Powe, Karl	WR	6-2	178	2	Alabama State
75	Pozderac, Phil	T	6-9	283	6	Notre Dame
64	Rafferty, Tom	C	6-3	262	12	Penn State
82	Renfro, Mike	WR	6-0	187	10	Texas Christian
70	Richards, Howard	T	6-6	269	7	Missouri
50	Rohrer, Jeff	LB	6-2	227	6	Yale
4	Saxon, Mike	P	6-3	188	3	San Diego State
22	Scott, Victor	DB	6-0	203	4	Colorado
86	Sherrard, Mike	WR	6-2	187	2	UCLA
60	Smerek, Don	DT	6-7	262	6	Nevada-Reno
63	Titensor, Glen	G	6-4	270	7	Brigham Young
71	Tuinei, Mark	T-C	6-5	283	5	Hawaii
	Walen, Mark	DT	6-5	265	1	UCLA
34	Walker, Herschel	RB	6-1	223	2	Georgia
24	Walls, Everson	CB	6-1	193	7	Grambling State
11	White, Danny	QB	6-3	197	12	Arizona State
54	White, Randy	DT	6-4	265	13	Maryland
	Yancey, Lloyd	G	6-4	275	1	Temple

Mike Sherrard proved to be an excellent draft selection.

NEW YORK GIANTS

Address Giants Stadium, East Rutherford, New Jersey 07073.

Stadium Giants Stadium, East Rutherford.
Capacity 76,891 *Playing Surface* AstroTurf.

Team Colours Blue, Red, and White.

Head Coach Bill Parcells – fifth year.

Championships Division 1986; Conference 1986; NFL 1927, '34, '38, '56; Super Bowl 1986.

History NFL 1925-69, NFC 1970-

Offense

The Super Bowl Champion Giants have so much talent that it is difficult to find a weakness, but they gave us a clue to what they feel is an area in which they could improve by selecting wide receivers with three of their first four options in the draft. First-round pick Mark Ingram is the complete wide receiver. He has that priceless gift of acceleration, with the hands to match. It would be no surprise to see him in the starting lineup halfway through the season. Before then the Giants will probably pick-and-mix from Lionel Manuel, Phil McConkey, Bobby Johnson and Stacy Robinson. No club in the league has better strength at tight end, where Mark Bavaro is backed up by Zeke Mowatt. Bavaro is a superb blocker and, last year, only his second in the NFL, he started in the Pro Bowl. Mowatt is a former Giants starter who lost his place, initially, through injury. Quarterback Phil Simms has his detractors, but they were stunned into silence by the most impressive performance by any quarterback in the history of the Super Bowl, when he completed 22 of 25 passes. Like Bob Beamon's long jump, it's a record which could stand until human physical development catches up. As backups, the Giants have Jeff Rutledge and Jeff Hostetler, the latter who is coming back after injury. It has to be said that they would not be expected to maintain the momentum in the event of a significant injury to Simms. Only late last season did the Giants' offensive line begin to attract credit for the team's success. Brad Benson, Billy Ard, Bart Oates, Chris Godfrey and Karl Nelson have jelled to form a very handy unit. They are not the best pass protectors in the NFL (they allowed 46 quarterback sacks) but they combined to clear the way for the rushing game and, of course, they were rewarded by the incredible Joe Morris. The pocket battleship signed up only hours before the season opener, and he missed one game with a blood infection, but, in terms of rushing yardage, he was even more productive than in 1985. Furthermore, even when he isn't handed the ball, he's such a threat that teams now have to make special plans in the attempt to contain him. Maurice Carthon played a key role in blocking for Morris, and the acquisition of former Cardinals Pro Bowler Ottis Anderson, together with the emergence of Lee Rouson and the return from injury of former number one pick George Adams, completes a group which is the envy of most clubs in the league.

Defense

Only by a tiny margin were the Giants pipped by Chicago for the title of the NFL's top defense, but the Giants are deficient in the consistency of their coverage. Whereas the Bears ranked second against both rushing and passing, the Giants ranked first against the run but only 19th against the pass. They were not helped by an injury to their outstanding safety, Terry Kinard, who was lost for the season in early December. But also it is true that their cornerbacks, Perry Williams, Elvis Patterson and rookie Mark Collins, could be beaten. In addition, safeties Kenny Hill and Herb Welch would be described as solid pros as distinct from the sort who dominate their areas of responsibility. Kinard's return will be a boost, and second-round draftee Adrian White may play a significant part once he has adjusted to the demands of competing in the NFL. Looking at the front seven, though, there are no problems. In fact, the Giants have an over-abundance of talent, particularly at linebacker. Outside linebacker Lawrence Taylor is the finest, except in the eyes of the Giants, who, by their own grading system, put Carl Banks in the number-one spot. Whereas Taylor feeds on a diet of quarterbacks (he led the NFL with 20.5 sacks), Banks prefers running backs. On the inside, Harry Carson is a perennial Pro Bowler while his partner, Gary Reasons, hardly looks out of place in this company. Former second-round pick Pepper Johnson, Byron Hunt, Andy Headen and Robbie Jones keep sharp on special-teams duty while biding their time. It is a similar story of excellence on the defensive line. Both defensive end Leonard Marshall and nose tackle Jim Burt were selected to the Pro Bowl. Marshall had 12 quarterback sacks. Burt, Marshall and George Martin form the starting trio, but Erik Howard is ready to step in should Burt begin to lose his edge, and Eric Dorsey is a future starter at defensive end.

Special Teams

The talent spills over into the special teams, where former

1987 SCHEDULE OF GAMES	September	
	14 at Chicago (Mon.)	8:00
	20 DALLAS	4:00
	27 at Miami	1:00
	October	
	5 SAN FRANCISCO (Mon.)	9:00
	11 WASHINGTON	4:00
	18 at Buffalo	4:00
	25 ST LOUIS	4:00
	November	
	2 at Dallas (Mon.)	8:00
	8 NEW ENGLAND	8:00
	15 at Philadelphia	4:00
	22 at New Orleans	3:00
	29 at Washington	4:00
	December	
	6 PHILADELPHIA	1:00
	13 at St Louis	3:00
	19 GREEN BAY (Sat.)	12:30
	27 NEW YORK JETS	1:00

Colts placekicker Raul Allegre proved to be an excellent signing. Punter Sean Landeta went to the Pro Bowl after averaging a huge 44.8 gross yards, with 24 punts inside the 20-yard line. By contrast, on punt and kickoff returns the Giants were not impressive and were outgained in both areas by their opponents.

1987 DRAFT

Round	Name	Pos.	Ht.	Wt.	College
1.	Ingram, Mark	WR	5-10	186	Michigan State
2.	White, Adrian	S	6-0	200	Florida
3.	Baker, Stephen	WR	5-7	160	Fresno State
4.	Turner, Odessa	WR	6-2	205	N.W. State, Louisiana
5.	O'Connor, Paul	G	6-2	274	Miami
6.	Richardson, Tim	RB	5-11	210	Pacific
6.	Riesenberg, Doug	T	6-5	265	California
8.	Jones, Rod	TE	6-3	230	Washington
9.	Parker, Stan	G-T	6-5	272	Nebraska
9.	Wright, Dana	RB	6-0	206	Findlay College
10.	Faucette, Chuck	LB	6-2	238	Maryland
11.	Walter, Dave	QB	6-2	225	Michigan Tech
12.	Berthusen, Bill	DT	6-4	286	Iowa State
12.	Stark, Chad	RB	6-1	228	North Dakota State

VETERAN ROSTER

No.	Name	Pos.	Ht.	Wt.	NFL Year	College
33	Adams, George	RB	6-1	225	2	Kentucky
2	Allegre, Raul	K	5-10	167	5	Texas
24	Anderson, Ottis	RB	6-2	225	9	Miami
67	Ard, Bill	G	6-3	270	7	Wake Forest
58	Banks, Carl	LB	6-4	235	4	Michigan State
89	Bavaro, Mark	TE	6-4	245	3	Notre Dame
60	Benson, Brad	T	6-3	270	10	Penn State
64	Burt, Jim	NT	6-1	260	7	Miami
53	Carson, Harry	LB	6-2	240	12	South Carolina State
44	Carthon, Maurice	RB	6-1	225	3	Arkansas State
25	Collins, Mark	CB	5-10	190	2	Cal State-Fullerton
39	Davis, Tyrone	CB	6-1	190	2	Clemson
77	Dorsey, Eric	DE	6-5	280	2	Notre Dame
28	Flynn, Tom	S	6-0	195	4	Pittsburgh
30	Galbreath, Tony	RB	6-0	228	12	Missouri
61	Godfrey, Chris	G	6-3	265	5	Michigan
54	Headen, Andy	LB	6-5	242	5	Clemson
48	Hill, Kenny	S	6-0	195	7	Yale
15	Hostetler, Jeff	QB	6-3	212	4	West Virginia
74	Howard, Erik	NT	6-4	268	2	Washington State
57	Hunt, Byron	LB	6-5	242	7	Southern Methodist
88	Johnson, Bob	WR	5-11	171	4	Kansas
68	Johnson, Damian	T	6-5	290	2	Kansas State
52	Johnson, Thomas	LB	6-3	248	2	Ohio State
59	Johnston, Brian	C	6-3	275	2	North Carolina
51	Jones, Robbie	LB	6-2	230	4	Alabama
69	Jordan, David	G	6-6	276	3	Auburn
43	Kinard, Terry	S	6-1	200	5	Clemson
5	Landeta, Sean	P	6-0	200	3	Towson State
46	Lasker, Greg	S	6-0	200	2	Arkansas
86	Manuel, Lionel	WR	5-11	180	4	Pacific
70	Marshall, Leonard	DE	6-3	285	5	Louisiana State
75	Martin, George	DE	6-4	255	13	Oregon
80	McConkey, Phil	WR	5-10	170	4	Navy
76	McGriff, Curtis	DE	6-5	276	7	Alabama
87	Miller, Solomon	WR	6-1	185	2	Utah State
20	Morris, Joe	RB	5-7	195	6	Syracuse
84	Mowatt, Zeke	TE	6-3	240	4	Florida State
63	Nelson, Karl	T	6-6	285	4	Iowa State
65	Oates, Bart	C	6-3	265	3	Brigham Young
34	Patterson, Elvis	CB	5-11	188	4	Kansas
55	Reasons, Gary	LB	6-4	234	4	N.W. State, Louisiana
66	Roberts, Bill	T	6-5	280	3	Ohio State
81	Robinson, Stacy	WR	5-11	186	3	North Dakota State
22	Rouson, Lee	RB	6-1	222	3	Colorado
17	Rutledge, Jeff	QB	6-1	195	9	Alabama
78	Sally, Jerome	NT	6-3	270	6	Missouri
11	Simms, Phil	QB	6-3	214	9	Morehead State
56	Taylor, Lawrence	LB	6-3	243	7	North Carolina
73	Washington, John	DE	6-4	275	2	Oklahoma State
27	Welch, Herb	DB	5-11	180	3	UCLA
23	Williams, Perry	CB	6-2	203	4	North Carolina State

Mark Bavaro has emerged as NFC's premier tight end.

PHILADELPHIA EAGLES

NFC EASTERN DIVISION

Address Philadelphia Veterans Stadium, Broad St. and Pattison Ave., Philadelphia, Pa. 19148.

Stadium Veterans Stadium, Philadelphia.
Capacity 69,417 *Playing Surface* AstroTurf.

Team Colours Kelly Green, Silver, and White.

Head Coach Buddy Ryan – second year.

Championships Division 1980; Conference 1980; NFL 1948, '49, '60.

History NFL 1933-69, NFC 1970-

Offense

Before the Eagles can begin to think of contending for a title they need to solve the problems of an offensive line which, last year, gave up an all-time league record 104 quarterback sacks. They had a chance to draft top-class help but chose instead to pick a defensive lineman. Only in the third round (they had no second-round pick) did they attend to a clear need by selecting center Ben Tamburello. Entering the April mini-camp, the starting lineup had Ken Reeves at left tackle, Bob Landsee at left guard, Gerry Feehery at center, Ron Baker at right guard and Joe Conwell at right tackle. There could be changes before September, with Matt Darwin, who started the last ten games, moving permanently ahead of Feehery. Interestingly, last year's 12th-round pick, defensive tackle Reggie Singletary, will try to make the conversion to guard. After a great deal of shuffling around, two rookies, Keith Byars and Anthony Toney, ended up as the starting running backs. Byars was still in the process of recovering from a foot injury he sustained in college, and he performed way below his best collegiate form. There is still every prospect that he could become a franchise running back but, sadly, he has needed surgery on his other foot for an injury in training camp and will have to go through the rehabilitation process of all over again. Toney has the class to be productive and is a fine blocker. With Junior Tautalatasi questionable because of knee problems, Toney's partner while Byars recovers is likely to be Michael Haddix, who is coming off the best of his four modest years in the league. The departure of Ron Jaworski has left Randall Cunningham in charge at quarterback. A big, scrambling player, Cunningham has learned the hard way – he was sacked 72 times last year. There are those who feel that he could rise to the level of greatness. He is backed up by Matt Cavanaugh. The one area where the Eagles are in fine shape is at wide receiver, with the outstanding Mike Quick and Kenny Jackson as the starters. Quick has just been to his fourth straight Pro Bowl. Ron Johnson is the senior backup and comes on when the Eagles go into a three-receiver set. Tight end John Spagnola's productivity as a receiver fell away as, increasingly, he was required to lend his shoulder to help solve the blocking problems. But there is no doubt that he is a pass receiver of great competence.

Defense

With the drafting of the awesome Jerome Brown, head coach Ryan now has enough linemen to begin thinking of reproducing the dominance he established at Chicago with the '46' defense. Defensive end Reggie White, who came back into his own after some unhappy games at defensive tackle, had 18 sacks and was voted MVP in the last Pro Bowl. But he is just the start of it. Defensive end Greg Brown (nine sacks) and defensive tackle Ken Clarke (eight sacks) play different roles in the scheme but are not far behind White in effectiveness. One imagines Ryan using five defensive linemen, blowing the bugle and sitting back to watch the fun. The Eagles took a chance by starting rookie Alonzo Johnson at outside linebacker, and he stayed alive. He is expected to be a force in the coming season. In the middle position, Mike Reichenbach learned the new system quickly and has emerged as a leader, while the veteran Garry Cobb is at left linebacker. In addition, Cobb plays a vital role when the Eagles shift to their 'nickel' formation. Last year's rookie, Seth Joyner, is a good reserve. The secondary spent most of the season without its best player, All-Pro free safety Wes Hopkins, who injured his left knee on Week Four. He is expected back by August but his recovery may take longer. His replacement, Terry Hoage, did a respectable job. Andre Waters really came to prominence in his first full year as the starting strong safety. Waters tied for the club lead in both tackles (129 with Reichenbach) and interceptions (6) with Roynell Young. Young was voted the club's defensive MVP after a super season at left cornerback. Elbert Foules will continue to start at right cornerback, ahead of the man he displaced, Evan Cooper.

Special Teams

Gregg Garrity may have earned himself a job after averaging 11 yards on 17 punt returns when taking over from Evan Cooper for the last eight games. The club needs to find a kickoff returner. Rookie punter John

1987 SCHEDULE OF GAMES	September	
	13 at Washington	1:00
	20 NEW ORLEANS	1:00
	27 at San Francisco	1:00
	October	
	4 CHICAGO	1:00
	11 at Dallas	12:00
	18 at Green Bay	12:00
	25 DALLAS	1:00
	November	
	1 at St Louis	12:00
	8 WASHINGTON	1:00
	15 NEW YORK GIANTS	4:00
	22 ST LOUIS	1:00
	29 at New England	1:00
	December	
	6 at New York Giants	1:00
	13 MIAMI	1:00
	20 at New York Jets	1:00
	27 BUFFALO	1:00

Teltschik proved to be an excellent acquisition after being signed off waivers. He averaged 41.6 yards, including 20 punts inside the 20-yard line. Placekicker Paul McFadden had a poor year but the Eagles know that they have a good one and they'll stay with him.

1987 DRAFT

Round	Name	Pos.	Ht.	Wt.	College
1.	Brown, Jerome	DT	6-2	290	Miami
3.	Tamburello, Ben	C	6-2	268	Auburn
4.	Evans, Byron	LB	6-2	217	Arizona
5.	Alexander, David	G	6-2	270	Tulsa
6.	Moten, Ron	LB	6-0	225	Florida
6.	Pike, Chris	DT	6-7	285	Tulsa
7.	Williams, Brian	T	6-6	280	Central Michigan
9.	Lambiotte, Ken	QB	6-3	198	William & Mary
10.	Carberry, Paul	DT	6-3	262	Oregon State
12.	Morse, Bobby	RB	5-10	200	Michigan State

VETERAN ROSTER

No.	Name	Pos.	Ht.	Wt.	NFL Year	College
63	Baker, Ron	G	6-4	274	10	Oklahoma State
77	Black, Mike	T-G	6-4	290	2	Cal State-Sacramento
98	Brown, Greg	DE	6-5	265	7	Kansas State
42	Byars, Keith	RB	6-1	230	2	Ohio State
6	Cavanaugh, Matt	QB	6-2	212	10	Pittsburgh
71	Clarke, Ken	DT	6-2	275	10	Syracuse
50	Cobb, Garry	LB	6-2	230	9	Southern California
79	Conwell, Joe	T	6-5	275	2	North Carolina
21	Cooper, Evan	CB-KR	5-11	184	4	Michigan
45	Crawford, Charles	RB-KR	6-2	235	2	Oklahoma State
12	Cunningham, Randall	QB	6-4	192	3	Nevada-Las Vegas
84	Darby, Byron	TE	6-4	262	5	Southern California
78	Darwin, Matt	C	6-4	260	2	Texas A&M
67	Feehery, Gerry	C	6-2	270	5	Syracuse
29	Foules, Elbert	CB	5-11	185	5	Alcorn State
33	Frizzell, William	S	6-3	198	4	North Carolina Central
86	Garrity, Gregg	WR-PR	5-10	169	5	Penn State
26	Haddix, Michael	RB	6-2	227	5	Mississippi State
62	Haden, Nick	G-C	6-2	270	2	Penn State
34	Hoage, Terry	S	6-3	199	4	Georgia
48	Hopkins, Wes	S	6-1	212	5	Southern Methodist
81	Jackson, Kenny	WR	6-0	180	4	Penn State
53	Jiles, Dwayne	LB	6-4	242	3	Texas Tech
54	Johnson, Alonzo	LB	6-3	222	2	Florida
85	Johnson, Ron	WR	6-3	186	3	Long Beach State
59	Joyner, Seth	LB	6-2	241	2	Texas-El Paso
52	Kraynak, Rich	LB	6-1	230	5	Pittsburgh
65	Landsee, Bob	G-C	6-4	273	2	Wisconsin
58	Lee, Byron	LB	6-2	230	2	Ohio State
89	Little, Dave	TE	6-2	236	4	Middle Tennessee St.
11	Mackey, Kyle	QB	6-3	219	2	East Texas State
8	McFadden, Paul	K	5-11	163	4	Youngstown State
74	Mitchell, Leonard	T	6-7	295	7	Houston
82	Quick, Mike	WR	6-2	190	6	North Carolina State
	Redick, Cornelius	WR-PR	5-11	185	1	Cal State-Fullerton
66	Reeves, Ken	T-G	6-5	275	3	Texas A&M
55	Reichenbach, Mike	LB	6-2	238	4	East Stroudsburg State
76	Schreiber, Adam	G-C	6-4	270	4	Texas
95	Schulz, Jody	LB	6-3	235	4	East Carolina
96	Simmons, Clyde	DT-DE	6-6	258	2	Western Carolina
68	Singletary, Reggie	G-T	6-3	272	2	North Carolina State
83	Smith, Phil	WR	6-3	188	4	San Diego State
88	Spagnola, John	TE	6-4	242	8	Yale
93	Strauthers, Tom	DT-DE	6-4	264	5	Jackson State
37	Tautalatasi, Junior	RB	5-10	205	2	Washington State
10	Teltschik, John	P	6-2	215	2	Texas
25	Toney, Anthony	RB	6-0	227	2	Texas A&M
69	Tupper, Jeff	DE	6-5	269	2	Oklahoma
20	Waters, Andre	S	5-11	185	4	Cheyney State
92	White, Reggie	DE	6-5	285	3	Tennessee
22	Wilson, Brenard	S	6-0	185	9	Vanderbilt
43	Young, Roynell	CB	6-1	185	8	Alcorn State

Running back Keith Byars will hope to make a speedy recovery from his foot injury.

ST LOUIS CARDINALS

Address Busch Stadium, Box 888, St Louis, Missouri 63188.
Stadium Busch Stadium, St Louis.
   Capacity 51,392 *Playing Surface* Astro Turf-8.
Team Colours Cardinal Red, Black, and White.
Head Coach Gene Stallings – second year.
Championships Division 1974, '75; NFL 1925, '47.
History NFL 1920-69, NFC 1970-
   (Until 1960, they were known as the Chicago Cardinals.)

Offense

On the face of it, the Cardinals are in trouble, after stumbling to their worst record since the franchise moved to St Louis in 1960. However, inspection of their results shows a series of narrow losses, including those to the Rams (16-10), the Giants (13-6) and Washington (28-21 and 20-17). They had bad luck on the offensive line, where only left tackle Luis Sharpe started all sixteen games, as injuries to good veterans required a collection of draftees and first-year players to be conscripted into duty. Center Gene Chilton did beat out Randy Clark, who has subsequently been released, while Ray Brown moved in at left guard when first-year man Derek Kennard switched to right guard towards the end of the season. The return of injured guards Doug Dawson and Joe Bostic will give the unit a sorely-needed boost. There was uncertainty at quarterback, where the normal starter, Neil Lomax, was benched for two and a half games in favour of the former Steelers quarterback Cliff Stoudt. Lomax re-established his seniority but there's little doubt that he'll have to do it all over again in training camp, where the pair will be joined in the competition by first-round draftee Kelly Stouffer. How things change. In 1984, Lomax formed a tremendous partnership with wide receiver Roy Green but now, both players are struggling to find the magic formula. Green has been troubled by a series of nagging injuries and it is as well that the veteran J.T. Smith, formerly of Kansas City, chose last season to have the best campaign of his career. Smith is a really solid pro, but a return to top form by Green is critical if the Cardinals are to break out of the doldrums. The likelihood that Pat Tilley will not return from injury leaves only a group of inexperienced players in reserve. At tight end, Doug Marsh is expected to turn in his usual solid performance but now he comes under threat from draftee Robert Awalt, who was among the top two or three tight ends available. A great deal more might be anticipated from the offensive backfield, where, following the trade of Ottis Anderson, Stump Mitchell has become the senior running back. Last season, Mitchell and fullback Earl Ferrell ground out 1,348 yards between them, averaging 4.6 and 4.4 yards respectively. It could be that they were just warming up.

Defense

Overall, the Cardinals do not have a problem on defense and it will surprise many people to learn that they rated fourth in the NFL. Even more astonishing, they were rated best against the pass. It begins to appear that with the cushion of just a few more points from the offense, this unit could bring the club back into contention. Defensive ends Al 'Bubba' Baker and Bob Clasby, and nose tackle David Galloway started for most of the season, but Scott Bergold and former starter Curtis Greer will return from injury to challenge for playing time. It was the linebacking quartet which attracted the flak for the Cardinals' poor showing against the run – they rated 25th in the NFL – and it is rumoured that head coach Gene Stallings is thinking of reverting to the 4-3 system in 1987. This may be the reason that he selected defensive linemen Colin Scotts and Rod Saddler in the upper half of the draft. Almost every player in the linebacking corps has an excellent pedigree, with all three of E.J. Junior, Freddie Joe Nunn and Anthony Bell having been first-round draft choices. Bell could not displace either of Nunn or Charlie Baker, who started in all sixteen games on the outsides. Similarly, Junior and Niko Noga are the established starters on the inside, with Ron Monaco as the backup. The secondary is the real strength of the defense. Leonard Smith and Lonnie Young built a terrific combination in the safety positions, while Cedric Mack and rookie Carl Carter closed down on the corners. The maintenance of quality is ensured by the selection of safety Tim McDonald, the former USC star.

Special Teams

Another area in which the Cardinals excel is in some aspects of special teams play. Vai Sikahema, a rookie 10th-round pick, tied an NFL record by returning two punts for touchdowns in the final game, on the way to leading the NFC. In addition, he came third in the NFC on kickoff returns, clinching a spot on the Pro Bowl roster. Another surprise name on that roster was that of Ron Wolfley, who developed into a notorious wedge-buster and special-teams tackler. By contrast, placekicker John Lee, on whom the Cardinals used a second-round option,

1987 SCHEDULE OF GAMES	September	
	13 DALLAS	12:00
	20 at San Diego	1:00
	27 INDIANAPOLIS	12:00
	October	
	4 at Washington	1:00
	11 NEW ORLEANS	12:00
	18 at San Francisco	1:00
	25 at New York Giants	4:00
	November	
	1 PHILADELPHIA	12:00
	8 TAMPA BAY	12:00
	15 LOS ANGELES RAMS	12:00
	22 at Philadelphia	1:00
	29 at Atlanta	1:00
	December	
	6 WASHINGTON	12:00
	13 NEW YORK GIANTS	3:00
	20 at Tampa Bay	4:00
	27 at Dallas	12:00

was a disappointment before being injured on Week Eleven. Lee will be retained but punter Greg Cater may have to fight for his place in training camp.

1987 DRAFT

Round	Name	Pos.	Ht.	Wt.	College
1.	Stouffer, Kelly	QB	6-3	211	Colorado State
2.	McDonald, Tim	S	6-2	205	Southern California
3.	Awalt, Robert	TE	6-5	243	San Diego State
3.	Scotts, Colin	DT	6-5	262	Hawaii
4.	Saddler, Rod	DE	6-5	273	Texas A&M
5.	Swarn, George	RB	5-11	205	Miami, Ohio
5.	Bruno, John	P	6-1	200	Penn State
5.	Jarostchuk, Ilia	LB	6-3	230	New Hampshire
6.	Garalczyk, Mark	DT	6-5	267	Western Michigan
7.	Peoples, Tim	S	6-0	194	Washington
7.	Harris, William	TE	6-4	245	Bishop College
8.	Alvord, Steve	DT	6-4	268	Washington
9.	Davis, Wayne	LB	6-2	217	Alabama
10.	Wright, Charles	DB	5-10	179	Tulsa
11.	Peat, Todd	G	6-2	298	Northern Illinois

VETERAN ROSTER

No.	Name	Pos.	Ht.	Wt.	NFL Year	College
16	Austin, Kent	QB	6-1	195	2	Mississippi
60	Baker, Al	DE	6-6	270	10	Colorado State
52	Baker, Charlie	LB	6-2	234	8	New Mexico
55	Bell, Anthony	LB	6-3	231	2	Michigan State
74	Bergold, Scott	DE	6-7	263	2	Wisconsin
89	Boso, Cap	TE	6-3	224	1	Illinois
71	Bostic, Joe	G	6-3	268	9	Clemson
62	Brown, Ray	T-G	6-5	257	2	Arkansas State
41	Carter, Carl	CB	5-11	180	2	Texas Tech
14	Cater, Greg	P	6-0	191	6	Tennessee-Chattanooga
58	Chilton, Gene	C	6-3	271	2	Texas
79	Clasby, Bob	DE	6-5	260	3	Notre Dame
66	Dawson, Doug	G	6-2	267	3	Texas
56	DiBernardo, Rick	LB	6-3	225	2	Notre Dame
73	Duda, Mark	NT	6-3	279	5	Maryland
31	Ferrell, Earl	RB	6-0	224	6	East Tennessee State
65	Galloway, David	NT	6-3	279	6	Florida
81	Green, Roy	WR	6-0	195	9	Henderson State
75	Greer, Curtis	DE	6-4	258	7	Michigan
82	Holmes, Don	WR	5-10	180	2	Mesa, Colorado
78	Hughes, Van	DE	6-3	280	2	Southwest Texas
87	Johnson, Troy	WR	6-1	175	2	Southern
54	Junior, E.J.	LB	6-3	235	7	Alabama
70	Kennard, Derek	G	6-3	285	2	Nevada-Reno
10	Lee, John	K	5-11	182	2	UCLA
15	Lomax, Neil	QB	6-3	215	7	Portland State
47	Mack, Cedric	CB	6-0	194	5	Baylor
80	Marsh, Doug	TE	6-3	238	8	Michigan
76	Mays, Stafford	DE	6-2	255	8	Washington
30	Mitchell, Stump	RB	5-9	188	7	Citadel
59	Monaco, Ron	LB	6-1	225	2	South Carolina
38	Nelson, Lee	S	5-10	185	11	Florida State
57	Noga, Niko	LB	6-1	235	4	Hawaii
85	Novacek, Jay	WR	6-4	217	3	Wyoming
53	Nunn, Freddie Joe	LB	6-4	228	3	Mississippi
63	Robbins, Tootie	T	6-5	302	6	East Carolina
51	Ruether, Mike	C	6-4	275	2	Texas
39	Sargent, Broderick	RB	5-10	215	2	Baylor
67	Sharpe, Luis	T	6-4	260	6	UCLA
36	Sikahema, Vai	RB-KR	5-9	191	2	Brigham Young
84	Smith, J.T.	WR	6-2	185	10	North Texas State
61	Smith, Lance	T	6-2	262	3	Louisiana State
45	Smith, Leonard	S	5-11	202	5	McNeese State
44	Smith, Wayne	CB	6-0	170	8	Purdue
18	Stoudt, Cliff	QB	6-4	215	9	Youngstown State
86	Swanson, Eric	WR	5-11	186	2	Tennessee
32	Thurman, Dennis	S	5-11	179	10	Southern California
83	Tilley, Pat	WR	5-10	178	11	Louisiana Tech
24	Wolfley, Ron	RB	6-0	222	3	West Virginia
43	Young, Lonnie	S	6-1	182	3	Michigan State

Stump Mitchell enters his first campaign as the Cardinals' senior running back.

WASHINGTON REDSKINS

NFC EASTERN DIVISION

Address Redskin Park, P.O. Box 17247, Dulles International Airport, Washington, D.C. 20041.

Stadium Robert F. Kennedy Stadium, Washington. *Capacity* 55,750 *Playing Surface* Grass (Prescription Athletic Turf).

Team Colours Burgundy and Gold.

Head Coach Joe Gibbs – seventh year.

Championships Division 1972,'83,'84;
Conference 1972,'82,'83;
NFL 1937,'42; Super Bowl 1982.

History NFL 1932-69, NFC 1970-
(Originally named the Boston Braves for the 1932 season only, they were renamed the Boston Redskins until, in 1937, they moved to Washington.)

Offense

There can be little doubt that the Redskins have now settled in with that group of six or so clubs from whom one would expect the Super Bowl Champion to emerge. It has been the result of careful management, building on those outstanding drafts and free-agent signings beginning in 1980. It was in 1981 that they obtained three future starters for the offensive line in tackles Joe Jacoby and Mark May, and guard Russ Grimm. Center Jeff Bostic had arrived the year before and, subsequently, R.C. Thielemann, who was a three-time Pro Bowler and occasional All-Pro when with the Falcons, was acquired to fill a gap at right guard. The starters, then, may even be the best in the NFC. However, the backups are modest and inexperienced at that. There's no lack of either experience or potential at running back, where the great George Rogers is the senior player in the Redskins' one-back system. Rogers appears to have lost a step of open-field speed over his six years in the trenches, but he still has explosive power through the line of scrimmage. Last year, he rushed for more than 1,000 yards for the fourth time in his career and scored a league-leading 18 touchdowns, all by rushing. Behind Rogers waits Kelvin Bryant, a player of enormous potential whom one feels must soon be turned loose. The Redskins have bided their time, allowing him to feel his way into the NFL mostly as a pass receiver, but we may not have to wait long for confirmation of his rushing ability. In reserve, Keith Griffin is joined by fifth-round draftee Tim Smith. At quarterback, Schroeder has his big days and only the occasional poor outing, as against the Giants on Week Fourteen when six of his passes were intercepted. He will have improved after the experiences of his testing 1986 season. Individually, his wide receivers are of the first order, and in tandem they are devastating. Last year, Gary Clark surpassed his senior partner, Art Monk, by a touch in receptions, by 200 or so yards and by seven touchdowns to four, but, over the past three seasons, no wide receiver in pro football has caught as many passes for as many yards as the graceful Monk. The backup, first-year player Ricky Sanders was given few opportuni-

ties, but he showed his big-play talents with his first reception in the pros, which went for a 71-yard gain. At tight end, Clint Didier continued to improve as a pass receiver, averaging an astounding 20.3 yards on 34 receptions. He must surely come into the reckoning for a Pro Bowl spot this season. The second tight end in the normal set, Don Warren, is the better blocker.

Defense

It is difficult to establish the reason for the Redskins' lowly ranking of 21st in the NFL. They have a good pass rush, led by defensive ends Dexter Manley, who had a team-leading 18.5 quarterback sacks, and Charles Mann, who came second with 10. There's not much wrong with defensive left tackle Dave Butz, who started in all sixteen games, and when defensive right tackle Darryl Grant was injured, Dean Hamel stepped in to start eight games. It is probably fair to assert that the weakness lay at linebacker, and stemmed from injuries which kept Mel Kaufman out for the last fourteen games and restricted Monte Coleman to just four starts. The Redskins use only three line-backers, but Kaufman and Coleman would normally share time with Neal Olkewicz and Rich Milot. For the third time in his career, Olkewicz led the club in tackles (183). In the secondary the starting lineup is projected to have Darrell Green at cornerback, with Curtis Jordan at free safety and Ken Coffey at strong safety. Green, who is the NFL's fastest player, led the club with five interceptions and was selected to his second Pro Bowl. The other cornerback position will be filled by Vernon Dean or Tim Morrison, the latter who replaced Dean as the starter for the last five games of the regular season. Conceivably, second-round draftee Brian Davis could leapfrog them both. Another player who will challenge for more starting time is Alvin Walton, nicknamed the 'Crushin' Kansan', who started at strong safety when Coffey was injured.

1987 SCHEDULE OF GAMES		
September		
13 PHILADELPHIA		1:00
20 at Atlanta		1:00
27 NEW ENGLAND		1:00
October		
4 ST LOUIS		1:00
11 at New York Giants		4:00
19 at Dallas (Mon.)		8:00
25 NEW YORK JETS		1:00
November		
1 at Buffalo		1:00
8 at Philadelphia		1:00
15 DETROIT		1:00
23 LOS ANGELES RAMS (Mon.)		9:00
29 NEW YORK GIANTS		4:00
December		
6 at St Louis		12:00
13 DALLAS		1:00
20 at Miami		8:00
26 at Minnesota (Sat.)		3:00

Special Teams

Placekicking was a Redskins weakness and it's possible that Max Zendejas, who missed five extra point attempts, may not hold onto the job he was given when Mark Moseley was released after six weeks of the season. Jess Atkinson looked much more secure when he replaced the injured Zendejas in mid-December. Steve Cox is both a powerful punter and a valuable long-range field goal specialist. Ken Jenkins, Green and Eric Yarber combined to give the Redskins an excellent punt return average of 10.8 yards but the club averaged only 19.6 returning kickoffs and could use a big-play performer.

1987 DRAFT

Round	Name	Pos.	Ht.	Wt.	College
2.	Davis, Brian	CB	6-1	194	Nebraska
2.	Kleine, Wally	DL-T	6-8	290	Notre Dame
5.	Smith, Tim	RB	5-10	213	Texas Tech
6.	Gage, Steve	S	6-3	209	Tulsa
6.	Simmons, Ed	T	6-4	270	Eastern Washington
7.	Thomas, Johnny	DB	5-9	188	Baylor
8.	Vaughn, Clarence	S	6-0	202	Northern Illinois
9.	Jenkins, Alfred	QB-RB	6-3	215	Arizona
10.	Wilson, Ted	WR	5-8	160	Central Florida
11.	Brown, Laron	WR	5-10	171	Texas
12.	Hitchcock, Ray	C	6-2	285	Minnesota

VETERAN ROSTER

No.	Name	Pos.	Ht.	Wt.	NFL Year	College
4	Atkinson, Jess	K	5-9	162	3	Maryland
26	Badanjek, Rick	RB	5-8	217	2	Maryland
67	Beasley, Tom	DE	6-5	248	10	Virginia Tech
53	Bostic, Jeff	C	6-2	260	8	Clemson
23	Bowles, Todd	S	6-2	203	2	Temple
29	Branch, Reggie	RB	5-11	227	3	East Carolina
24	Bryant, Kelvin	RB	6-2	195	2	North Carolina
58	Burks, Shawn	LB	6-1	230	2	Louisiana State
65	Butz, Dave	DT	6-7	295	15	Purdue
50	Caldwell, Ravin	LB	6-3	229	1	Arkansas
84	Clark, Gary	WR	5-9	173	3	James Madison
48	Coffey, Ken	S	6-0	198	4	Southwest Texas State
51	Coleman, Monte	LB	6-2	230	9	Central Arkansas
12	Cox, Steve	P	6-4	195	7	Arkansas
56	Daniels, Calvin	LB	6-3	241	6	North Carolina
32	Dean, Vernon	CB	5-11	178	6	San Diego State
86	Didier, Clint	TE	6-5	240	6	Portland State
30	Garner, Dwight	RB	5-8	183	2	California
77	Grant, Darryl	DT	6-1	275	7	Rice
28	Green, Darrell	CB	5-8	170	5	Texas A&I
35	Griffin, Keith	RB	5-8	185	4	Miami
68	Grimm, Russ	G	6-3	275	7	Pittsburgh
78	Hamel, Dean	DT	6-3	275	3	Tulsa
64	Hamilton, Steve	DE-DT	6-4	255	3	East Carolina
88	Holloway, Derek	WR	5-7	166	2	Arkansas
66	Jacoby, Joe	T	6-7	305	7	Louisville
31	Jenkins, Ken	RB-KR	5-8	185	5	Bucknell
82	Jones, Anthony	TE	6-3	248	4	Wichita State
22	Jordan, Curtis	S	6-2	205	11	Texas Tech
55	Kaufman, Mel	LB	6-2	218	6	Cal Poly-SLO
74	Koch, Markus	DE	6-5	275	2	Boise State
72	Manley, Dexter	DE	6-3	257	7	Oklahoma State
71	Mann, Charles	DE	6-6	270	5	Nevada-Reno
73	May, Mark	T	6-6	295	7	Pittsburgh
63	McKenzie, Raleigh	G	6-2	262	3	Tennessee
60	McQuaid, Dan	T	6-7	278	3	Nevada-Las Vegas
57	Milot, Rich	LB	6-4	237	9	Penn State
81	Monk, Art	WR	6-3	209	8	Syracuse
41	Morrison, Tim	CB	6-1	195	2	North Carolina
52	Olkewicz, Neal	LB	6-0	233	9	Maryland
87	Orr, Terry	TE	6-3	227	2	Texas
38	Rogers, George	RB	6-2	229	7	South Carolina
11	Rypien, Mark	QB	6-4	234	2	Washington State
46	Sanders, Ricky	WR-RB	5-11	180	2	Southwest Texas State
10	Schroeder, Jay	QB	6-4	215	4	UCLA
75	Slater, Bob	DT	6-4	265	1	Oklahoma
69	Thielemann, R.C.	G	6-4	262	11	Arkansas
76	Tilton, Ron	G	6-4	250	2	Tulane
89	Verdin, Clarence	WR-KR	5-8	160	2	Southwest Louisiana
40	Walton, Alvin	S	6-0	180	2	Kansas
85	Warren, Don	TE	6-4	242	9	San Diego State
45	Wilburn, Barry	CB	6-3	186	3	Mississippi
17	Williams, Doug	QB	6-4	220	7	Grambling State
80	Yarber, Eric	WR-KR	5-8	156	1	Idaho
14	Zendejas, Max	K	5-11	184	2	Arizona

Jay Schroeder established himself as Redskins' leader.

CHICAGO BEARS

Address 250 N. Washington, Lake Forest, Illinois 60045.
Stadium Soldier Field, Chicago.
Capacity 65,790 *Playing Surface* AstroTurf.
Team Colours Navy Blue, Orange, and White.
Head Coach Mike Ditka – sixth year.
Championships Division 1984,'85,'86; Conference 1985;
NFL 1921,'32,'33,'40,'41,'43,'46,'63; Super Bowl 1985.
History NFL 1920-69, NFC 1970-
(Before 1922, they were known as firstly the Decatur
Staleys and then the Chicago Staleys.)

Offense

Such are the standards set by the football world for the reigning Super Bowl Champion, that the Bears were seen as a failure, even though they went 14-2 over the regular season. In reality, the Bears did not succeed, simply because, at a vital stage in their playoff loss to the Redskins, they fumbled away their chances to win. They have one of the best offensive lines in football and the best rushing attack – in 1986 they became the first club to lead the league in rushing for four straight years since the great Bears teams of the period, 1939-42. The offensive line features the Pro Bowlers, left tackle Jim Covert and center Jay Hilgenberg, who start alongside left guard Mark Bortz, right tackle Keith Van Horne and right guard Tom Thayer, the latter who held off the challenge of returning veteran Kurt Becker. Fourth-round draftee Paul Blair survived the rigours of training camp and became the senior backup at both tackle positions. Running back Walter Payton is talking more seriously about retirement but it may take a precipitous decline to give him the final push. For this outstanding footballer, the most productive backfield player of all time, there always will be new challenges on the football field. He'll play this season, his thirteenth, with all the enthusiasm and commitment of a rookie fighting for his place. It is likely that Neal Anderson, who is Payton's heir apparent, will be given more time. At fullback, Matt Suhey may have to concede time to Calvin Thomas. The situation at quarterback has been clouded by a war of words, mostly the undignified variety and emanating from quarterback Jim McMahon. It boils down to this. McMahon has had shoulder surgery but will probably be back to somewhere near his best. And that would be good enough to lead the club to another title. However, the diminutive Doug Flutie has a special admirer in head coach Mike Ditka. He is inexperienced but very talented. Add the fact that Jim Harbaugh was drafted in the first round to join Steve Fuller and Mike Tomczak, and we have the makings of a training camp which could attract as much attention as the regular season. At wide receiver, there can be few doubts remaining about Willie Gault, though his detractors will continue to say that he lacks fortitude. Dennis McKinnon should be back after the injury which kept him out for the whole of 1986, and you have to like the look of second-round draftee Ron Morris,

who has outstanding speed and natural ability. At tight end, Emery Moorehead retains a distinct edge over Tim Wrightman.

Defense

All those experts who predicted disaster for the Bears' defense after the replacement of Buddy Ryan by Vince Tobin, were silenced when the unit retained its status as the NFL's best and set the league record for fewest points conceded in a sixteen-game season. The reasons are clear. Tobin didn't make as many changes as expected and the same personnel did what they'd done the year before, namely, play outstanding football. Defensive end Richard Dent did not dominate as much as expected but he led the club with 11.5 sacks, ahead of Dan Hampton, who had 10. The media attention faded away from William 'Refrigerator' Perry, thank goodness, and he was able (mostly) to concentrate on playing football. Steve McMichael completes a tremendous four-man line, which has Henry Waechter, Mike Hartenstine, Al Harris, and draftees Sean Smith and Steve Bryan in support. There were no changes at linebacker, just the same level of excellence from starters Otis Wilson, Mike Singletary and Wilber Marshall, backed up mainly by Harris and Ron Rivera. For the umpteenth time, free safety Gary Fencik led the secondary in tackles, and strong safety Dave Duerson held off the challenge of Todd Bell, a former Pro Bowler, who rejoined the club after a year out of football. It was good to see cornerback Mike Richardson shake off the label that he was a weak link and, equally, it was refreshing to see rookie Vestee Jackson move in to start. Richardson led the club with seven interceptions, one more than Duerson. Shaun Gayle, Maurice Douglass and Reggie Phillips are the reserves.

Special Teams

The Bears' kicking game is secure in the hands of placekicker Kevin Butler and punter Maury Buford.

1987 SCHEDULE OF GAMES	September	
	14 NEW YORK GIANTS (Mon.)	8:00
	20 TAMPA BAY	12:00
	27 at Detroit	1:00
	October	
	4 at Philadelphia	1:00
	11 MINNESOTA	12:00
	18 NEW ORLEANS	12:00
	25 at Tampa Bay	1:00
	November	
	1 KANSAS CITY	12:00
	8 at Green Bay	12:00
	16 at Denver (Mon.)	7:00
	22 DETROIT	12:00
	29 GREEN BAY	12:00
	December	
	6 at Minnesota	7:00
	14 at San Francisco (Mon.)	6:00
	20 SEATTLE	12:00
	27 at Los Angeles Raiders	1:00

Rookie Lew Barnes found a niche as a punt returner, averaging a solid 8.5 yards. Also, he chipped in with an 85-yard touchdown on a kickoff return. But pride of place went to Dennis Gentry, who led the NFL with a kickoff return average of 28.8 yards, including a 91-yard touchdown return.

1987 DRAFT

Round	Name	Pos.	Ht.	Wt.	College
1.	Harbaugh, Jim	QB	6-2	204	Michigan
2.	Morris, Ron	WR	6-1	190	Southern Methodist
4.	Smith, Sean	DE	6-4	268	Grambling State
5.	Bryan, Steve	DE	6-2	257	Oklahoma
5.	Johnson, Will	LB	6-4	222	Northeast Louisiana
6.	Adickes, John	C	6-2	270	Baylor
7.	Harris, Archie	T	6-5	267	William & Mary
8.	Migliazzo, Paul	LB	6-1	222	Oklahoma
9.	Heimuli, Lakei	RB	5-11	216	Brigham Young
10.	Chapura, Dick	DT	6-3	271	Missouri
11.	Jessie, Tim	WR-RB	5-11	197	Auburn
12.	Jeffries, Eric	CB	5-10	165	Texas

VETERAN ROSTER

No.	Name	Pos.	Ht.	Wt.	NFL Year	College
35	Anderson, Neal	RB	5-11	210	2	Florida
81	Barnes, Lew	WR	5-8	163	2	Oregon
79	Becker, Kurt	G	6-5	267	6	Michigan
25	Bell, Todd	S	6-1	205	6	Ohio State
68	Blair, Paul	T	6-4	295	2	Oklahoma State
62	Bortz, Mark	G	6-6	269	5	Iowa
8	Buford, Maury	P	6-1	191	6	Texas Tech
6	Butler, Kevin	K	6-1	195	3	Georgia
74	Covert, Jim	T	6-4	271	5	Pittsburgh
95	Dent, Richard	DE	6-5	263	5	Tennessee State
37	Douglass, Maurice	DB	5-11	200	2	Kentucky
22	Duerson, Dave	S	6-1	203	5	Notre Dame
45	Fencik, Gary	S	6-1	196	12	Yale
2	Flutie, Doug	QB	5-9	176	2	Boston College
21	Frazier, Leslie	CB	6-0	187	6	Alcorn State
4	Fuller, Steve	QB	6-4	195	9	Clemson
83	Gault, Willie	WR	6-1	183	5	Tennessee
23	Gayle, Shaun	CB	5-11	193	4	Ohio State
29	Gentry, Dennis	RB	5-8	181	6	Baylor
99	Hampton, Dan	DE-DT	6-5	267	9	Arkansas
90	Harris, Al	LB	6-5	253	8	Arizona State
73	Hartenstine, Mike	DE	6-3	254	13	Penn State
63	Hilgenberg, Jay	C	6-3	258	7	Iowa
75	Humphries, Stefan	G	6-3	268	4	Michigan
24	Jackson, Vestee	CB	6-0	186	2	Washington
88	Kozlowski, Glen	WR	6-1	193	1	Brigham Young
	Lush, Mike	S	6-2	195	2	East Stroudsburg State
58	Marshall, Wilber	LB	6-1	225	4	Florida
85	McKinnon, Dennis	WR	6-1	185	4	Florida State
9	McMahon, Jim	QB	6-1	190	6	Brigham Young
76	McMichael, Steve	DT	6-2	260	8	Texas
87	Moorehead, Emery	TE	6-2	220	11	Colorado
51	Morrissey, Jim	LB	6-3	215	3	Michigan State
89	Ortego, Keith	WR	6-0	180	3	McNeese State
34	Payton, Walter	RB	5-10	202	13	Jackson State
72	Perry, William	DT	6-2	325	3	Clemson
48	Phillips, Reggie	CB	5-10	170	3	Southern Methodist
53	Rains, Dan	LB	6-1	222	4	Cincinnati
27	Richardson, Mike	CB	6-0	188	5	Arizona State
59	Rivera, Ron	LB	6-3	239	4	California
52	Rubens, Larry	C	6-2	262	4	Montana State
20	Sanders, Thomas	RB	5-11	203	3	Texas A&M
50	Singletary, Mike	LB	6-0	228	7	Baylor
26	Suhey, Matt	FB	5-11	216	8	Penn State
57	Thayer, Tom	G	6-4	261	3	Notre Dame
33	Thomas, Calvin	FB	5-11	245	6	Illinois
18	Tomczak, Mike	QB	6-1	195	3	Ohio State
78	Van Horne, Keith	T	6-6	280	7	Southern California
70	Waechter, Henry	DT	6-5	275	6	Nebraska
82	Walton, Riley	TE	6-3	230	1	Tennessee State
55	Wilson, Otis	LB	6-2	232	8	Louisville
80	Wrightman, Tim	TE	6-3	237	3	UCLA

Jim McMahon could take the Bears to the Super Bowl.

DETROIT LIONS

NFC CENTRAL DIVISION

Address Pontiac Silverdome, 1200 Featherstone Road –
Box 4200, Pontiac, Michigan 48057.

Stadium Pontiac Silverdome.
Capacity 80,638 *Playing Surface* AstroTurf.

Team Colours Honolulu Blue and Silver.

Head Coach Darryl Rogers – third year.

Championships Division 1983; NFL 1935, '52, '53, '57.

History NFL 1930-69, NFC 1970-
(Until 1934, they were known as the Portsmouth (Ohio)
Spartans.)

Offense

Injuries to key players and a susceptibility to losing on big plays, broken plays and mistakes dropped the Lions to yet another net-losing season – they have had only five net-winning campaigns since the NFL was reorganised in 1970. It's not that they are woefully bad but, rather, that they can't seem to shake off the tag of being 'ordinary'. One always has the feeling that just a couple of impact players – perhaps even the lucky types who make those one-handed catches which bounce off a defender's helmet – would do the trick. By selecting defensive players with his first six draft options, head coach Rogers clearly indicated where his priorities lay, meaning that, in the absence of a major trade, the offense will be unchanged. It's an offense which does have its bright spots, and, in quarterback Chuck Long, limitless potential. Long, who was the twelfth player selected overall in the 1986 draft, signed for the Lions only three weeks before the regular season began and, not having the benefit of a training camp, it was late November before he played. Let's hope that it is a sign for the future that his first pass was for a 34-yard touchdown. It's probable that Long will be the starter, leaving veterans Joe Ferguson and Eric Hipple to battle for the backup spot. Detroit has one bona fide wide receiver in Jeff Chadwick, who seemed set to gain 1,000 yards receiving in a season for the first time in his four-year career. However, he missed the last two games with injury and was left marooned on 995. He'll be back, probably with Carl Bland as his starting partner and Leonard Thompson as the senior reserve. The passing offense was given a lift by the arrival of former Pro Bowl tight end Jimmie Giles who, surprisingly, had been waived by Tampa Bay. The rushing offense is workmanlike and reliable. As expected, rookie Garry James added his acceleration and sparkle to the known power of James Jones, the latter also who led the club with 54 pass receptions. It's an interesting combination which could develop. The offensive line is a Detroit strength, with all of tackles Lomas Brown and Rich Strenger, guards Harvey Salem and Keith Dorney, and center Steve Mott well respected around the league. Salem, who is a former second-round draft pick, came via a trade with Houston and fitted in smoothly to cushion the loss of injured starter Chris Dieterich.

Defense

It has been a similar story on defense, where there are many competent players throughout the unit and no obvious weakness. The good times may be just around the corner if first-round draftee defensive end Reggie Rogers can reproduce the form he showed at the University of Washington. A remarkably versatile athlete, he must surely add fire to the pass rush, which wasn't that bad anyway but which now may make the difference in those close games. Veteran defensive end Keith Ferguson was outstanding, leading the club with 9.5 quarterback sacks, and nose tackle Eric Williams has settled down nicely. The other defensive end, Bill Gay, is a fierce competitor and a former starter, Curtis Green, backs up in all three positions. The starting linebackers should be Mike Cofer and Jimmy Williams on the outsides, with Shelton Robinson and James Harrell on the insides. Williams is the driving force, and his unavailability through injury for much of last year was a blow. His return will release Vernon Maxwell for his best role as a specialist pass rusher. After struggling as an undersized defensive end for much of his career, Cofer has found a home as a very quick outside linebacker who is equally comfortable rushing the passer and dropping back into pass coverage. The secondary was disturbed by an injury to starting left cornerback Bobby Watkins, but first-year man Duane Galloway stepped in and held his position throughout the season. It was widely felt that draftee Devon Mitchell was a bargain fourth-round draft selection, and he showed it by moving up to start at free safety with all the assurance of a seasoned veteran. Mitchell led the club with five interceptions, one more than Galloway and right cornerback Bruce McNorton. Strong safety Demetrious Johnson is entering his third campaign as a starter.

Special Teams

The Lions have good special teams. Eddie Murray is one

1987 SCHEDULE OF GAMES		
September		
13 at Minnesota		12:00
20 at Los Angeles Raiders		1:00
27 CHICAGO		1:00
October		
4 TAMPA BAY		1:00
11 at Green Bay		12:00
18 SEATTLE		1:00
25 GREEN BAY		1:00
November		
1 at Denver		2:00
8 DALLAS		1:00
15 at Washington		1:00
22 at Chicago		12:00
26 KANSAS CITY (Thanksgiving)		12:30
December		
6 LOS ANGELES RAMS		1:00
13 at Tampa Bay		4:00
20 MINNESOTA		1:00
27 at Atlanta		1:00

of the NFL's top placekickers and new punter Jim Arnold found the Silverdome to his liking as he averaged a good 42.6 gross yards. Pete Mandley ranked third in the NFC returning the punts, and while Herman Hunter's kickoff return average was a modest 20.6 yards, he tied for the NFL lead with 1,007 return yards.

1987 DRAFT

Round	Name	Pos.	Ht.	Wt.	College
1.	Rogers, Reggie	DE	6-5	268	Washington
3.	Ball, Jerry	NT	6-0	280	Southern Methodist
4.	Rivers, Garland	S	6-0	185	Michigan
6.	Lockett, Danny	LB	6-2	224	Arizona
7.	Saleaumua, Dan	DT	6-1	308	Arizona State
8.	Gibson, Dennis	LB	6-2	230	Iowa State
9.	Calhoun, Rick	RB	5-7	188	Cal State-Fullerton
10.	Brown, Raynard	WR-RB	5-9	185	South Carolina
11.	Siverling, Brian	TE	6-6	246	Penn State
12.	Lee, Gary	WR	6-1	191	Georgia Tech

VETERAN ROSTER

No.	Name	Pos.	Ht.	Wt.	NFL Year	College
6	Arnold, Jim	P	6-3	211	5	Vanderbilt
68	Baack, Steve	NT-G	6-4	265	4	Oregon
61	Barrows, Scott	G-T	6-2	278	2	West Virginia
80	Bland, Carl	WR	5-11	182	4	Virginia Union
42	Bostic, John	CB	5-10	178	3	Bethune-Cookman
23	Brown, Arnold	CB	5-10	185	2	No. Carolina Central
75	Brown, Lomas	T	6-4	282	3	Florida
96	Butcher, Paul	LB	6-0	219	2	Wayne State
89	Chadwick, Jeff	WR	6-3	190	5	Grand Valley State
55	Cofer, Mike	LB	6-5	245	5	Tennessee
50	Curley, August	LB	6-3	235	5	Southern California
72	Dieterich, Chris	G-T	6-3	275	8	North Carolina State
70	Dorney, Keith	G-T	6-5	285	9	Penn State
37	Elder, Donnie	CB	5-9	175	3	Memphis State
66	Evans, Leon	DE	6-5	282	3	Miami
12	Ferguson, Joe	QB	6-1	195	15	Arkansas
77	Ferguson, Keith	DE	6-5	260	7	Ohio State
40	Galloway, Duane	CB-S	5-8	181	2	Arizona State
79	Gay, William	DE	6-5	260	10	Southern California
81	Giles, Jimmie	TE	6-3	240	11	Alcorn State
53	Glover, Kevin	C-G	6-2	267	3	Maryland
33	Graham, William	S	5-11	191	6	Texas
62	Green, Curtis	DE-NT	6-3	265	7	Alabama State
34	Griffin, James	S	6-2	197	5	Middle Tennessee St.
58	Harrell, James	LB	6-1	230	8	Florida
47	Hill, Rod	CB	6-0	188	5	Kentucky State
17	Hipple, Eric	QB	6-2	198	8	Utah State
36	Hunter, Herman	RB-KR	6-1	193	3	Tennessee State
32	James, Garry	RB	5-10	214	2	Louisiana State
	Jamison, George	LB	6-1	230	1	Cincinnati
21	Johnson, Demetrious	S	5-11	190	5	Missouri
54	Johnson, James	LB	6-2	236	2	San Diego State
30	Jones, James	RB	6-2	229	5	Florida
	Kearse, Tim	WR	5-11	192	1	San Jose State
63	Kenney, Steve	G·	6-4	262	8	Clemson
92	King, Angelo	LB	6-1	222	7	South Carolina State
87	Lewis, David	TE	6-3	235	4	California
16	Long, Chuck	QB	6-4	211	2	Iowa
82	Mandley, Pete	WR-KR	5-10	191	4	Northern Arizona
57	Maxwell, Vernon	LB	6-2	235	5	Arizona State
29	McNorton, Bruce	CB	5-11	175	6	Georgetown, Kentucky
74	Milinichik, Joe	T	6-5	300	1	North Carolina State
31	Mitchell, Devon	S	6-1	194	2	Iowa
24	Moore, Alvin	RB	6-0	194	5	Arizona State
52	Mott, Steve	C	6-3	270	5	Alabama
3	Murray, Ed	K	5-10	175	8	Tulane
86	Nichols, Mark	WR	6-2	208	6	San Jose State
51	Robinson, Shelton	LB	6-2	236	6	North Carolina
84	Rubick, Rob	TE	6-3	234	6	Grand Valley State
64	Sanders, Eric	T	6-7	280	7	Nevada-Reno
25	Smith, Oscar	RB	5-9	203	2	Nicholls State
71	Strenger, Rich	T	6-7	285	4	Michigan
39	Thompson, Leonard	WR	5-11	192	13	Oklahoma State
27	Watkins, Bobby	CB	5-10	184	6	Southwest Texas State
76	Williams, Eric	NT	6-4	280	4	Washington State
59	Williams, Jimmy	LB	6-3	230	6	Nebraska
38	Williams, Scott	FB	6-2	234	2	Georgia

Chuck Long and the Lions are aiming high.

MINNESOTA VIKINGS

NFC CENTRAL DIVISION

Address 9520 Viking Drive, Eden Prairie, Minnesota 55344.
Stadium Hubert H. Humphrey Metrodome, Minneapolis.
  Capacity 62,345 *Playing Surface* Super Turf.
Team Colours Purple, Gold, and White.
Head Coach Jerry Burns – second year.
Championships Division 1970,'71,'73,'74,'75,'76,'77,'78,'80;
  Conference 1973,'74,'76; NFL 1969.
History NFL 1961-69, NFC 1970-

Offense

The six full seasons which have gone by since the Vikings last won the NFC Central division title have seen a major reconstruction. And while no one is suggesting that they will unseat the Bears, they enter 1987 with the distinct prospect of securing a playoff spot. Victories in the final two games against Houston and New Orleans could have been enough last year, but they lost to Houston. Earlier, they'd traded wins with the Bears, and, against the Giants, they lost to a last-second field goal which came after Phil Simms had completed a 21-yard pass on fourth-and-17. The grounds for optimism start with an offensive line which, though not great, is very solid. Both left guard Jim Hough and center Dennis Swilley are seasoned nine-year veterans while, on the right side, guard Terry Tausch and tackle Tim Irwin have been in the league five and six years respectively. Former USFL star Gary Zimmerman was a major acquisition for that most vital of line positions, left tackle. He played with the authority of an all-pro. Quarterback Tommy Kramer enjoyed the best campaign of his ten-year career, winning the league passing title. He's a player of courage and talent who has overcome major disappointments. Reassuringly, in Wade Wilson, the club has a fine backup. Wilson stood in when Kramer was injured and won games against Tampa Bay and New Orleans, in those two outings passing for a total of 700 yards and six touchdowns without an interception. The excellence of wide receiver Anthony Carter we can take for granted, and Leo Lewis must now be feared after producing figures of similar dimensions, most notably in yards receiving (600) and average per reception (18.8). On slightly fewer pass receptions, rookie Hassan Jones showed himself to be the club's finest deep threat (28 catches at an average of 20.4 yards), and he could well move up to start. It was in the Vikings' tradition that running back Darrin Nelson caught 53 passes, coming second in the club, but the form of tight end Steve Jordan was one of the major shocks of the year. 58 receptions at an average of 14.8 yards, and six touchdowns, was a haul which earned his first Pro Bowl selection, and he must now be taken very seriously. In the search for power at running back, the Vikings drafted D.J. Dozier in the first round. Each of last year's starters, Nelson and fullback Alfred Anderson, averaged a fine 4.2 yards per carry. Ted Brown and Allen Rice would rank amongst the NFL's better backups.

Defense

From appearing not much more than a collection of solid pros, the Vikings defense can now point to a growing number of impact players spread throughout the unit. The starting four-man line features three former first-round draftees in defensive ends Doug Martin and Chris Doleman, and defensive tackle Keith Millard. Tim Newton, who starts at defensive left tackle, was the Vikings' equivalent of 'The Refrigerator' but, wisely, he has trimmed down to 287 pounds. On its day, this line is as good as any in the league. And there is ample depth, with last year's first-round draftee, Gerald Robinson, at defensive end, while Joe Phillips and Mike Stensrud are the backups at defensive tackle. The starting linebackers, Chris Martin, Scott Studwell and David Howard, are primarily run-stuffers. Scott Studwell is the most experienced and, for only the first time in the last seven seasons, he failed to lead the club in tackles (he came second). Martin is unchallenged for the left-side position and Howard, who played in the USFL, was an excellent acquisition in the 1984 supplemental draft. Former Seattle player John Harris was acquired in a trade to fill a vacancy at free safety and he did a fine job, coming fourth in tackles and intercepting three passes. Four-year veteran Joey Browner has been selected to the last two Pro Bowls, first as a special-teamer and then in his own right as a safety. Both Browner and cornerback Issiac Holt are ferocious competitors. Holt's daring brought him the club lead with eight interceptions but his very enthusiasm led to his undoing when, on occasion, he was beaten badly. The other starter is the reliable Carl Lee, who matched Harris in interceptions. Rufus Bess and Willie Teal are the most experienced backups.

Special Teams

Placekicker Chuck Nelson has found a home after being cut by both the Rams and Buffalo. He's a reliable kicker with a strong leg and plenty of nerve. Punter Greg

1987 SCHEDULE OF GAMES		
September		
13 DETROIT		12:00
20 at Los Angeles Rams		1:00
27 at Kansas City		12:00
October		
4 GREEN BAY		12:00
11 at Chicago		12:00
18 TAMPA BAY		12:00
25 DENVER		12:00
November		
1 at Seattle		1:00
8 LOS ANGELES RAIDERS		12:00
15 at Tampa Bay		1:00
22 ATLANTA		12:00
26 at Dallas (Thanksgiving)		3:00
December		
6 CHICAGO		7:00
13 vs. Green Bay at Milwaukee		12:00
20 at Detroit		1:00
26 WASHINGTON (Sat.)		3:00

Coleman is a solid veteran of nine years with the Vikings. Rufus Bess is the senior punt returner and will continue to share the kickoffs with Buster Rhymes, the latter who spent much of 1986 on injured reserve.

1987 DRAFT

Round	Name	Pos.	Ht.	Wt.	College
1.	Dozier, D.J.	RB	6-0	204	Penn State
2.	Berry, Ray	LB	6-2	225	Baylor
3.	Thomas, Henry	DT	6-2	260	Louisiana State
4.	Rutland, Reginald	S	6-2	195	Georgia Tech
6.	Richardson, Greg	WR-KR	5-7	168	Alabama
8.	Fenney, Rick	RB	6-2	244	Washington
9.	Jones, Leonard	S	6-1	185	Texas Tech
10.	Riley, Bob	T	6-5	274	Indiana
11.	Pease, Brent	QB	6-3	203	Montana
12.	Williams, Keith	DT	6-4	255	Florida

VETERAN ROSTER

No.	Name	Pos.	Ht.	Wt.	NFL Year	College
46	Anderson, Alfred	RB	6-1	220	4	Baylor
58	Ashley, Walker Lee	LB	6-0	237	4	Penn State
21	Bess, Rufus	CB	5-9	189	9	South Carolina State
62	Boyd, Brent	G	6-3	280	7	UCLA
23	Brown, Ted	RB	5-10	212	9	North Carolina State
47	Browner, Joey	S	6-2	212	5	Southern California
81	Carter, Anthony	WR	5-11	175	3	Michigan
8	Coleman, Greg	P	6-0	184	11	Florida A&M
56	Doleman, Chris	LB	6-5	250	3	Pittsburgh
26	Evans, David	CB	6-0	178	2	Central Arkansas
	Freeman, Steve	S	5-11	185	13	Mississippi State
41	Guggemos, Neal	S	6-0	187	2	St Thomas
80	Gustafson, Jim	WR	6-1	181	2	St Thomas
44	Harris, John	S	6-2	198	10	Arizona State
82	Hilton, Carl	TE	6-3	232	2	Houston
30	Holt, Issiac	CB	6-1	200	3	Alcorn State
51	Hough, Jim	C-G	6-2	269	10	Utah State
99	Howard, David	LB	6-2	232	3	Long Beach State
72	Huffman, David	T	6-6	284	8	Notre Dame
76	Irwin, Tim	T	6-7	288	7	Tennessee
84	Jones, Hassan	WR	6-0	195	2	Florida State
83	Jordan, Steve	TE	6-3	239	6	Brown
9	Kramer, Tommy	QB	6-2	205	11	Rice
39	Lee, Carl	CB	5-11	187	5	Marshall
87	Lewis, Leo	WR	5-8	170	7	Missouri
63	Lowdermilk, Kirk	C	6-3	269	3	Ohio State
71	MacDonald, Mark	G	6-4	267	3	Boston College
57	Martin, Chris	LB	6-2	239	5	Auburn
79	Martin, Doug	DE	6-3	264	8	Washington
75	Millard, Keith	DT	6-6	262	3	Washington State
86	Mularkey, Mike	TE	6-4	234	5	Florida
77	Mullaney, Mark	DE	6-6	248	13	Colorado State
1	Nelson, Chuck	K	5-11	172	4	Washington
20	Nelson, Darrin	RB	5-9	189	6	Stanford
96	Newton, Tim	DT	6-0	287	3	Florida
91	Phillips, Joe	DT	6-4	278	2	Southern Methodist
88	Rhymes, Buster	WR	6-1	218	3	Oklahoma
36	Rice, Allen	RB	5-10	204	4	Baylor
95	Robinson, Gerald	DE	6-3	256	2	Auburn
68	Rouse, Curtis	G	6-3	335	6	Tennessee-Chattanooga
78	Schippang, Gary	T	6-4	279	2	West Chester
53	Schuh, Jeff	LB	6-3	234	7	Minnesota
54	Solomon, Jesse	LB	6-0	235	2	Florida State
74	Stensrud, Mike	DT	6-5	280	9	Iowa State
55	Studwell, Scott	LB	6-2	230	11	Illinois
67	Swilley, Dennis	C	6-3	266	10	Texas A&M
66	Tausch, Terry	G	6-5	276	6	Texas
37	Teal, Willie	CB	5-10	192	8	Louisiana State
11	Wilson, Wade	QB	6-3	213	7	East Texas State
65	Zimmerman, Gary	T	6-6	277	2	Oregon

Anthony Carter.

ATLANTA FALCONS

Address Suwanee Road at I-85, Suwanee, Georgia 30174.
Stadium Atlanta-Fulton County Stadium.
Capacity 60,748 *Playing Surface* Grass.
Team Colours Red, Black, White, and Silver.
Head Coach Marion Campbell – first year.
Championships Division 1980.
History NFL 1966-69, NFC 1970-

Offense

For the first four weeks of the 1986 campaign, the Falcons were the hottest team in the NFC West, but a mid-season slump after they had battled to a 10-10 tie with the 49ers put paid to their playoff hopes. Just a little more firepower on offense could have done the trick in three close losses and we'd all have been talking about the new kid on the block. Earlier in the year, at draft time, the decision had been made to use both first-round options to boost the defense, and it was only in the sixth round that the Falcons had their next pick. However, in the 1987 draft it was the turn of the offense, for which quarterback Chris Miller, running back Kenny Flowers and tackle Ralph Van Dyke were selected with the Falcons' first three options. Coming into the season, the probable starting offensive line will have Mike Kenn and Brett Miller at tackle, John Scully and Bill Fralic at guard, and Wayne Radloff at center. Kenn has been selected to five Pro Bowls and one has the feeling that had it not been for an injury on Week Eleven of the 1985 season, his streak might still be alive. He's a super player who only rarely is called for holding. Fralic has become the blue-chipper which everyone expected and has just celebrated the first of what should be many All-Pro and Pro Bowl selections. Radloff eased in as the starter ahead of the respected Jeff Van Note, who has subsequently retired. New head coach Marion Campbell is thinking of changing from the one- to a more orthodox two-back offense, and in Flowers he has obtained a player with the speed to match the power of the indestructible Gerald Riggs, the latter who rushed for over 1,000 yards for the third year in a row. The arrival of Flowers has secured the future for a rushing offense which, though having Cliff Austin and the former great William Andrews in reserve, would look a little thin were Riggs to be injured. Charlie Brown has brought poise and speed to the wide receiving corps, and sixth-round draftee Floyd Dixon proved to be an inspired selection as he caught 42 passes for 617 yards. Injuries meant that Stacey Bailey would not be a factor but he will make a bid to start in the coming season. Billy 'White Shoes' Johnson, also who was injured, may just be back for a cameo performance. If the Falcons do adopt the two-back system, Arthur Cox, who has the edge on Ken Whisenhunt both catching passes and as a blocker, would be the senior tight end. Miller joins Turk Schonert, Scott Campbell and the incumbent, Dave Archer, in the competition to start at quarterback.

Defense

With Marion Campbell as defensive coordinator, the defense made a dramatic improvement in 1986. It doesn't yet look frightening but it certainly looks tough. They do need to improve their pass rushing, a skill which first-round draftee Tony Casillas has not yet mastered and led to his replacement on obvious passing downs by Mike Pitts. The leading sackers were starting defensive ends Rick Bryan (7), who played on despite a cracked bone in his leg, Mike Gann (5.5) and reserve Pitts (5.5). In fairness, the Falcons don't place a great emphasis on the pass rush, and they don't often blitz. It was a disappointing season for the Falcons' second pick in the first round, linebacker Tim Green, who injured a calf muscle in training camp and didn't make his first start until the final game of the season. The starters for almost the entire campaign were Reggie Wilkes and Joel Williams on the outsides, with the pairing of Buddy Curry and John Rade on the inside. Curry had 157 tackles to lead the club for the seventh year in a row. It is a steady unit and it is not clear how Green is going to fit in. His best spot is at inside linebacker but he could hardly displace either of the starters. In the secondary, Scott Case was superb at right cornerback after playing two years at safety. The opposition challenged him until it dawned on them that here was an outstanding player. The other starting cornerback, Bobby Butler, was restricted to seven games because of injury. First-year safety Bret Clark proved to be a good acquisition from the Raiders, as he led the team with five interceptions, and rookie safety Robert Moore came through to start nine games.

Special Teams

Placekicker Mick Luckhurst saw his season end with injury after ten games, and he faces competition in training camp from Ali Haji-Sheikh, who did little wrong after taking over. Punter Rick Donnelly averaged an excellent 43.9 yards to rank fourth in the league. By contrast, the kick-return specialists were no better than par, though,

1987 SCHEDULE OF GAMES	September	
	13 at Tampa Bay	1:00
	20 WASHINGTON	1:00
	27 at New Orleans	12:00
	October	
	4 PITTSBURGH	1:00
	11 at San Francisco	1:00
	18 LOS ANGELES RAMS	1:00
	25 at Houston	12:00
	November	
	1 NEW ORLEANS	1:00
	8 at Cleveland	1:00
	15 CINCINNATI	4:00
	22 at Minnesota	12:00
	29 ST LOUIS	1:00
	December	
	6 at Dallas	12:00
	13 at Los Angeles Rams	1:00
	20 SAN FRANCISCO	1:00
	27 DETROIT	1:00

'White Shoes' showed some of his old speed and elusiveness, returning eight punts for 87 yards.

1987 DRAFT

Round	Name	Pos.	Ht.	Wt.	College
1.	Miller, Chris	QB	6-1	190	Oregon
2.	Flowers, Kenny	RB	6-0	210	Clemson
4.	Van Dyke, Ralph	T	6-5	265	Southern Illinois
5.	Mraz, Mark	DE	6-3	255	Utah State
6.	Kiser, Paul	G	6-3	278	Wake Forest
7.	Reid, Michael	LB	6-1	217	Wisconsin
8.	Taliaferro, Curtis	LB	6-2	223	Virginia Tech
9.	Anthony, Terrence	CB	5-10	186	Iowa State
10.	Reese, Jerry	TE	6-1	220	Illinois
11.	Shelley, Elbert	S	5-11	180	Arkansas State
12.	Emery, Larry	RB	5-9	190	Wisconsin

VETERAN ROSTER

No.	Name	Pos.	Ht.	Wt.	NFL Year	College
85	Allen, Anthony	WR	5-11	182	3	Washington
31	Andrews, William	RB	6-0	220	7	Auburn
16	Archer, Dave	QB	6-2	208	4	Iowa State
39	Austin, Cliff	RB	6-1	213	5	Clemson
82	Bailey, Stacey	WR	6-0	157	6	San Jose State
26	Britt, James	CB	6-0	185	4	Louisiana State
52	Brown, Aaron	LB	6-2	238	5	Ohio State
89	Brown, Charlie	WR	5-10	184	6	South Carolina State
77	Bryan, Rick	DE	6-4	265	4	Oklahoma
23	Butler, Bobby	CB	5-11	182	7	Florida State
10	Campbell, Scott	QB	6-0	195	4	Purdue
25	Case, Scott	CB	6-0	178	4	Oklahoma
75	Casillas, Tony	NT	6-3	280	2	Oklahoma
20	Cason, Wendell	CB	5-11	197	3	Oregon
28	Clark, Bret	S	6-3	198	2	Nebraska
56	Costello, Joe	LB	6-3	250	2	Central Connecticut
88	Cox, Arthur	TE	6-2	262	5	Texas Southern
30	Croudip, David	CB	5-8	185	4	San Diego State
50	Curry, Buddy	LB	6-4	222	8	North Carolina
86	Dixon, Floyd	WR	5-9	170	2	Stephen F. Austin
3	Donnelly, Rick	P	6-0	190	3	Wyoming
73	Dukes, Jamie	G	6-1	270	2	Florida State
79	Fralic, Bill	G-T	6-5	280	3	Pittsburgh
76	Gann, Mike	DE	6-5	265	3	Notre Dame
99	Green, Tim	LB	6-2	249	2	Syracuse
6	Haji-Sheikh, Ali	K	6-0	172	5	Michigan
68	Harrison, Dennis	DE	6-8	280	10	Vanderbilt
66	Hinson, Billy	G	6-1	278	1	Florida
71	Howe, Glen	T	6-7	298	3	Southern Mississippi
81	Johnson, Billy	WR	5-9	170	12	Widener
84	Jones, Joey	WR	5-8	165	2	Alabama
78	Kenn, Mike	T	6-7	277	10	Michigan
63	Kiewel, Jeff	G	6-3	277	2	Arizona
80	Landrum, Mike	TE	6-2	231	2	Southern Mississippi
18	Luckhurst, Mick	K	6-1	178	7	California
83	Matthews, Aubrey	WR	5-7	165	2	Delta State
87	Middleton, Ron	TE	6-2	252	2	Auburn
62	Miller, Brett	T	6-7	300	5	Iowa
34	Moore, Robert	S	5-11	190	2	N.W. State, Louisiana
64	Pellegrini, Joe	G-C	6-4	265	6	Harvard
74	Pitts, Mike	DE	6-5	277	5	Alabama
72	Provence, Andrew	DE	6-3	267	5	South Carolina
59	Rade, John	LB	6-1	240	5	Boise State
55	Radloff, Wayne	C	6-5	277	3	Georgia
42	Riggs, Gerald	RB	6-1	232	6	Arizona State
14	Schonert, Turk	QB	6-1	196	8	Stanford
61	Scully, John	G	6-6	270	7	Notre Dame
97	Sharp, Dan	TE	6-2	235	1	Texas Christian
29	Stamps, Sylvester	RB	5-7	175	3	Jackson State
21	Turner, Jimmy	CB	6-0	187	5	UCLA
45	Whisenhunt, Ken	TE	6-2	233	3	Georgia Tech
51	Wilkes, Reggie	LB	6-4	242	10	Georgia Tech
54	Williams, Joel	LB	6-1	227	9	Wisconsin-La Crosse
35	Williams, Keith	WR-RB	5-10	173	2	Southwest Missouri
22	Woodberry, Dennis	CB	5-10	183	2	Southern Arkansas

Bill Fralic guards while Turk Schonert picks a target.

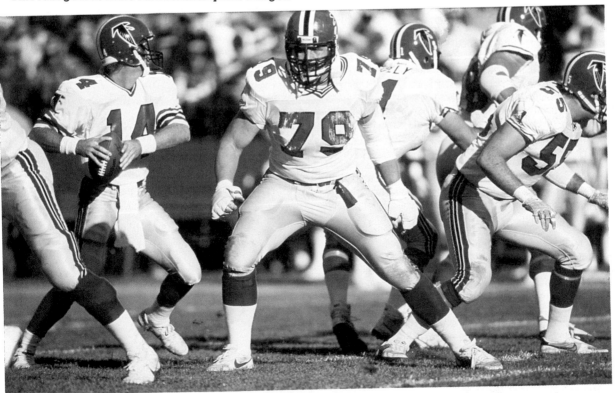

LOS ANGELES RAMS

NFC WESTERN DIVISION

Address 2327 West Lincoln Avenue, Anaheim, California 92801.

Stadium Anaheim Stadium, Anaheim.
Capacity 69,007 *Playing Surface* Grass.

Team Colours Royal Blue, Gold, and White.

Head Coach John Robinson – fifth year.

Championships Division 1973,'74,'75,'76,'77,'78,'79,'85; Conference 1979; NFL 1945,'51.

History NFL 1937-69, NFC 1970-
(Until 1946, they were known as the Cleveland Rams.)

Offense

It is a pro football axiom that the Rams always are tough, and in support of this assertion one can point to eight NFC Western division titles, seven of which were in consecutive years (1973-79), and a further four trips to the playoffs as a wild card, all coming in the seventeen years since the NFL was reorganised. And even allowing for the flood of optimism which always comes when one considers this well-run club, it's difficult not to conclude that the squad which enters the 1987 season may be their best in recent memory. A great deal depends upon the development of second-year quarterback Jim Everett, for whose rights the Rams paid a high price to Houston. On his debut, albeit in a losing cause, he was spectacularly successful, completing 12 of 19 passes for 193 yards and three touchdowns, without an interception. He came down from the clouds the following week against New Orleans, when he could manage only seven completions for 56 yards, no touchdowns and was intercepted twice, but there is no doubting his class. In the coming season, the Rams need no more than a steady performance from him, just enough to provide an alternative to the rushing game. The starting wide receivers will be Henry Ellard and, probably, Kevin House, the latter who could be the long-ball target with Ellard adopting the role of possession receiver. Ron Brown and Michael Young are the backups. The senior tight end, David Hill, has a safe pair of hands, but he is used more for his blocking than his pass receiving. Everyone knows that Eric Dickerson will be given the ball on seven out of ten rushing plays, and it is equally certain that he will average somewhere between 4.5 and five yards per carry. He'll probably win the league rushing title. It is easy to overlook the fact that, behind Dickerson, there are players such as Barry Redden and Charles White who, in the appropriate circumstances, could be 1,000-yard rushers. Providing the platform for the assault, the Rams' offensive line is very powerful and on a par with those units in Chicago, Miami, San Francisco and Washington. Second-round draftee Tom Newberry slipped easily into the place vacated by the departed Kent Hill (he was traded to Houston as part of the Everett deal), inbetween left tackle Irv Pankey and center Doug Smith. Guard Dennis Harrah and tackle Jackie Slater are the other starters. Collectively, Smith, Harrah and Slater have been selected to the Pro Bowl eleven times. Tony Slaton is a first-class backup at both guard and center while Duval Love is the senior reserve at tackle.

Defense

In 1986, the Rams' defense ranked fifth in the NFL and, importantly, it was well balanced. By using a bewildering variety of rapid personnel changes, the club has made its contribution to the strategic novelties of a widespread modern philosophy which has placed emphasis on what might be called 'special-situation substitution'. As an option to their normal first-down alignment, which is an orthodox 3-4-4 arrangement, they use their own brand of 'nickel' defense, in which Vince Newsome is the linchpin. Jerry Gray becomes the 'slot' man, marking the third wide receiver, while Johnnie Johnson comes in for Gray as the orthodox left cornerback. Nolan Cromwell shifts from strong safety to free safety, the position vacated by Newsome, with a new face coming in at strong safety (it was former Pro Bowler Tim Fox, but he has been released). LeRoy Irvin remains at right cornerback. Of the starting linebackers, only Mike Wilcher stays on the field. The other three orthodox starters, Mel Owens, Jim Collins and Carl Ekern, watch from the sideline. Up front, Reggie Doss leaves the field as Kevin Greene and Gary Jeter come on to join Shawn Miller and Doug Reed. Collins and Cromwell are former Pro Bowlers, while Ekern, Gray and Irvin currently enjoy that status. It is a squad littered with impact players. Any one of the front-line pass rushers can have a big day, and the secondary always seems to come up with more than its share of big interception returns, as last year when Cromwell went 80 yards for a touchdown, Irvin rambled 50 yards to score, and even inside linebacker Mark Jerue scored on a 22-yard return. Collins, Steve Busick and Charles DeJurnett ended the season on injured reserve, but all three are expected to be ready for the 1987 season.

1987 SCHEDULE OF GAMES	September	
	13 at Houston	12:00
	20 MINNESOTA	1:00
	27 CINCINNATI	1:00
	October	
	4 at New Orleans	12:00
	11 PITTSBURGH	1:00
	18 at Atlanta	1:00
	26 at Cleveland (Mon.)	9:00
	November	
	1 SAN FRANCISCO	1:00
	8 NEW ORLEANS	1:00
	15 at St Louis	12:00
	23 at Washington (Mon.)	9:00
	29 TAMPA BAY	1:00
	December	
	6 at Detroit	1:00
	13 ATLANTA	1:00
	21 DALLAS (Mon.)	6:00
	27 at San Francisco	5:00

Special Teams

1986 was not a good year for the Rams' special teams. Punter Dale Hatcher was down on his excellent 1985 showing, placekicker Mike Lansford was no better than steady, while Ron Brown might have been expected to average better than 22.1 yards returning kickoffs. However, punt returners Mickey Sutton and Ellard combined for a good 8.6-yard average.

1987 DRAFT

Round	Name	Pos.	Ht.	Wt.	College
2.	Evans, Donald	DE	6-2	256	Winston-Salem State
3.	Hicks, Clifford	CB	5-9	187	Oregon
4.	Bartlett, Doug	NT	6-2	252	Northern Illinois
4.	Kelm, Larry	LB	6-3	223	Texas A&M
5.	Mersereau, Scott	NT	6-2	265	Southern Connecticut
6.	Embree, Jon	TE	6-2	227	Colorado
8.	Stewart, Michael	S	5-10	190	Fresno State
9.	Ham, Tracy	RB	5-10	185	Georgia Southern
10.	Smith, David	LB	6-5	220	Northern Arizona
12.	Williams, Alonzo	RB	5-10	185	Mesa, Colorado
12.	Stokes, Fred	DE	6-2	243	Georgia Southern

VETERAN ROSTER

No.	Name	Pos.	Ht.	Wt.	NFL Year	College
89	Brown, Ron	WR	5-11	181	4	Arizona State
53	Busick, Steve	LB	6-4	227	7	Southern California
50	Collins, Jim	LB	6-2	235	6	Syracuse
64	Cox, Robert	T	6-5	260	1	UCLA
21	Cromwell, Nolan	S	6-1	200	11	Kansas
70	DeJurnett, Charles	NT	6-4	260	11	San Jose State
29	Dickerson, Eric	RB	6-3	218	5	Southern Methodist
8	Dils, Steve	QB	6-1	191	8	Stanford
71	Doss, Reggie	DE	6-4	263	10	Hampton Institute
55	Ekern, Carl	LB	6-3	230	11	San Jose State
80	Ellard, Henry	WR	5-11	175	5	Fresno State
11	Everett, Jim	QB	6-5	212	2	Purdue
63	Goebel, Hank	T	6-7	270	1	Cal State-Fullerton
25	Gray, Jerry	CB	6-0	185	3	Texas
91	Greene, Kevin	LB	6-3	238	3	Auburn
44	Guman, Mike	RB	6-2	218	8	Penn State
60	Harrah, Dennis	G	6-5	265	13	Miami
3	Hatcher, Dale	P	6-2	200	3	Clemson
81	Hill, David	TE	6-2	240	12	Texas A&I
83	House, Kevin	WR	6-1	185	8	Southern Illinois
87	Hunter, Tony	TE	6-4	237	5	Notre Dame
47	Irvin, LeRoy	CB	5-11	184	8	Kansas
59	Jerue, Mark	LB	6-3	232	5	Washington
77	Jeter, Gary	DE	6-4	260	11	Southern California
86	Johnson, Damone	TE	6-4	230	2	Cal Poly-SLO
20	Johnson, Johnnie	S	6-1	183	8	Texas
1	Lansford, Mike	K	6-0	183	6	Washington
57	Laughlin, Jim	LB	6-1	222	8	Ohio State
45	Long, Darren	TE	6-3	240	2	Long Beach State
67	Love, Duval	G	6-3	263	3	UCLA
90	McDonald, Mike	LB	6-1	230	4	Southern California
69	Meisner, Greg	NT	6-3	253	7	Pittsburgh
12	Millen, Hugh	QB	6-5	215	1	Washington
98	Miller, Shawn	NT	6-4	255	4	Utah State
66	Newberry, Tom	G	6-2	279	2	Wisconsin-La Crosse
22	Newsome, Vince	S	6-1	179	5	Washington
58	Owens, Mel	LB	6-2	224	7	Michigan
75	Pankey, Irv	T	6-4	267	7	Penn State
30	Redden, Barry	RB	5-10	205	6	Richmond
93	Reed, Doug	DE	6-3	262	4	San Diego State
76	Schad, Mike	T	6-5	290	1	Queen's, Canada
	Schamel, Duke	LB	6-2	220	1	South Dakota
84	Scott, Chuck	WR	6-2	202	2	Vanderbilt
78	Slater, Jackie	T	6-4	271	12	Jackson State
61	Slaton, Tony	C	6-4	265	4	Southern California
56	Smith, Doug	C	6-3	253	10	Bowling Green
49	Sutton, Mickey	CB	5-8	165	2	Montana
52	Thrift, Cliff	LB	6-2	235	9	East Central, Oklahoma
32	Tyrrell, Tim	RB	6-1	201	4	Northern Illinois
51	Vann, Norwood	LB	6-1	225	4	East Carolina
33	White, Charles	RB	5-10	190	7	Southern California
54	Wilcher, Mike	LB	6-2	235	5	North Carolina
99	Wright, Alvin	NT	6-2	285	2	Jacksonville State
88	Young, Michael	WR	6-1	185	3	UCLA

Wide receiver Henry Ellard is a key player in the Rams' receiving corps.

NEW ORLEANS SAINTS

Address 1500 Poydras Street, New Orleans, Louisiana 70112.

Stadium Louisiana Superdome, New Orleans. *Capacity* 69,723 *Playing Surface* AstroTurf.

Team Colours Old Gold, Black, and White.

Head Coach Jim Mora – second year.

Championships None.

History NFL 1967-69, NFC 1970-

Offense

Jim Mora's first term at the helm should be seen as a year of organising his resources, installing new players and tailoring the system to his liking in preparation for the big push in 1987. It would be ridiculous to suggest that he wasn't looking for a winning season last year, but it's probably true that he was satisfied with what he got. One benefit from Mora's USFL experience was that he had good knowledge of that league's players. All told, he signed eight former USFL players, four of whom came through to start. One of them, Chuck Commiskey, started at right guard in what developed into a really fine offensive line. The other starting offensive linemen at the end of the season were left tackle Bill Contz, a former Cleveland player who was signed off waivers, left guard Joel Hilgenberg, center Steve Korte and right tackle Stan Brock. They will be strengthened by the return of both rookie first-round pick Jim Dombrowski, who had won the starting job at left tackle before going on injured reserve in late September, and Brad Edelman, who should regain his starting spot at left guard. They allowed only 27 quarterback sacks and, of equal importance, gave their young backfield players the time to express themselves. Of these, the running backs, third-round draftee Rueben Mayes was a sensation, rushing for 1,353 yards at a blue-chip average of 4.7 per carry. Another of Mora's ex-USFL imports, Buford Jordan, started all year as an effective blocking fullback, while Dalton Hilliard, the club's second-round draftee, settled in as reserve to Mayes. Hokie Gajan, who has a sparkling 5.4-yard career rushing average, may be back after a year-long injury and would be expected to displace Jordan. At quarterback, Bobby Hebert has an edge over Dave Wilson, the latter who is a battler but is not the most mobile and has modest range with his passing. The Saints have not had a league-ranking wide receiver since the days of Wes Chandler in 1980, but second-round draftee Lonzell Hill could be that man. Also, it would be wrong to overlook the development of the pairing of Mike Jones and Eric Martin, which brought in 1,300 yards and eight touchdowns in 1986. Hoby Brenner and John Tice will compete for the starting spot at tight end.

Defense

'Think carefully before you run,' would be good advice to the Saints' 1987 opposition. Last year, the defense led the NFL in lowest average gain per rush (3.2 yards). They adopt the 3-4 formation on first down with Bruce Clark and Jim Wilks at defensive end and Tony Elliot at nose tackle. First-round pick Shawn Knight was an excellent acquisition. Of the veterans, Clark, who is also a former first-round draftee, is the class player. He's had knee surgery during the offseason and will be back at full speed after being slowed by the problem for much of last season. The specialist pass rushers are James Geathers and Frank Warren. Geathers registered nine quarterback sacks to share the club lead with left outside linebacker Rickey Jackson. Nine sacks would not be regarded as anything special for Jackson, who had 12, 12 and 11 respectively in the previous three seasons, and has been selected to the last four Pro Bowls. In Mora's system, Jackson's role was modified and it did lead to some frustration on the part of the player. However, he was happy after the Week Fifteen game against Atlanta, when the club gave him free rein and he registered four sacks, the last one coming as the clock ran out and preserving the Saints' five-point lead. Sam Mills, another of Mora's ex-USFL imports, played well, James Haynes was steady and, thankfully, former first-round draftee Alvin Toles began to play up to his potential. Former starter Jack Del Rio and Vaughan Johnson are the senior backups. Antonio Gibson was the fourth of Mora's ex-USFL imports to start. He blended in smoothly at strong safety in place of Russell Gary, who subsequently was released. The other starters, Dave Waymer, Frank Wattelet and Johnnie Poe, have been regulars for the last five seasons. Waymer fell only one short of the club record with nine pass interceptions in 1986. None of the starters is likely to be displaced but the reserve strength is modest and it made sense to select Mike Adams in round three of the draft.

Special Teams

The Saints have super special teams. Placekicker Morten Andersen has a very strong leg and went to the Pro Bowl.

1987 SCHEDULE OF GAMES		
September		
13 CLEVELAND		12:00
20 at Philadelphia		1:00
27 ATLANTA		12:00
October		
4 LOS ANGELES RAMS		12:00
11 at St Louis		12:00
18 at Chicago		12:00
25 SAN FRANCISCO		12:00
November		
1 at Atlanta		1:00
8 at Los Angeles Rams		1:00
15 at San Francisco		1:00
22 NEW YORK GIANTS		3:00
29 at Pittsburgh		1:00
December		
6 TAMPA BAY		3:00
13 HOUSTON		12:00
20 at Cincinnati		1:00
27 GREEN BAY		12:00

Punter Brian Hansen, who is a former Pro Bowler, would be expected to average over 42 yards. Mel Gray scored a touchdown on a 101-yard kickoff return, helping his average to 27.9 yards, a figure which gave him second place in the NFL list. In addition to his role as a wide receiver, Eric Martin returned 24 punts at the fine average of 9.5 yards.

1987 DRAFT

Round	Name	Pos.	Ht.	Wt.	College
1.	Knight, Shawn	DE	6-6	288	Brigham Young
2.	Hill, Lonzell	WR	5-11	183	Washington
3.	Adams, Mike	CB	5-9	195	Arkansas State
4.	Trapilo, Steve	G	6-4	280	Boston College
5.	Mack, Milton	CB	5-11	182	Alcorn State
6.	Henley, Thomas	WR	5-9	175	Stanford
7.	Atkins, Gene	S	6-0	190	Florida A&M
8.	Cook, Toi	CB	5-10	183	Stanford
9.	Leach, Scott	LB	6-2	220	Ohio State
10.	Clark, Robert	WR	5-10	180	North Carolina Central
11.	Wells, Arthur	TE	6-3	238	Grambling State
12.	Sorrells, Tyrone	G	6-3	260	Georgia Tech

VETERAN ROSTER

No.	Name	Pos.	Ht.	Wt.	NFL Year	College
7	Andersen, Morten	K	6-2	221	6	Michigan State
85	Brenner, Hoby	TE	6-4	245	7	Southern California
67	Brock, Stan	T	6-6	292	8	Colorado
75	Clark, Bruce	DE	6-3	274	6	Penn State
66	Commiskey, Chuck	G	6-4	290	2	Mississippi
70	Contz, Bill	T	6-5	270	5	Penn State
50	Del Rio, Jack	LB	6-4	238	3	Southern California
72	Dombrowski, Jim	T	6-5	289	2	Virginia
06	Dumbauld, Jonathan	DE	6-4	259	2	Kentucky
63	Edelman, Brad	G	6-6	270	6	Missouri
83	Edwards, Kelvin	WR	6-2	197	2	Liberty Baptist
99	Elliott, Tony	NT	6-3	295	6	North Texas State
43	Fowler, Bobby	RB	6-2	230	2	Louisiana Tech
46	Gajan, Hokie	RB	5-11	226	5	Louisiana State
97	Geathers, James	DE	6-7	290	4	Wichita State
27	Gibson, Antonio	S	6-3	204	2	Cincinnati
77	Gilbert, Daren	T	6-6	295	3	Cal State-Fullerton
88	Goodlow, Eugene	WR	6-2	186	5	Kansas State
37	Gray, Mel	RB	5-9	166	2	Purdue
10	Hansen, Brian	P	6-3	209	4	Sioux Falls, S.D.
80	Harris, Herbert	WR	6-1	200	2	Lamar
92	Haynes, James	LB	6-2	233	4	Mississippi Valley St.
3	Hebert, Bobby	QB	6-4	215	2	N.W. State, Louisiana
61	Hilgenberg, Joel	C-G	6-3	252	4	Iowa
40	Hilliard, Dalton	RB	5-8	204	2	Louisiana State
57	Jackson, Rickey	LB	6-2	243	7	Pittsburgh
22	Jakes, Van	DB	6-0	190	4	Kent State
24	Johnson, Bobby	S	6-0	187	5	Texas
53	Johnson, Vaughan	LB	6-3	235	2	North Carolina State
86	Jones, Mike	WR	5-11	183	5	Tennessee State
23	Jordan, Buford	RB	6-0	223	2	McNeese State
55	Kohlbrand, Joe	LB	6-4	242	3	Miami
60	Korte, Steve	C	6-2	269	5	Arkansas
84	Martin, Eric	WR	6-1	207	3	Louisiana State
39	Maxie, Brett	DB	6-2	194	3	Texas Southern
36	Mayes, Rueben	RB	5-11	200	2	Washington State
42	McLemore, Dana	CB-KR	5-10	183	6	Hawaii
51	Mills, Sam	LB	5-9	225	2	Montclair State
25	Poe, Johnnie	CB	6-1	194	7	Missouri
68	Saindon, Pat	G	6-3	260	2	Vanderbilt
27	Sutton, Reggie	CB	5-10	175	1	Miami
56	Swilling, Pat	LB	6-3	242	2	Georgia Tech
41	Thompson, Robert	WR	5-9	174	1	Youngstown State
82	Tice, John	TE	6-5	249	5	Maryland
54	Toles, Alvin	LB	6-1	227	3	Tennessee
73	Warren, Frank	DE	6-4	290	7	Auburn
49	Wattelet, Frank	S	6-0	186	7	Kansas
44	Waymer, Dave	CB	6-1	188	8	Notre Dame
94	Wilks, Jim	DE	6-5	266	7	San Diego State
45	Williams, John A.	RB	5-11	213	3	Wisconsin
79	Williams, Ralph	G	6-3	298	4	Southern
18	Wilson, Dave	QB	6-3	206	6	Illinois

Morten Andersen is one of the NFL's finest kickers.

SAN FRANCISCO 49ers

Address 711 Nevada Street, Redwood City, California 94061.

Stadium Candlestick Park, San Francisco.
Capacity 61,499 *Playing Surface* Grass.

Team Colours Forty Niners Gold and Scarlet.

Head Coach Bill Walsh – ninth year.

Championships Division 1970,'71,'72,'81,'83,'84,'86; Conference 1981,'84; Super Bowl 1981,'84.

History AAFC 1946-49, NFL 1950-69, NFC 1970-

Offense

It is consistent with the fact that the 49ers have won the NFC Western division title in four of the last five full seasons, that they have one of the best squads in the NFL. They are well organised and always seem to have a good draft. The latter was true in April, when they ensured the continuity of their authority on the offensive line by selecting Harris Barton and Jeff Bregel. Neither rookie is likely to start immediately but, equally, they may not have to wait long since, of the existing starters, only left tackle William 'Bubba' Paris will be under thirty by the beginning of the season. For the moment though, head coach Bill Walsh is pleased with his senior players. He describes left guard John Ayers as 'one of the best pass-blocking guards of the '80s'. Right guard Randy Cross has been selected to three Pro Bowls and right tackle Keith Fahnhorst is a really fine technician. Center Fred Quillan is a solid fulcrum. The 49ers' second option in the first round of the draft brought them running back Terrence Flagler, who made astonishing progress in his senior year, moving ahead of his Clemson teammate, Kenny Flowers. Flagler's selection becomes all the more significant following the retirement of Wendell Tyler. Again, though, he's not likely to displace the incumbent at halfback, Joe Cribbs, who took time to settle after his arrival from Buffalo but is a genuine candidate to rush for 1,000 yards in a season. The starting fullback, Roger Craig, made a slow start but he warmed up as the campaign wore on. Craig, who in 1985 became the first player in NFL history to gain over 1,000 yards in each of rushing and pass receiving, remains as one of the finest dual-purpose backs in the league. With the powerful Tom Rathman as his backup, the 49ers are well set to handle all eventualities. In a mini-reorganisation at quarterback, the 49ers released Mike Moroski, traded Jeff Kemp to Seattle and acquired Steve Young from Tampa Bay. Young is seen as the ideal person for the 49ers' innovative passing offense and he will be given time to unravel its complexities. He is not expected to challenge the incumbent, Joe Montana, who remains the key player. Without him, the club may win regular-season games, but it's unlikely that they'd win a title game. Last season, wide receiver Jerry Rice was the NFL's unchallenged leader in most categories, completely overshadowing his more experienced teammate, Dwight Clark. The tall, rangy Clark has adopted the role of possession receiver. Mike

Wilson is a fine third receiver and the club feels that John Taylor is a future starter. At tight end, Russ Francis is a model of consistency and should stay ahead of John Frank.

Defense

On the front line, the 49ers use several combinations of players according to circumstances. Nominally, Michael Carter is the starting nose tackle, Dwaine Board starts at defensive right end, and though Manu Tuiasosopo is listed ahead of Jeff Stover, it is only because he is the more effective against the run. Stover has been troubled throughout his career with minor injuries but, when fit, he is an outstanding pass rusher. With 11 sacks, he came second on the team behind rookie linebacker Charles Haley (12), who was a 'steal' in the fourth round. The 49ers' first draft pick in 1986, Larry Roberts (he came in the second round), reported late and it was around mid-season before· he began to penetrate the opposing backfields. He had 5.5 sacks. The depth of talent is equally evident at linebacker. Former first-round pick Todd Shell has recovered from the thigh muscle injury which kept him out for most of last season. He'll compete with Keena Turner for a starting spot. In fact, the situation is very fluid, with Mike Walter expected to challenge Jim Fahnhorst to start at right inside linebacker, and the former Buccaneers player, Keith Browner, involved in a battle with Milt McColl at left outside linebacker. Riki Ellison would appear to be the only certain starter. Two rookies, Tim McKyer and Don Griffin, started at cornerback and did exceptionally well. Free safety Ronnie Lott led the NFL in interceptions with 10, while McKyer had six. Strong safety Carlton Williamson remains as one of the NFL's most respected tacklers. McKyer should continue to start ahead of Tory Nixon, but Griffin will be displaced if, as anticipated, former starter Eric Wright makes a full recovery from injury.

1987 SCHEDULE OF GAMES		
September		
13	at Pittsburgh	1:00
20	at Cincinnati	1:00
27	PHILADELPHIA	1:00
October		
5	at New York Giants (Mon.)	9:00
11	ATLANTA	1:00
18	ST LOUIS	1:00
25	at New Orleans	12:00
November		
1	at Los Angeles Rams	1:00
8	HOUSTON	1:00
15	NEW ORLEANS	1:00
22	at Tampa Bay	1:00
29	CLEVELAND	5:00
December		
6	at Green Bay	12:00.
14	CHICAGO (Mon.)	6:00
20	at Atlanta	1:00
27	LOS ANGELES RAMS	5:00

Special Teams

The club is pleased with the performance of punter Max Runager, and they must be relieved that placekicker Ray Wersching was able to battle his way out of a poor spell in mid-season. Don Griffin proved to be a fine punt returner, averaging 9.9 yards to rank second in the NFC, but, in common with several others, he was not effective as a kickoff returner. Perhaps it's in this role that Flagler will cut his teeth.

1987 DRAFT

Round	Name	Pos.	Ht.	Wt.	College
1.	Barton, Harris	T	6-4	275	North Carolina
1.	Flagler, Terrence	RB	5-11	200	Clemson
2.	Bregel, Jeff	G	6-3	280	Southern California
5.	Jokisch, Paul	TE	6-7	238	Michigan
6.	White, Bob	LB	6-2	245	Penn State
7.	DeLine, Steve	K	5-10	175	Colorado State
8.	Grayson, David	LB	6-2	227	Fresno State
9.	Shelley, Jonathan	DB	6-0	190	Mississippi
10.	Paye, John	QB	6-2	200	Stanford
11.	Nicholas, Calvin	WR	6-2	200	Grambling State

VETERAN ROSTER

No.	Name	Pos.	Ht.	Wt.	NFL Year	College
68	Ayers, John	G	6-5	265	11	West Texas State
76	Board, Dwaine	DE	6-5	248	8	North Carolina A&T
59	Browner, Keith	LB	6-6	245	4	Southern California
95	Carter, Michael	NT	6-2	285	4	Southern Methodist
87	Clark, Dwight	WR	6-4	215	9	Clemson
69	Collie, Bruce	T-G	6-6	275	3	Texas-Arlington
57	Cousineau, Tom	LB	6-3	225	6	Ohio State
33	Craig, Roger	RB	6-0	224	5	Nebraska
83	Crawford, Derrick	WR-KR	5-10	185	2	Memphis State
28	Cribbs, Joe	RB	5-11	193	7	Auburn
51	Cross, Randy	G	6-3	265	12	UCLA
64	Durrette, Michael	G	6-4	280	2	West Virginia
50	Ellison, Riki	LB	6-2	225	5	Southern California
79	Fagan, Kevin	DT	6-3	260	1	Miami
55	Fahnhorst, Jim	LB	6-4	230	4	Minnesota
71	Fahnhorst, Keith	T	6-6	273	14	Minnesota
54	Ferrari, Ron	LB	6-0	215	6	Illinois
81	Francis, Russ	TE	6-6	242	12	Oregon
86	Frank, John	TE	6-3	225	4	Ohio State
49	Fuller, Jeff	S-LB	6-2	216	4	Texas A&M
11	Gagliano, Bob	QB	6-3	195	4	Utah State
29	Griffin, Don	CB	6-0	176	2	Middle Tennessee St.
94	Haley, Charles	LB-DE	6-5	230	2	James Madison
24	Harmon, Derrick	RB-KR	5-10	202	4	Cornell
75	Harty, John	DE	6-4	260	6	Iowa
46	Holmoe, Tom	S	6-2	195	4	Brigham Young
67	Kugler, Pete	NT	6-4	255	5	Penn State
42	Lott, Ronnie	S	6-0	200	7	Southern California
84	Margerum, Ken	WR	6-0	180	6	Stanford
53	McColl, Milt	LB	6-6	230	7	Stanford
62	McIntyre, Guy	G	6-3	264	4	Georgia
22	McKyer, Tim	CB	6-0	174	2	Texas-Arlington
32	Monroe, Carl	WR	5-8	180	5	Utah
16	Montana, Joe	QB	6-2	195	9	Notre Dame
20	Nixon, Tory	CB	5-11	186	3	San Diego State
77	Paris, Bubba	T	6-6	299	5	Michigan
56	Quillan, Fred	C	6-5	266	10	Oregon
44	Rathman, Tom	RB	6-1	232	2	Nebraska
80	Rice, Jerry	WR	6-2	200	3	Mississippi Valley St.
30	Ring, Bill	RB	5-10	205	7	Brigham Young
91	Roberts, Larry	DE	6-3	264	2	Alabama
65	Rogers, Doug	DE	6-5	280	5	Stanford
25	Rogers, Jimmy	RB	5-10	190	6	Oklahoma
4	Runager, Max	P	6-1	189	9	South Carolina
61	Sapolu, Jesse	G-C	6-4	260	2	Hawaii
90	Shell, Todd	LB	6-4	225	3	Brigham Young
72	Stover, Jeff	DE	6-5	275	6	Oregon
82	Taylor, John	WR	6-1	185	1	Delaware State
78	Tuiasosopo, Manu	NT	6-3	262	9	UCLA
58	Turner, Keena	LB	6-2	222	8	Purdue
74	Wallace, Steve	T	6-5	276	2	Auburn
99	Walter, Mike	LB	6-3	238	5	Oregon
14	Wersching, Ray	K	5-11	215	15	California
27	Williamson, Carlton	S	6-0	204	7	Pittsburgh
85	Wilson, Mike	WR	6-3	215	7	Washington State
21	Wright, Eric	CB	6-1	185	7	Missouri
8	Young, Steve	QB	6-2	200	3	Brigham Young

Linebacker Charles Haley (# 94) had an outstanding rookie season.

CHAPTER EIGHT

1987 NATIONAL FOOTBALL LEAGUE SCHEDULE

(All times local)

FIRST WEEK

Sunday, September 13	Kickoff
Atlanta at Tampa Bay	1:00
Cincinnati at Indianapolis	12:00
Cleveland at New Orleans	12:00
Dallas at St Louis	12:00
Detroit at Minnesota	12:00
Los Angeles Raiders at Green Bay	3:00
Los Angeles Rams at Houston	12:00
Miami at New England	1:00
New York Jets at Buffalo	1:00
Philadelphia at Washington	1:00
San Diego at Kansas City	12:00
San Francisco at Pittsburgh	1:00
Seattle at Denver	2:00

Monday, September 14	
New York Giants at Chicago	8:00

SECOND WEEK

Sunday, September 20	
Dallas at New York Giants	4:00
Denver vs. Green Bay at Milwaukee	12:00
Detroit at Los Angeles Raiders	1:00
Houston at Buffalo	1:00
Kansas City at Seattle	1:00
Miami at Indianapolis	12:00
Minnesota at Los Angeles Rams	1:00
New Orleans at Philadelphia	1:00
Pittsburgh at Cleveland	1:00
St Louis at San Diego	1:00
San Francisco at Cincinnati	1:00
Tampa Bay at Chicago	12:00
Washington at Atlanta	1:00

Monday, September 21	
New England at New York Jets	9:00

THIRD WEEK

Sunday, September 27	
Atlanta at New Orleans	12:00
Buffalo at Dallas	12:00
Chicago at Detroit	1:00
Cincinnati at Los Angeles Rams	1:00
Green Bay at Tampa Bay	1:00
Indianapolis at St Louis	12:00
Los Angeles Raiders at Houston	12:00
Minnesota at Kansas City	12:00
New England at Washington	1:00
New York Jets at Pittsburgh	4:00
New York Giants at Miami	1:00
Philadelphia at San Francisco	1:00
Seattle at San Diego	1:00

Monday, September 28	
Denver at Cleveland	9:00

FOURTH WEEK

Sunday, October 4	
Chicago at Philadelphia	1:00
Cleveland at New England	1:00
Dallas at New York Jets	4:00
Green Bay at Minnesota	12:00
Houston at Denver	2:00
Indianapolis at Buffalo	1:00
Kansas City at Los Angeles Raiders	1:00
Los Angeles Rams at New Orleans	12:00
Miami at Seattle	1:00
Pittsburgh at Atlanta	1:00
St Louis at Washington	1:00
San Diego at Cincinnati	1:00
Tampa Bay at Detroit	1:00

Monday, October 5	
San Francisco at New York Giants	9:00

FIFTH WEEK

Sunday, October 11	
Atlanta at San Francisco	1:00
Buffalo at New England	1:00

Cincinnati at Seattle	1:00
Detroit at Green Bay	12:00
Houston at Cleveland	1:00
Kansas City at Miami	1:00
Minnesota at Chicago	12:00
New Orleans at St Louis	12:00
New York Jets at Indianapolis	12:00
Philadelphia at Dallas	12:00
Pittsburgh at Los Angeles Rams	1:00
San Diego at Tampa Bay	1:00
Washington at New York Giants	4:00

Monday, October 12

Los Angeles Raiders at Denver	7:00

SIXTH WEEK
Sunday, October 18

Cleveland at Cincinnati	1:00
Denver at Kansas City	3:00
Indianapolis at Pittsburgh	1:00
Los Angeles Rams at Atlanta	1:00
Miami at New York Jets	1:00
New England at Houston	12:00
New Orleans at Chicago	12:00
New York Giants at Buffalo	4:00
Philadelphia at Green Bay	12:00
St Louis at San Francisco	1:00
San Diego at Los Angeles Raiders	1:00
Seattle at Detroit	1:00
Tampa Bay at Minnesota	12:00

Monday, October 19

Washington at Dallas	8:00

SEVENTH WEEK
Sunday, October 25

Atlanta at Houston	12:00
Buffalo at Miami	1:00
Chicago at Tampa Bay	1:00
Cincinnati at Pittsburgh	1:00
Dallas at Philadelphia	1:00
Denver at Minnesota	12:00
Green Bay at Detroit	1:00
Kansas City at San Diego	1:00
New England at Indianapolis	1:00
New York Jets at Washington	1:00
St Louis at New York Giants	4:00
San Francisco at New Orleans	12:00
Seattle at Los Angeles Raiders	1:00

Monday, October 26

Los Angeles Rams at Cleveland	9:00

EIGHTH WEEK
Sunday, November 1

Cleveland at San Diego	1:00
Detroit at Denver	2:00
Houston at Cincinnati	1:00
Indianapolis at New York Jets	1:00
Kansas City at Chicago	12:00
Los Angeles Raiders at New England	1:00

Minnesota at Seattle	1:00
New Orleans at Atlanta	1:00
Philadelphia at St Louis	12:00
Pittsburgh at Miami	1:00
San Francisco at Los Angeles Rams	1:00
Tampa Bay vs. Green Bay at Milwaukee	12:00
Washington at Buffalo	1:00

Monday, November 2

New York Giants at Dallas	8:00

NINTH WEEK
Sunday, November 8

Atlanta at Cleveland	1:00
Chicago at Green Bay	12:00
Dallas at Detroit	1:00
Denver at Buffalo	1:00
Houston at San Francisco	1:00
Los Angeles Raiders at Minnesota	12:00
Miami at Cincinnati	4:00
New England at New York Giants	8:00
New Orleans at Los Angeles Rams	1:00
Pittsburgh at Kansas City	12:00
San Diego at Indianapolis	1:00
Tampa Bay at St Louis	12:00
Washington at Philadelphia	1:00

Monday, November 9

Seattle at New York Jets	9:00

TENTH WEEK
Sunday, November 15

Buffalo at Cleveland	1:00
Cincinnati at Atlanta	4:00
Dallas at New England	1:00
Detroit at Washington	1:00
Green Bay at Seattle	1:00
Houston at Pittsburgh	1:00
Indianapolis at Miami	1:00
Los Angeles Raiders at San Diego	5:00
Los Angeles Rams at St Louis	12:00
Minnesota at Tampa Bay	1:00
New Orleans at San Francisco	1:00
New York Giants at Philadelphia	4:00
New York Jets at Kansas City	12:00

Monday, November 16

Chicago at Denver	7:00

ELEVENTH WEEK
Sunday, November 22

Atlanta at Minnesota	12:00
Buffalo at New York Jets	1:00
Cleveland at Houston	12:00
Denver at Los Angeles Raiders	1:00
Detroit at Chicago	12:00
Green Bay at Kansas City	12:00
Indianapolis at New England	1:00
Miami at Dallas	7:00
New York Giants at New Orleans	3:00
Pittsburgh at Cincinnati	1:00

St Louis at Philadelphia	1:00
San Diego at Seattle	1:00
San Francisco at Tampa Bay	1:00

Monday, November 23

Los Angeles Rams at Washington	9:00

TWELFTH WEEK
Thursday, November 26 (Thanksgiving Day)

Kansas City at Detroit	12:30
Minnesota at Dallas	3:00

Sunday, November 29

Cincinnati at New York Jets	1:00
Cleveland at San Francisco	5:00
Denver at San Diego	1:00
Green Bay at Chicago	12:00
Houston at Indianapolis	1:00
Miami at Buffalo	1:00
New Orleans at Pittsburgh	1:00
New York Giants at Washington	4:00
Philadelphia at New England	1:00
St Louis at Atlanta	1:00
Tampa Bay at Los Angeles Rams	1:00

Monday, November 30

Los Angeles Raiders at Seattle	6:00

THIRTEENTH WEEK
Sunday, December 6

Atlanta at Dallas	12:00
Buffalo at Los Angeles Raiders	1:00
Chicago at Minnesota	7:00
Indianapolis at Cleveland	1:00
Kansas City at Cincinnati	1:00
Los Angeles Rams at Detroit	1:00
New England at Denver	2:00
Philadelphia at New York Giants	1:00
San Diego at Houston	12:00
San Francisco at Green Bay	12:00
Seattle at Pittsburgh	1:00
Tampa Bay at New Orleans	3:00
Washington at St Louis	12:00

Monday, December 7

New York Jets at Miami	9:00

FOURTEENTH WEEK
Sunday, December 13

Atlanta at Los Angeles Rams	1:00
Buffalo at Indianapolis	1:00
Cincinnati at Cleveland	1:00
Dallas at Washington	1:00
Denver at Seattle	5:00
Detroit at Tampa Bay	4:00
Houston at New Orleans	12:00
Los Angeles Raiders at Kansas City	3:00
Miami at Philadelphia	1:00
Minnesota vs. Green Bay at Milwaukee	12:00
New York Giants at St Louis	3:00
New York Jets at New England	1:00

Pittsburgh at San Diego	1:00

Monday, December 14

Chicago at San Francisco	6:00

FIFTEENTH WEEK
Saturday, December 19

Green Bay at New York Giants	12:30
Kansas City at Denver	2:00

Sunday, December 20

Cleveland at Los Angeles Raiders	1:00
Indianapolis at San Diego	1:00
Minnesota at Detroit	1:00
New England at Buffalo	1:00
New Orleans at Cincinnati	1:00
Philadelphia at New York Jets	1:00
Pittsburgh at Houston	12:00
St Louis at Tampa Bay	4:00
San Francisco at Atlanta	1:00
Seattle at Chicago	12:00
Washington at Miami	8:00

Monday, December 21

Dallas at Los Angeles Rams	6:00

SIXTEENTH WEEK
Saturday, December 26

Cleveland at Pittsburgh	12:30
Washington at Minnesota	3:00

Sunday, December 27

Buffalo at Philadelphia	1:00
Chicago at Los Angeles Raiders	1:00
Cincinnati at Houston	12:00
Detroit at Atlanta	1:00
Green Bay at New Orleans	12:00
Los Angeles Rams at San Francisco	5:00
New York Jets at New York Giants	1:00
St Louis at Dallas	12:00
San Diego at Denver	2:00
Seattle at Kansas City	12:00
Tampa Bay at Indianapolis	1:00

Monday, December 28

New England at Miami	9:00

Postseason

Sunday, Jan. 3	AFC and NFC First Round Playoffs
Saturday, Jan. 9	AFC and NFC Divisional Playoffs
Sunday, Jan. 10	AFC and NFC Divisional Playoffs
Sunday, Jan. 17	AFC and NFC Championship Games
Sunday, Jan. 31	Super Bowl XXII at San Diego Jack Murphy Stadium, San Diego, California
Sunday, Feb. 7	AFC-NFC Pro Bowl at Honolulu, Hawaii

STOP PRESS

The discussion of teams is based upon information available up to early July. Below are listed several subsequent player movements which we were unable to incorporate into the main body of text but which, in some cases, could have significance for the strengths of the clubs.

Underlining his commitment to rebuilding the Chargers' rushing offense, head coach Al Saunders traded a fourth-string running back, Buford McGee, together with the Chargers' 1988 second-round draft option and a conditional 1988 middle-round draft option, to the Los Angeles Rams in exchange for Barry Redden. Redden, who was the Rams' first-round pick in 1982, is a genuine pro starter but has seen only limited action behind the great Eric Dickerson. He could be just what the Chargers need, and his arrival is a further pointer to the likely conversion of Gary Anderson to wide receiver. The middle-round draft option will be a fourth, fifth or sixth, conditional on Redden's productivity.

In what might be called the 'Boz' supplemental draft, held on June 12th, the Seattle Seahawks acquired the rights to Brian Bosworth, the former University of Oklahoma All-America linebacker. Bosworth is probably the best inside linebacker to come out of college for several years and is projected to have an impact similar to that of the retired Hall of Famer, Dick Butkus of the Chicago Bears. The downside is that, thus far, he has shown himself to be 'difficult' (some would say he was downright arrogant). Before the supplemental draft, he publicly stated that he'd play for one of only six teams, the Raiders, Rams, Giants, Jets, Buccaneers and Eagles. At the time of writing he is said to be 'prepared' to listen to a once-only offer from the Seahawks. However, when he does sign for a club, all the nonsense will disappear. And if that club happens to be Seattle, its name can be pencilled in for the playoffs – Bosworth is that good.

It was a major surprise when the Cowboys placed their third-string quarterback, Reggie Collier, and tackle Howard Richards on recallable waivers in mid-June. Richards was quickly claimed by the New York Jets but, at the time of writing, Collier is still available and one wonders why. It is true that he has not done anything worthwhile in the NFL, but he abounds with talent and you'd imagine that he'd fit in well with the Bears – though they already have more than enough involved in the shuffle.

Following the retirement of former All-Pro punter Ray Guy, the Raiders signed Stan Talley, formerly of the USFL's Oakland Invaders.

Two veterans, running back Curtis Dickey (Cleveland) and tight end Doug Marsh (St Louis) have been waived. On a happier note, the former Miami and Pittsburgh quarterback, David Woodley, is attempting a comeback. The Steelers traded his rights to the Green Bay Packers in exchange for an undisclosed draft option.

ALL-TIME HEAD-TO-HEAD RESULTS

	Buffalo	Indianapolis	Miami	New England	N.Y. Jets	Cincinnati	Cleveland	Houston	Pittsburgh	Denver	Kansas City	L.A. Raiders	San Diego	Seattle
Buffalo		16-16-1	7-34-1	23-30-1	26-27-0	5-9-0	2-6-0	9-18-0	4-6-0	13-9-1	15-12-1	11-12-0	9-17-2	0-2-0
Indianapolis	16-16-1		9-26-0	15-18-0	16-18-0	5-4-0	5-11-0	5-4-0	4-9-0	1-6-0	3-6-0	3-4-0	2-5-0	2-0-0
Miami	34-7-1	26-9-0		25-17-0	23-19-1	7-3-0	3-4-0	10-10-0	7-3-0	5-2-1	6-7-0	3-15-1	5-9-0	3-1-0
New England	30-23-1	18-15-0	17-25-0		23-30-1	6-4-0	2-6-0	14-13-1	3-5-0	12-13-0	7-11-3	12-12-1	13-12-2	5-2-0
N.Y. Jets	27-26-0	18-16-0	19-23-1	30-23-1		7-4-0	3-8-0	10-15-1	0-9-0	11-10-1	12-13-0	11-12-2	7-14-1	2-7-0
Cincinnati	9-5-0	4-5-0	3-7-0	4-6-0	4-7-0		17-16-0	21-14-1	15-18-0	6-9-0	7-9-0	4-12-0	7-10-0	4-2-0
Cleveland	6-2-0	11-5-0	4-3-0	6-2-0	8-3-0	16-17-0		22-11-0	43-31-0	3-9-0	5-5-1	1-10-0	5-5-1	2-7-0
Houston	18-9-0	4-5-0	10-10-0	13-14-1	15-10-1	14-21-1	11-22-0		9-26-0	18-10-1	12-21-0	10-22-0	12-17-1	3-2-0
Pittsburgh	6-4-0	9-4-0	3-7-0	5-3-0	9-0-0	18-15-0	31-43-0	26-9-0		5-8-1	9-5-0	6-9-0	8-4-0	3-3-0
Denver	9-13-1	6-1-0	2-5-1	13-12-0	10-11-1	9-6-0	9-3-0	10-18-1	8-5-1		19-34-0	16-36-2	25-28-1	12-8-0
Kansas City	12-15-1	6-3-0	7-6-0	11-7-3	13-12-0	9-7-0	5-5-1	21-12-0	5-9-0	34-19-0		22-31-2	26-26-1	9-8-0
L.A. Raiders	12-11-0	4-3-0	15-3-1	12-12-1	12-11-2	12-4-0	10-1-0	22-10-0	9-6-0	36-16-2	31-22-2		35-18-2	10-10-0
San Diego	17-9-2	5-2-0	9-5-0	12-13-2	14-7-1	10-7-0	5-5-1	17-12-1	4-8-0	28-25-1	26-26-1	18-35-2		9-8-0
Seattle	2-0-0	0-2-0	1-3-0	2-5-0	7-2-0	2-4-0	7-2-0	2-3-0	3-3-0	8-12-0	8-9-0	10-10-0	8-9-0	
Dallas	3-1-0	6-3-0	2-3-0	5-0-0	3-0-0	2-1-0	9-15-0	4-1-0	11-12-0	3-2-0	2-1-0	1-3-0	3-1-0	3-1-0
N.Y. Giants	2-1-0	3-7-0	0-1-0	1-1-0	2-2-0	0-3-0	16-26-2	3-0-0	41-26-3	3-2-0	4-1-0	1-3-0	3-2-0	3-2-0
Philadelphia	3-1-0	5-5-0	2-3-0	3-2-0	3-0-0	0-4-0	11-29-1	3-0-0	42-25-3	3-2-0	1-0-0	2-3-0	2-2-0	2-1-0
St. Louis	3-2-0	5-4-0	0-5-0	4-1-0	2-1-0	1-2-0	10-30-3	3-1-0	20-29-3	0-1-1	1-3-1	1-1-0	1-2-0	2-0-0
Washington	2-2-0	6-15-0	2-4-0	3-1-0	3-0-0	3-1-0	8-31-1	2-2-0	40-27-3	2-2-0	1-2-0	2-4-0	4-0-0	3-1-0
Chicago	2-1-0	14-21-0	0-4-0	3-2-0	2-1-0	1-2-0	3-6-0	2-2-0	14-4-1	4-3-0	2-1-0	2-3-0	1-4-0	1-3-0
Detroit	1-1-1	16-17-2	1-2-0	2-2-0	2-2-0	2-2-0	12-4-0	2-2-0	13-9-1	2-3-0	2-2-0	2-3-0	3-2-0	1-2-0
Green Bay	1-2-0	18-17-1	0-4-0	1-2-0	1-4-0	2-4-0	8-5-0	2-3-0	16-11-0	1-3-0	1-1-1	1-4-0	3-1-0	3-1-0
Minnesota	4-1-0	5-12-1	1-4-0	1-2-0	1-3-0	2-3-0	7-2-0	2-2-0	6-4-0	2-2-0	2-2-0	1-5-0	3-3-0	1-2-0
Tampa Bay	3-1-0	1-2-0	1-2-0	0-2-0	1-3-0	1-2-0	0-3-0	1-2-0	0-3-0	0-2-0	2-4-0	0-2-0	0-2-0	0-2-0
Atlanta	2-2-0	0-9-0	1-4-0	2-3-0	2-2-0	1-4-0	1-6-0	4-1-0	1-6-0	3-3-0	0-2-0	1-4-0	2-0-0	0-3-0
L.A. Rams	3-1-0	15-20-2	1-4-0	1-3-0	3-2-0	2-3-0	7-8-0	3-1-0	12-4-2	3-2-0	3-0-0	1-4-0	2-1-0	3-0-0
New Orleans	1-2-0	1-3-0	1-4-0	0-5-0	1-4-0	2-3-0	1-8-0	2-2-1	4-4-0	0-4-0	2-2-0	0-3-1	0-3-0	1-2-0
San Francisco	1-2-0	15-21-0	2-4-0	4-1-0	4-1-0	4-1-0	4-8-0	3-2-0	6-6-0	2-3-0	3-1-0	2-3-0	1-3-0	2-1-0